Readings & Case Studies in
MEDIATION

Jerry Bagnell • Bruce C. McKinney
University of North Carolina Wilmington

Kendall Hunt
publishing company

Cover image © Shutterstock, Inc.

Kendall Hunt
publishing company

www.kendallhunt.com
Send all inquiries to:
4050 Westmark Drive
Dubuque, IA 52004-1840

This book is dedicated to our friends and colleagues who have inspired us by their example and dedication to the profession of mediation, and to our wives—Amy and Jess—who inspire us to be better at everything we do.

Contents

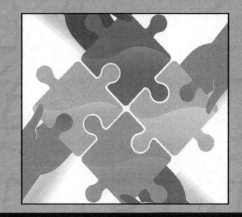

About the Contributors

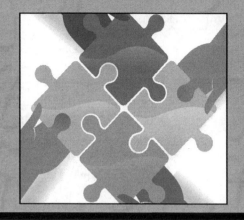

Jerry Bagnell has been a mediator and trainer since 1979. He has a Master of Education from the University of Delaware and a Master of Social Work from the University of Georgia. He has presented more than 200 programs to professional organizations throughout the United States for almost 30 years and has been a featured presenter for national and state conferences sponsored by the Academy of Family Mediators, The Association of Family and Conciliation Courts, and The Association for Conflict Resolution. Jerry was designated as a Mentor and Certified Mediator by the Supreme Court of Virginia from 1993–2003 and was Director of the Divorce Mediation Service from 1989–2001. Jerry has taught courses in Negotiation as well as Mediation & Conflict Management at the University of North Carolina Wilmington since 2004 and has presented training in "Intercultural Dispute Resolution" for the United States Marine Corps Special Operations Command (MARSOC) at Camp Lejeune, NC since 2006. He is a trainer and mentor-mediator of work place disputes for the Department of the Navy and the Department of Veterans Affairs. He also serves as Chairman of the Board of Directors for The ADR Center in Wilmington, NC.

Bruce C. McKinney is a professor of communication studies at the University of North Carolina Wilmington. He teaches undergraduate and graduate courses in mediation and conflict resolution and has served as a community and divorce mediator. He received his graduate degrees (M.A., Ph.D.) in speech communication from The Pennsylvania State University. He is co-author of *Mediator Communication Competencies: Problem Solving and Transformative Practices* 5th edition, and has co-authored four other books. McKinney has published over forty articles including articles in *Communication Education, Communication Quarterly, Conflict Resolution Quarterly, Communication Research Reports, Asian Profile,* and *Canadian Journal of Peace Studies.* Since 1999 he has been teaching short courses in negotiation and decision-making in Vietnam for Vietnam National University and the Ho

Chi Minh City Development Learning in Ho Chi Minh City, Hanoi, and Vung Tau. McKinney also works with the United States Marine Corps Special Operations Command teaching officers intercultural and negotiation skills.

Amanda Jordan-Brainard is the Director of Development at the Alternative Dispute Resolution Center, Inc. in Wilmington, North Carolina. She began mediating for the center in 2002 in the district court setting and has served in a number of capacities at the center including Peer Mediation and Conflict Resolution trainer for grades 3–12, Teen Court Coordinator for two counties, and intern supervisor. She has facilitated over one thousand Child and Family Team Meetings for Department of Social Services and has mediated numerous child custody cases. Amanda holds a Master's Degree in Psychology from University of North Carolina Wilmington.

Noa M. Broder graduated from the University of North Carolina Wilmington with a Bachelor of Arts in Communication Studies. She initially became interested in conflict resolution while taking a Mediation and Conflict Management class during her sophomore year at UNCW. The following year, she took a class on Negotiation that solidified her interest in pursuing the field of dispute resolution. Her role as Vice President of Operations for her sorority at UNCW provided her with invaluable experience working with a large number of people with diverse personalities who did not always see eye to eye on all issues. In the fall of her senior year, Noa became a Facilitation and Mediation Intern at the Alternative Dispute Resolution Center in Wilmington. There she observed ADR Center staff members mediating and facilitating disputes such as Child and Family Team Meetings with the Department of Social Services, Medicaid cases, as well as a few special cases involving disputes among local community organizations as well as local schools. The majority of her internship experience involved observing and eventually co-mediating Child and Family Team Meetings. Over the course of her internship, she observed 30 CFTMs and co-mediated ten. She currently works on the Cardiology Team at Weatherby Healthcare in Cary, North Carolina where she utilizes her mediation and negotiation skills on a daily basis to engage with doctors and clients to understand their needs and then place them in a position that mutually satisfies both parties' needs and desires.

Julius Z. Frager has been a mediator since 1992. He has a J.D. from Washington University Law School and a M.B.A. from Harvard University Graduate School of Business. He was an Advanced Practitioner Member of Family Mediation in the Association for Conflict Resolution. He has been trained in Transformative Mediation by the U.S. Postal Service for REDRESS I and REDRESS II and has been doing mediation for them in the St. Louis, Missouri; Kansas City, Missouri; and the West Coast of Florida areas since the beginning of the REDRESS® program in St. Louis, Missouri in 1999. He taught Negotiation at Keller Graduate School of Management for two summer semesters. Currently, besides doing mediation for the U.S. Postal Service, Mr. Frager does mediation and arbitration for American Arbitration Association and arbitration for FINRA (Financial Industry Regulatory Authority).

Merri L. Hanson is the Director of Peninsula Mediation & ADR in Williamsburg and Hampton Virginia. Her education achievements include a Bachelor of Arts in Speech Communication, a Master of Arts in Communication and Conflict Management, and post-graduate work in organizational psychology. Peninsula Mediation & ADR provides a comprehensive range of mediation services for family, workplace, EEO, ADA, business, and commercial disputes. Under Merri's direction, Peninsula Mediation & ADR manages ADR contracts and service delivery throughout the United States and Hawaii for the Navy, the Department of Homeland Security, the Veterans Administration, NASA HQ, and the Department of Transportation. Merri also serves on the mediation and ADR training rosters for NASA, the U.S. Air Force, the U.S. Army, the Department of Energy, and the Department of Justice ADA Program (through the Key Bridge Foundation), and el Centro Interdisciplinario para el Manejo de Conflictos, A.C. in Mexico City.

Jessica Katz Jameson is Associate Head and Associate Professor in the Department of Communication at North Carolina State University where she teaches courses in organizational communication, conflict management, and nonprofit leadership. Her research focuses on organizational conflict management and she has published articles in *Negotiation Journal,* the *International Journal of Conflict Management, Conflict Resolution Quarterly,* the *Western Journal of Communication,* and the *Journal of Health Communication.* Professor Jameson is a mediator for NC State's employee mediation program and she recently co-developed a mediation training for university administrators, staff, and faculty.

William D. Kimsey is a Professor Emeritus at James Madison University and he received his Ph.D. from Southern Illinois University. He is a co-author of CONFLICTALK, an instrument used for measuring conflict styles of elementary, middle, and high school students and he is a co-author of Mediator Communication Competencies: Problem Solving and Transformative Practices, *5th edition.* He has published articles on communication and conflict in a variety of journals including *Communication Monographs, Conflict Resolution Quarterly, Canadian Journal of Peace Studies,* and *Asian Profile.* He has served as a community mediator for over thirty years.

Cynthia Mazur, M Div, JD, LLM, PhD is the ADR Director at FEMA. She earned her PhD in conflict resolution from George Mason University's School for Conflict Analysis and Resolution. She has been mediating family cases for the D.C. Superior Court and arbitrating legal malpractice and fee dispute cases for the D.C. Bar since 1991. She has been the Chair of the Interagency Alternative Dispute Resolution Working Group, Workplace Conflict Management Section since 2003. She has been a mentor/mediator in the Federal Shared Neutrals program since its inception in 1995.

Lawrie Parker is Executive Director, Piedmont Dispute Resolution Center (PDRC). Ms. Parker has been involved in mediation and restorative justice for 23 years as a certified mediator, trainer, and program developer. She is the current president of the Restorative Justice Association of Virginia (RJAV). Ms. Parker is a founder of the Piedmont Dispute Resolution Center and sits on the Supreme Court of

Virginia's Dispute Resolution Advisory Council and its Mediator Complaint Panel, the Board of Directors of the Virginia Mediation Network, and the Virginia Association for Community Conflict Resolution as well as numerous local boards. She developed her agency's restorative justice program in 1996. She trains students in school peer mediation programs and was involved in the Fauquier Schools 2010 strategic planning which adopted restorative justice as a long range goal. In 2001, Ms. Parker received the Supreme Court of Virginia Award for Outstanding Achievement in Community Mediation, in 2010 she was named one of Virginia's 50 Influential Women by Virginia Lawyers Media and in 2011 she received the Distinguished Mediator Award from the Virginia Mediation Network. Ms. Parker holds a B.A. from the University of Michigan and an M.B.A. from the University of Mary Washington.

Catherine S. Powell is founder and director of CPowell & Associates, Human Resource Management and Training Consultants. She holds a Masters in Public Administration and a doctorate in Curriculum & Instruction from the University of West Florida. She began mediating Discrimination and Equal Opportunity cases at the University in 1998, and advanced to become director of the University's Office for Informal Dispute Resolutions (Ombudsman) and ADA Compliance in 2002. While continuing in that role, she also worked as an adjunct professor, teaching alternative dispute resolution/mediation classes for graduate and undergraduate students. Throughout her tenure, the recipients of her services as a mediator and trainer included faculty, students, and staff until she retired from the University in 2011. Her formal mediation training includes successful completion of graduate and undergraduate coursework in Alternative Dispute Resolution and Mediation, the state of Florida's Supreme Court Mediation Training Program, and Campus Mediation Training with the state of Georgia's Consortium on Negotiation and Conflict Resolution. She has also presented mediation training at annual conferences for the Association for Conflict Resolution and the Center for Alternative Dispute Resolution in Greenbelt, Maryland.

Sallye S. Trobaugh is the owner of Mediation Associates, LLC and a Broker Associate for ERA Kline and May Realty in Harrisonburg, Virginia. She has served as a mediator in domestic and business disputes for over twenty years. She is a licensed Real Estate Broker, licensed Virginia Real Estate Instructor, Certified Residential Broker, a Certified Ethics Instructor, Education Director for ERA Kline and May Realty, and is a trainer in real estate negotiation, mediation, and problem solving facilitation. She has published in *Conflict Resolution Quarterly*.

Aubrey Waddell is Vice President Counsel for Jones Lang LaSalle, a firm that provides property management and agency leasing services for approximately 200 shopping centers nationwide. Her responsibilities include negotiating commercial contracts, as well as claim and litigation management. Prior to joining Jones Lang LaSalle, Ms. Waddell was in private practice with the firms of DLA Piper, specializing in Real Estate and Construction Litigation, and Alston & Bird, specializing in Construction and Government Contracts. She received her undergraduate degree in Commerce from the McIntire School of Commerce of the University of Virginia, and a J.D. from Vanderbilt University Law School.

Chapter 1

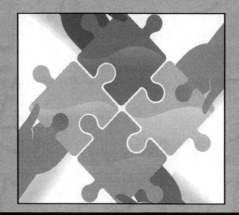

Introduction

Jerry Bagnell

In this our second edition, Bruce and I have focused on providing more information from practitioners. Readers of our first edition asked us to give them more insight about how practitioners actually conduct mediation than what the theoretical basis is for conducting mediation.

Our contributors for this edition range from a recent undergraduate who just began practicing as a mediator, to a number of professionals with years of experience as mediators. We have included chapters from mediators who practice within local communities, for colleges and universities, and those who practice as mediators for national organizations.

Ever mindful of emerging thought about alternative dispute resolution, we have included discussions of the latest trends within the subject matter area. Our overall purpose remains as one that encourages persons with little or no experience in mediation to explore what practice modalities exist and how practitioners function within those modalities.

We hope that the insight our contributors provide will peak the curiosity of both those interested in becoming mediators as well as those who seek more efficient ways to resolve disputes. We make no claim that mediation is always a better alternative than other dispute resolution processes but only hope that when searching for ways to resolve disputes, people will consider the full range of alternatives.

If we have succeeded in arousing the curiosity of our readers about any particular type of dispute resolution process, we hope you will either contact our contributors or do more scholarly research to learn more about mediation and other available dispute resolution processes.

We ask you to accept that the opinions and perspectives of our contributors are theirs alone and do not represent the policy or philosophy of the agencies or organizations they represent.

Professor McKinney and I have used the following assignment in our undergraduate as well as graduate classes at UNCW.

> Choose two chapters from *Readings and Case Studies in Mediation*. Then, prepare a comparison of similarities and differences in the conduct of each practice modality by answering the following questions.

1. Which two chapters are you analyzing? What is the general focus **and** target population for each of the two practice modalities you will compare and contrast? Why did you choose them?
2. What training and/or experience do the authors say are necessary to be a credible and competent practitioner in each area?
3. Why do you personally believe that such training and/or experience are necessary? What other training and/or experience do you think might be necessary?
4. What are the similarities and differences of typical problems encountered by the practitioner in each area?
5. How does the practitioner handle the problems unique to each area? Which might you find difficult to handle as a practitioner and why? If you were the practitioner, how do you think they might be handled? Would you do something differently? If so, what, how, and why?
6. How and why do you think each type of mediation practice presents a better alternative than the way in which the disputes they concern might be handled such as arbitration, litigation, or another ADR process? Consider the four underlying principles of mediation: voluntariness, confidentiality, self-determination, and informed consent. Consider other factors such as cost, enforceability or durability of the agreement, or any others that might be relevant. If you think mediation would not a better alternative, why? What process would you use or recommend?

Bruce and I thank you for accepting *Readings and Case Studies in Mediation* as a text without equal that presents information and insight about mediation as a possible alternative for resolving disputes. Our intent is not to provide detailed information about how to conduct mediation but merely to provide enough of an appetizer to encourage further exploration and research on the part of those who might be interested in learning more about the process.

Chapter 2

Getting Started as a Mediator

Noa M. Broder

When I was in fifth grade, my elementary school had a volunteer program for students to mediate disputes between kindergarten students that arose on the playground during recess. As a ten-year-old playground mediator, I was responsible for strolling around and overseeing the playground area to ensure that all of the kindergarteners were playing fairly and peacefully. If I witnessed any sort of conflict or argument between children such as a squabble over whose turn it was to ride down the slide, I would step in and ask, "Is there a problem here?" After a few minutes of sitting under a tree or talking it out in the sandbox, the children would apologize to each other, agree on some sort of resolution that we developed, (sometimes hug each other), and then scamper off to play again. I remember feeling an immense sense of power and pride as I patrolled the recess grounds sporting my bright white trucker hat with the word "MEDIATOR" printed across the front in large neon green letters. While some of my fellow mediators quickly lost interest in spending their free time on the blacktop watching six year olds play freeze tag and ride down the slide, I felt a sense of purpose knowing that these young children were coming to me to assist them in resolving their disputes.

My early exposure to what I thought was mediation, peaked my interest in the conflict resolution field. As a natural problem solver, I thought that helping other people solve their problems was something that I was skilled at and therefore wanted to pursue in some way. In my freshman year of college, I was thrilled to take an entire course devoted to the subject and practice of Mediation and Conflict

Management. I prematurely jumped to the conclusion that my innate ability to help people solve problems would make this class a breeze for me. I was wrong. I quickly realized that my fifth grade mediator experience combined with my own personal "mediations" of disputes between my friends in high school did not make me an expert nor did it make me a natural in this field. Learning about this topic from a professional with extensive mediation experience opened my eyes to the reality of what it takes to be an effective mediator in a challenging field. For me, one of the biggest challenges of the class was wrapping my head around the idea that mediators do not give suggestions, advice, ideas, or solutions to their clients. As someone who previously prided myself on my advice-giving ability, which in my mind would make me a successful mediator, this was quite a reality check. The very definition of my position as a mediator in fifth grade was to help five and six year olds fix the issues that they were arguing about, figure out a solution to the problem, and release them to play freely and fairly on the playground once again. If only mediating disputes on the kindergarten playground was that simple. My introduction to mediation and conflict management taught me that if the parties in conflict do not feel included and involved in the conflict resolution process, there is little to no chance that either party will make an effort to solve the issues with each other. However, if the mediator assists the parties in generating their own solutions by simply facilitating communication between the parties, they will be more likely to take an active role in working toward their goals.

Although my confidence in my abilities as a mediator was slightly shaken in the beginning, I committed myself to improving as a student and practitioner of this field. I realized that just because I did not possess all of the essential mediator skills I was learning about at the time, it did not mean I was incapable of practicing and developing these skills. Additionally, I learned how to enhance and adapt some of the skills that I already possessed to make them more powerful as a mediator. Watching my fellow classmates mediate disputes in their assigned role-plays during class helped me recognize and discern between effective and ineffective mediator behaviors. Observing others make the same mistakes that I made during my own role-plays enabled me to understand why certain skills are so essential when mediating.

A semester later, I was thrilled once again when I enrolled in Negotiation, a course designed to be the next level of the conflict resolution curriculum after Mediation and Conflict Management. Negotiation taught me additional skills while simultaneously reinforcing many of the essential skills taught in Mediation and Conflict Management, such as active listening, attentiveness, discerning listening with sensitivity to hidden agendas, persuasiveness, and empathy. The Negotiation class included similar in-class role-plays that were critiqued, evaluated, and ultimately graded by my peers. The feedback I received from my classmates about the strengths and weaknesses of my performance and future improvements to consider was both constructive and practical.

With these two courses under my belt, I continued on the path of conflict resolution by securing a position as the Facilitation and Mediation Intern at the Alternative Dispute Resolution Center (ADR) in Wilmington, North Carolina during the fall of my senior year. I was interested to see how I could apply the skills and tools that I learned in the classroom to situations outside of the academic arena. The ADR Center provides alternative dispute resolution services to various businesses and residents of the Cape Fear region through mediation, facilitation, arbitration, and negotiation. The majority of my experience at the ADR Center focused on co-mediating Child Family Team Meetings (CFT) as required by the Department of Social Services (DSS). The internship certainly put my knowledge and skills to the test and I quickly became aware that CFT Meetings were an entirely different ball game than any practice role-play or even real life dispute that I had encountered. Because the classes I took did not focus on or delve into explicit detail on CFT Meetings, I was not directly trained for this type of family conferencing before starting my internship.

Child Family Team Meetings, sometimes referred to as family conferencing, are structured meetings that are arranged by a caseworker from DSS who is assigned to the case and facilitated by a professional, neutral, and non-biased third party. The meetings are intended to bring family members together with the additional support of professionals and community resources to collectively create a plan that addresses the identified issues of the child's (or children's) welfare. Mediation can be an effective means to developing family plans such as custody and visitation schedules. As stated on the ADR Center website, "As children get older or other circumstances change, revising the plan through mediation offers a non-confrontation forum to express concerns and develop a mutually satisfactory plan for the future." CFT Meetings aim to engage and work with all of the people who are involved with the family to build a strong support system for the family even once the case is closed with DSS.

Although I was not specifically taught how to mediate CFT Meetings prior to my internship at the ADR Center, it was apparent after observing only a handful of cases that facilitating family conferences called on all of the essential mediator skills that I had become familiar with. According to the North Carolina Department of Health and Human Services in regards to CFT Meetings, "It is the responsibility of the DSS social worker and/or the facilitator to assure that the ideas of the family and their natural supports will be considered with the same weight as those of the professionals in the room. If the family (and natural supports) is not given the power to make choices and put forth ideas, they may not feel respected or heard, and may find the meeting to be a waste of their time. This may also affect the extent to which the family invests in the plan that results from the meeting, potentially adversely affecting child welfare outcomes." Maximizing the extent to which the family invests in the plan is one of the ultimate goals of family conferencing. To effectively achieve this goal, the mediator is largely responsible for encouraging and engaging in open and honest communication between all present parties. By encouraging and respecting this type of communication the mediator can articulate, both verbally and in writing, a specific case plan that has been agreed upon, understood, and accepted by the family and their supports. The mediator helps the family develop the case plan by building on the family's strengths as well as addressing each family member's needs, desires, goals, and expectations for the future.

TRAINING AND EXPERIENCE NEEDED TO MEDIATE CHILD FAMILY TEAM MEETINGS

When I began my internship at the ADR Center I lacked experience facilitating and mediating real-life cases. My only relevant experience at the time was limited to the role-plays I had done in class that were loosely scripted and based on real-life conflict situations that had once occurred. I was able to prepare for my role the day before I performed in class. Individual grades were based on the language we used (or failed to use), our body language and other observable non-verbal behaviors, the types of questions we asked, when and how we asked them, as well as several other elements of our performance. Preparing for the role-plays the night before was usually stressful and tedious. At times it even seemed silly to prepare to mediate a conflict that was so scripted and contrived. However, the experience later proved to be invaluable preparation for when I co-mediated a CFT Meeting for the first time during my internship.

Both of the classes that I took continually emphasized the importance of not using verbal fillers such as "um" or "uh" when speaking. While it may have seemed utterly ridiculous at the time to receive point deductions from my grade for saying the word "um" too many times during a role-play, it forced me to adjust the way I spoke, which in turn helped me to project more confidence during the cases I co-mediated. Another relevant lesson from the classroom that I found extremely applicable and useful during my internship was the effective and appropriate use of open ended questions during mediations. Questions are the mediator's primary mode of communication during meetings. As the mediator of the CFT Meeting, asking questions gives you the power to re-frame something somebody said or redirect the focus of the meeting in a more productive direction. My classroom education about mediation emphasized that mediators should not give advice, suggestions, or instructions to the parties. This includes asking questions in such a way that implies any sort of suggestion or instruction. Instead, by asking different types of questions during different stages of the meeting, the mediator can help focus the content of the meeting while allowing the family members and other supports to maintain control of the decisions and answers.

My transition from mediating semi-scripted role-plays in the classroom to co-mediating emotionally heavy and often painful cases was not an easy one. However, the material that I learned from my coursework enabled me to feel more confident and prepared as a mediator in the highly stressful and emotional environment of CFT Meetings. My academic background in this field served as a means of training for my internship in the sense that it clarified what my role as a mediator and facilitator was. When I sat down in the family conferencing room each morning at my internship, I knew that my purpose was to facilitate conversation between family members and other supports in a way that would assist and encourage them to generate mutually satisfactory outcomes and decisions on their own. Without the degree of knowledge about mediation that I had and the practice and development of some of the essential mediator skills, I would have been lost and extremely overwhelmed when faced with the challenge of co-mediating a CFT Meeting.

While academic experience, knowledge of the field, and relevant skills are all extremely important in order to advance as a mediator, having a hands-on internship experience is the most useful and effective form of training that a novice mediator can receive. I spent the first few weeks of my internship shadowing staff members in their daily routines at work. I quietly observed the cases they mediated while taking notes on certain behaviors that I noticed. I paid attention to the types of questions that they asked different people and made note on what stage(s) of the meeting they asked them. I became familiar with phrases and terms that were part of a vocabulary that I had never been exposed to prior to working with DSS. I quickly grew restless from quietly observing cases in the corner of the room, however. I felt myself wanting to speak up during CFT Meetings and would suppress my desire to jump in and ask a question at times. After less than a month of observing, I was eager and ready to co-mediate a CFT Meeting with the help of an ADR staff member in the room with me. My first case was intimidating and slightly uncomfortable initially, but with each case that I co-mediated, I became increasingly more confident in myself and more comfortable with the process. Without my desire, willingness, and curiosity to jump into the process headfirst, I would have finished my internship feeling inexperienced and incapable of co-mediating, nonetheless mediating, an actual case. It is vital to realize that grasping the concepts and understanding the language of mediation is not enough to be an effective mediator. Applying the concepts to complex situations and utilizing the language as you communicate with individuals who are struggling to communicate with each other is how you can truly enhance your skills and abilities as a mediator. Because every individual person is different and thus every case is different, it is imperative to have hands-on mediating experience because it teaches you to not only apply concepts, but also adapt the concepts so that they correspond to the unique situation at hand. People are not stagnant and the heart of conflict resolution revolves around people. Therefore, there is no better training or experience to prepare for working with a variety of personalities than actually experiencing it firsthand.

HOW DO YOU PREPARE FOR THIS TYPE OF MEDIATION?

Once I began co-mediating CFT Meetings, I gradually began to discover and develop routines that helped me feel as prepared as possible for the cases that lay ahead for the day. An essential part of preparing for any case is to become familiar with the circumstances of the case itself ahead of time. During my internship, I usually spent about fifteen to twenty minutes prior to the CFT Meeting reading over any material or information available about the case. The ADR staff members that I shadowed usually read over the information the day before the case as well as the day of the case. If the CFT Meeting was a follow-up meeting that had met with the ADR Center before, Memoranda of Understanding (MOUs) from the previous meetings were available to look at. Reading the MOUs from previous meetings enabled me to familiarize myself with the circumstances of the case and allowed me to look at the identified strengths, goals, current services, and case plan elements of the family. If the meeting was not a follow-up and therefore had no MOU to look at, the only information available to prepare with ahead of time were the official forms sent by DSS to request and schedule the CFT Meeting. These forms typically contained the names of the family members and other supports involved in the case and a vague purpose for the meeting. Having some degree of knowledge or awareness of the case prior to the CFT Meeting can certainly be useful, but even if a meeting is a follow-up, it is guaranteed to be different than previous meetings. It is possible that a different DSS caseworker will be assigned to the case and therefore the dynamics of the group itself will be different. Since a follow-up meeting usually occurs at least one month after the previous meeting, there are probably going to be new developments, stories, conflicts, progress reports, etc. that are impossible for the mediator to predict and prepare for.

One of the most important ways a mediator can prepare for this type of mediation is also one of the most difficult. Mediating CFT Meetings requires individual mediators who possess a high tolerance for stress and a strong ability to control emotional reactions. The content of many CFT Meetings and the circumstances of the cases can be extremely disturbing, tragic, and uncomfortable. One of my mentors whom I shadowed during my internship told me about a case that she once mediated where a mother was told she had to make a decision between staying in a physically abusive relationship with a man and therefore losing custody of her two children, or promising to move out of the house with the abusive boyfriend and maintaining custody of her young boys. Right there in the conference room of the CFT Meeting, the woman made the choice of remaining with her boyfriend and losing her children. Everyone in the room had to sit and watch as the boys witnessed their own mother willingly give up her custody of them. As imagined, it was an extremely painful and emotional situation. Situations like these occur often during CFT Meetings and while there is no way to prepare for the exact situation that might occur, a mediator should prepare for almost any possibility. There is no single way to prepare for these types of situations. However, being aware of the emotional content of the meetings and being capable of controlling emotional reactions will make the process a bit easier for the mediator.

WHAT ARE SOME TYPICAL AND UNIQUE PROBLEMS ASSOCIATED WITH THIS TYPE OF MEDIATION?

It is somewhat difficult to speak about many of the more common as well as unique problems that are associated with family conferencing, as my experience both observing and co-mediating CFT Meetings is confined to a three month period at only one agency. Based on my own experience from my internship and from discussions with staff members at the agency that reaffirmed my perception, one of the biggest problems I noticed with this type of mediation stems from ineffective caseworkers from DSS.

In my three months as an intern, I witnessed a wide variety of personalities and styles from the caseworkers at DSS. Unfortunately and to my surprise, I felt many of the case workers that I encountered were not doing their jobs as well as I thought they should be. When DSS becomes involved with a family, a caseworker is assigned to the case. He or she begins working closely with the family to evaluate the family's strengths, weaknesses, and needs. During the time that DSS is involved with a family and the case is open, the caseworker as well as members of the family and other community supports meet with a facilitator/mediator for a CFT Meeting. As neutral third party facilitators, our role is to help everybody, including the caseworker, communicate more openly and effectively so that all parties are on the same page and all questions are answered. It is primarily the caseworker's responsibility to provide answers to many of the questions that the children, parents, and other supports might have about the case itself and the conditions and terms of it. In my experience co-mediating these meetings, I encountered several caseworkers who did not explain the conditions and terms of the case clearly to the family and supports they were working with. It would be very evident during the meeting that there was confusion and misunderstanding. It would take an extended period of time for each person to finally understand what was going on. Other times, passive caseworkers were not the problem. Some caseworkers came across as extremely aggressive and intimidating, which made it difficult to control the meeting. Caseworkers with strong and aggressive personalities tended to be seen by the family as the enemy, which was counterproductive to their case.

Caseworkers with quieter personalities were difficult to work with because they withheld information that was vital to the progress of the family's case and case plan. Many caseworkers seemed overwhelmed before, during, and after CFT Meetings and therefore did not come across as committed to the case we were dealing with, which was usually detrimental to the family.

CONCLUDING COMMENTS

As a student of mediation I used to sometimes wonder if I was actually capable of mediating the types of cases that I was learning about in class. Listening to stories of cases from divorce mediation and crisis negotiation fascinated me and yet seemed like a somewhat unattainable profession for someone at my level. As my abilities and confidence as a mediator grew exponentially while taking classes on the topic, I still felt unsure of how well I could perform in a mediation setting outside of the classroom. Interning at the ADR Center for a semester not only boosted my confidence to mediate outside of the academic arena but it also gave me unique insight into the field of mediation and conflict resolution through the lens of a professional.

I entered my internship without any prior knowledge of DSS cases or CFT Meetings. Initially, I was surprised and troubled by the content of the cases I observed and the types of people I encountered in these cases. The first few weeks were difficult because I had never been exposed to these types of family issues before. I had to learn to quickly come to terms with the reality that that these types of issues and people do exist if I wanted to succeed in this field. My experience observing and co-mediating CFT Meetings strongly enhanced my ability to project neutrality regardless of my biases—an essential mediator skill that I began to develop in the classroom.

Now that I have co-mediated a few cases, I feel that I need to continue to utilize what I have learned in order to grow in this field. After my internship, I am still not an expert nor am I qualified to mediate on my own yet. I was simply getting my feet wet by co-mediating CFT Meetings. The internship provided me with valuable hands-on experience that taught as much as it showed me how much I still have to learn. The skills that I developed through the internship will benefit me in many different aspects of my life. As an individual, I am more accepting and understanding of people's differences and I am more sensitive and capable of working with a diverse group of personalities.

My listening skills improved tremendously, and I know how to adapt my conflict style to different types of people depending on the situation and their communication style. I am more observant of other people as well as my own behavior now. I can objectively critique my own actions, which is crucial not only for mediators, but for any professional in the workforce.

The experience thus far in the conflict resolution field has helped me mature as a person. I encourage those who are interested in pursuing this field to become as involved in the process as possible for it is the only way to truly develop and hone the essential skills it takes to succeed. Mediating takes a certain type of person who maintains a balance of empathy and sensitivity with a neutral and tough exterior. One of the major things I realized when thinking about my experiences in retrospect is that the power and ability to effectively mediate disputes and manage conflicts is not confined to someone with the official title of "Mediator." These abilities are crucial to everyday life whether it be a small dispute in your personal life or a larger conflict in your workplace. With the small amount of experience I have had, I already feel a sense of power and control in my life that I know will only increase with additional experience.

Case Study

One of the first cases that I co-mediated during my internship I found to be particularly interesting because it strayed from the typical format of the CFT Meetings that I was accustomed to. In this case, custody of fifteen-year-old "Susan Jones" (a fictitious name) had previously been taken from her mother who was incarcerated. A few months prior to this meeting, Susan had been ordered by juvenile court to stay in a group home for youth with addictions, violence problems, and juvenile records. Susan had an upcoming court date to determine her future placement.

Because the terms of her placement were in the hands of the judge, this meeting served mostly to inform and update the family and supports of Susan's progress at her group home. Because there was no way to predict the outcome of Susan's upcoming court date, I felt the meeting was very tense and stressful.

Once everyone arrived at the conference room, we all took our seats and began introductions. My co-mediator and I introduced ourselves and explained our role as facilitators and mediators for the meeting in simple terms. Each person present introduced him or herself to the rest of the room by name and relationship to Susan. This allowed all persons present to understand who everyone was as well as enabling the mediator to prepare an accurate record in the MOU of who was present.

The family members present were Susan's aunt and Susan's maternal grandmother. Neither her mother nor her father was in attendance. Additional community supports present were her System of Care Coordinator, and a Behavioral and Psychological Support Professional from the group home that Susan was currently in. Both Susan and her psychologist attended the CFT Meeting via phone call from an office at the group home. The phone was placed in the center of the table in the conference room on speakerphone to ensure that all parties present at the conference table could hear. After introducing everyone at the table, we called Susan and her psychologist at the group home and informed them of who was present at the meeting. We briefly explained our role in this process once again, but adapted our language slightly so that it resonated with Susan, a teenager, who seemed as though she did not want to be on the phone call in the first place.

Before every CFT Meeting, DSS requires that the mediator read aloud a Confidentiality Agreement that all present members of the meeting must sign and comply with. The agreement is designed to protect the children and the family and states that any information discussed during the CFT Meeting must not be discussed or shared outside of the meeting itself. Before continuing the meeting, all persons present signed the agreement and Susan and her psychologist gave verbal consent for us to sign for them.

Just like every CFT Meeting, the meeting began by asking the DSS case worker what the strengths of this family were. The caseworker stated that this family's strength was support and love for Susan.

The next step is to identify the goals for the family, which guide the goals for the meeting. The case worker identified two goals: to discuss future placement for Susan, and to give a comprehensive update on Susan's progress since the last CFT Meeting that was one month ago.

Next, the caseworker identified any and all services that were currently in place for the child and for the family. In Susan's case, most services at the time were through her group home such as group therapy and individual counseling. Other services included Medicaid and an Individualized Education Program (IEP).

Susan's psychologist gave an update of Susan's progress at the group home as well as some regressions. She explained patterns of Susan's behavior and what she had observed to be triggers of Susan's anger and violent behavior. She explained that Susan was learning the difference between direct and indirect threats and she stated that Susan tended to threaten the people at the group home who made her mad. She described Susan's behavior as "explosive" and brought attention to the fact that this type of behavior was usually a result of Susan being told "no" to something she wanted to do or being told to do something she did not want to do.

Since she had been in the group home, the police had been called multiple times. The psychologist shared that Susan strategically calmed down when the police were called or were present. Susan was aware of an upcoming court date she had in a few weeks that would determine her future placement and whether she would return to the same group home or not.

Susan did not realize that there was a possibility that she would not be returning to the same group home after her court date. Others in the room tried to explain that her behavior and lack of progress would likely result in her being sent to a different home for high-risk teenagers. This began to upset Susan and she started to cry. She explained that she had learned from her mistakes and she believed she was "doing better now" at her group home. She shared that when she first got there, she behaved badly because she did not know she was going to be there and she was angry, upset, and hated it. Now that she was used to it however, she was following the rules and doing what she was supposed to. She shared that she did not want to go somewhere new.

Susan spoke in detail about how she had been improving and was working on her bad behaviors. She said that therapy had helped her work on calming herself down when she got angry with people. She said she knew how to walk away from a situation that was angering her instead of putting her hands on people. She shared that she had learned a lot at her group home and now she understood what was expected of her.

Susan's family members as well as the other supports in the room seemed to question Susan's claims of improvement. They explained that Susan did not seem to understand the severity of the consequences of her actions. They shared that her history of misbehaving would overshadow the short periods of time that Susan showed improvement. They stated that she must maintain her improved behavior for extended periods of time, which would demonstrate genuine progress. Susan's family members emphasized how important it was for Susan to behave herself between now and her court date, which meant no yelling, fighting, or disrespecting the staff at the group home.

Susan began crying hysterically. She continued to repeat how well she was doing now and how she had learned her lesson. Everyone tried to explain that at this point it would be up to a judge to evaluate Susan's progress and changes in behavior. The caseworker shared that a recommendation would be given to the court to temporarily place Susan in a different group home for high-risk teenagers.

The room was silent and Susan was hysterical and furious on the other end of the phone. Her psychologist suggested they hang up and her family said goodbye to Susan. A tentative follow-up CFT Meeting was arranged for a date after Susan's court date and placement decision. Each person received a copy of the MOU from the meeting as the meeting concluded.

This case was challenging for several reasons. As one of my first cases, it was difficult to facilitate communication while two of the parties were not present in person. The nature of this case made it additionally difficult because I was unsure how to go about developing a case plan when the ultimate decision of Susan's future placement lay in the hands of a judge. As an inexperienced mediator, I struggled to focus and redirect the conversation when it seemed that there was an outcome that was completely out of anyone's control.

QUESTIONS FOR DISCUSSION

1. What are some possible ways the mediator could have redirected the focus of the discussion when Susan began to get upset?

2. What types of questions could the mediator have asked Susan during different stages of the meeting and why?
3. What types of questions could the mediator have asked the case worker to ensure that everyone at the meeting understood what was going on in Susan's case in terms of future placement?
4. How might the meeting have been different if Susan and her psychologist had been in the room with everybody else?
5. What are some alternative or additional goals that could have been set for the family and/or for the meeting?

Chapter 3

The Most Essential Mediator Skill: Effective Questioning

Merri L. Hanson

Most professions have democratic test-based skills and knowledge criteria for admission. Yet admission doesn't equate to effectiveness. Those of us who educate and train mediators recognize the "it" factor when we see it; that person who possesses those key qualities for real effectiveness as a mediator. Yes, others can learn the necessary knowledge and skills and they will be effective to varying degrees.

During the last few decades, several attempts have been made to identify the essential skills, knowledge, competencies, or capacities that effective mediators must demonstrate. Christopher Moore's seminal book "The Mediation Process," first published in 1986 and reprinted several times since, cites the six key roles of mediators as:

* *Helping parties deal with feelings that are blocking them from focusing on constructive problem solving*
* *Designing and guiding a negotiation process*
* *Facilitating a creditable and useful exchange or presentation of substantive information*
* *Helping parties develop and evaluate alternatives*
* *Providing a workable problem frame for communicating and problem solving on key issues*
* *Closing the deal*

Mediator's Institute of Ireland (MII) has a more consolidated approach to this list of core mediator competencies:

* Managing the relationships
* Managing the process
* Managing the content
* Managing the self

Finally, the Association for Conflict Resolution (ACR) on October 10, 2011 adopted "Model Standards for Mediator Certification Programs" which are very similar to those promulgated by MII. Standard I is as follows:

STANDARD 1—BALANCED MEDIATOR CORE COMPETENCIES

Certifying programs will assess applicants for mediation certification based on their ability to:

* Attend to procedural justice (the parties' sense of having been dealt with fairly)
* Support self-determination, collaboration, and/or exchange among the parties
* Manage content and the issues discussed in mediation
* Appropriately deal with personal, emotional, and relational issues

Whether a mediator is managing relationships, the process, content, procedural justice, or party self-determination, one core skill that is essential is that of asking effective questions. Too often we forget what purpose those questions serve, and surely they need to serve relationships, content, procedural justice, and party self-determination and to do so through the promotion and facilitation of effective dialog and engagement.

For years I have sought solid guidance on effective questioning techniques in the context of mediation. This chapter will focus on what is indisputably one of the most fundamental mediator skills: effective questioning. We will explore how questions can take you down a Learner path or a Judger path (Adams, 2009), the necessity of asking emotion questions in addition to the pursuit of logic. We will examine standard question forms and add "The Six Thinking Hats" (DeBono, 1985) to our understanding of the content of questions. We will consider how various question forms and content are particularly useful in certain parts of the mediation process. Finally, we will consider the "how" of asking questions, the non-verbal part, which in the end is the weightiest factor in facilitating effective dialog.

Which Path Are You On? Which Path Do You Want to Be On?

Perhaps the most helpful general questioning tool that I have found in recent years is Marilee Adam's notion of questions taking a conversation down either a "Judger path" or a "Learner path." This analogy has useful face value and provides a simple conceptual frame to guide questioning. While Adam's construct is two-tailed, Judger path/bad and Learner path/good, it can be quite useful for a variety of questioning objectives (particularly if you forget the bad/good distinction).

The Judger Mindset is one that focuses on blame and domination. It tends to be inflexible and defensive. The Judger approach is characterized by debate to win at the expense of the other (Adams, 2009). While this approach would not be helpful in facilitating open dialogue, it certainly has value in proceedings in which allocating fault is important.

The Learner Mindset more closely aligns with the role of a mediator in facilitative processes in which the parties must make their own outcome decisions. Questions are asked from a win-win perspective, one that values dialogue and discussion of differences. The Learner perspective values listening for commonalities, facts, understanding, and seeks to resolve and create (Adams, 2009).

To follow are sample Learner/Judger Questions:

Judger	Learner
What's wrong?	What works?
Whose fault is it?	What are you responsible for?
What's wrong with you?	What do you need?
How can you prove you are right?	What can you learn?
How will this be a problem?	What are the facts? What's useful about this?
Why is that person so stupid and frustrating?	What is the other person thinking, feeling, and needing?
How can you be in control?	What's the big picture?
Why bother?	What's possible?
(Adapted from Adams, 2009)	

In facilitative mediation, parties typically find resolution because they learn things that they didn't previously know or understand. Facilitating the journey of others down a particular path—Judger or Learner—becomes the task of the mediator. For the participant already on a learner path, it simply requires asking questions that keep the person thinking along that path. For the participant trudging down the Judger path, the mediator needs to ask questions that engage Learner thinking and feeling. This shift makes a tremendous difference in mood in the mediation, but may be challenging for participants who have little experience with Learner thinking.

The general Judger/Learner Mindset distinction has tangible value for the mediator. You have a visceral sense of which path the dialog is on—hopefully it is the path you want to be on. If not, your work will be more challenging.

A Word about Persuasion: Ethos, Pathos, and Logos

At this juncture, it might be helpful to point out that the remainder of this chapter treads an old path in some new ways. Aristotle's notion that ethos, pathos, and logos were the three prongs of persuasion holds true when it comes to facilitating dialogue in which the participants must persuade one another to reach mutual, consensual outcome decisions. As such, ethos (credibility) will be discussed as a nonverbal construct; pathos (emotion/feeling) will be viewed from a neuropsychology perspective; and logos (reason) will be explained from a more classical perspective. But not in that sequence . . . .

First, emotions.

The Well of Emotion

The well is deep and the water can be wide when it comes to emotion in mediation. Whoever posited the myth that one could, or would want to take the emotion out of negotiations, sent us down a futile path. How can parties be moved to make decisions or change their minds without acknowledging the role of emotion? We even have strong feelings (emotions) about facts. During my early work with scientific organizations I thought that facts and reason would play a primary role in decision-making. What I learned, however, was that scientists have intense feelings about their formulae and theories (i.e., intense emotions).

What do we know now about the role of emotion in decision-making? We now know that emotion is a necessary component in making decisions. For instance, those with impairment to the emotion processing centers of the brain demonstrate impairment in the ability to make decisions (sometimes even simple ones like "do I take the road to the left or the road to the right to get home?"). As a result of the seeming magic of the fMRI *(functional Magnetic Resonance Image),* we can see the emotion processing centers alight with electrical activity in moments of sudden insight as well as in moments when we speak emotion words (Lehrer, 2009). There is ample research on the role of emotion in making decisions on game shows like "Deal or No Deal?" in which participants could calculate the mathematical probabilities of offers but routinely fail to do so because they are swept up in emotion.

In the "Upside of Irrationality," Dan Ariely (2010) argues that from a rational perspective, we should only make decisions that are in our best interest. But we don't. Think of the last major decision you made (a marriage, a divorce, a new home or car purchase, which university to attend, etc.). Walk back through the criteria you used in making that decision. How did you know you reached the decision you wanted? I'll bet that something made you feel some way that you wanted to feel (e.g., it just felt like "home," I felt like we were meant to be together, etc.). There is ample research on the role of mood in decision-making and one's satisfaction with negotiated outcomes as well as whether a moment will or won't be a teachable one (Lehrer, 2009; LaBar, 2012; Maddux, et al, 2007; Shapiro, 2004; Ubel, 2012). Good mood = satisfaction with outcomes.

Anchoring is another negotiation construct worth exploring. What emotional anchors have people developed in a negotiation? An emotional "anchor" is a subjective predisposition about something; for instance, that I can only agree to an outcome that meets a particular emotional need (revenge, dignity, growth, etc.), or must maintain the view that you are evil and not to be trusted, in order to meet my own need to feel correct or superior. In negotiations you can often spot emotional anchors at play when someone seems irrationally devoted to a particular view despite better objective evidence.

Framing becomes another important tool in understanding the role of emotion in mediation. How are ideas or offers being framed—as gains or losses? We know that gains boost positive emotions and losses generate negative emotions and avoidance. For example, Peter Ubel's recent work on doctors' framing of medical decisions really makes you think about the importance of the frame (Ubel, 2012). Ubel's study on options for prostate cancer treatment underscores how important the frame is for making medical decisions. Are outcome probabilities framed as likely successes with statistically minimal problems, or are the statistical probabilities of success overshadowed by complex lists of problems? In Ubel's studies patients often choose riskier treatment options largely because of the way they are framed.

Finally, Kevin LaBar of the Center for Cognitive Neuroscience at Duke University explains the important connection between memory and emotion (LaBar, 2012). LaBar says that memory is always a reconstructive process, and that emotion is more powerful in the reconstructive process than is neutral information. Hence, we remember the emotional parts of the story better than the neutral parts. LaBar also talks about reconsolidation of emotion (a current hot topic in memory research). In short, every time you recall an event, you are reconsolidating and restoring it for retrieval at a later time. The important thing for mediators to note is that how you ask for the memory to be recalled will result in a new reconsolidation. In other words, the memory continues to change over time. Are you asking about the "worst time . . . ," or "a time that worked . . ."?

Let's connect what we have learned about emotion with ways that mediators can ask questions that facilitate engagement with the kinds of emotion that will help parties find consensual solutions.

Here are some tips for effectively engaging emotion in mediation.

* Think of ways to attach emotion to messages you want a client to remember. Meaningful messages stick.
* Use narrative . . . telling and retelling of the story . . . to actually change how memory is stored.
* Ask questions that invite recollection of positive memories and then build upon those times that worked.
* Name the emotions you think are being expressed.
* Invite participants to name emotions they are experiencing.
* Frame questions appreciatively (what is desired, valued, etc).

The Basics of Logic

Thinking logically, analytically, and sequentially is easier for some than for others. In thinking about logic, we are essentially focusing on how to effectively encode messages, and in this case, how to effectively encode messages in facilitative mediation processes.

While Western logic is not the only logic system, it is the logic system with which we from Western European traditions are most familiar (if not proficient). As such, "logos" (logic/reason), is often done inductively or deductively. And while most of us may have hazy recollections of inductive and deductive forms of writing from 6th grade composition class, few could explain them now. And why is this relevant? Because the way you structure an idea and set it out for consideration can make it easier or harder for people to consider.

Inductive Reasoning

Inductive reasoning is when one argues an issue from a specific contention (claim) and then supports that contention with a series of specific proofs.

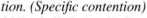

> **Example:** *Most EEO claims never reach the stage of full investigation. (Specific contention)*
> *93% of all claims filed are found to lack prima facie bases. (specific proof)*
> *Many claimants opt to resolve their claim through mediation or other less formal means than proceeding with investigation. (specific proof)*

Arguing inductively is most successful when your specific contention, or claim, is widely accepted and understood, and then followed with specific proofs that support the claim. One can think of inductive reasoning as pyramidal in "shape" . . . starting with your point, and then building a base of support.

Deductive Reasoning

Deductive reasoning is when one argues an issue from specific proofs and then arrives at a conclusion or contention (claim).

> ***Example:*** *93% of all EEO cases that opted for resolution through ADR were resolved. (specific proof)*
> *Those who participated in ADR processes to resolving EEO complaints express significantly higher satisfaction with outcomes than those who participated in the traditional investigative process. (specific proof)*
> *Therefore, ADR processes are more effective than the traditional EEO investigative process for resolving EEO complaints. (Specific contention; conclusion)*

Arguing deductively is generally more effective if your listener might not readily accept your specific contention or claim. You place your proofs up front where the listener will be more likely to listen rather than dismiss, and then conclude with your claim. Your listener will attend to what you say longer and will be less likely to automatically dismiss your claim.

So, how can mediators use inductive and deductive forms of reasoning to more effectively facilitate discussion in mediation?

* If a participant states controversial conclusions as "facts," ask them how they came to that conclusion. Ask them to walk you through their proofs or evidence. (Inductive) For instance, "I've been discriminated against because I am over 40 years of age" is a conclusion. Ask the person how they came to that conclusion. This will open up thinking and provide an opportunity for dialog and discussion of contravening proofs.
* When parties state conclusions as "facts," and they have difficulty providing a foundation of support, they are likely confusing "beliefs" with "facts." Beliefs are often not amenable to proofs. Sometimes participants are able to let go of an unsupported belief if their most important interests are being met; sometimes they are not. In situations when they still cling to unsupported beliefs, work the beliefs as you would emotions and try to understand the interests the belief is serving. (Inductive)
* Invite discussion of proofs or evidence before asking for conclusions. This will keep all listening longer than if you ask for a controversial conclusion followed by proofs. (Deductive)
* Spot the form of logic a participant seems to favor. Use that easy form of logic to facilitate dialogue. If there seems to be a disconnect between parties that is logic based (deductive vs. inductive), try to engage both forms of thinking and foster flexibility on the part of participants.

    ❋ Ask participants what evidence they would find meaningful, and see if you can facilitate disclosure thereof.

Inductive and Deductive forms of logic are important to robust dialog and problem understanding. Remember that one of the reasons Sherlock Holmes was so successful was because he never allowed himself to reach conclusions before he had all the evidence.

Standard Questions Forms

There are a variety of schemes for understanding question forms. In this section we will explore two general categories of questions: the open question, and the closed question. For each general category there are a variety of sub-categories: direct questions, indirect questions, leading questions, and probing questions. After clarifying these questions forms, we will explore the utility of particular question forms for particular tasks and parts of a facilitative mediation process (Adapted from Jandt, 1994). Bear with me for a bit; this will seem very technical, but it is critical to mediator success.

Open Questions
Open questions are broad and unstructured. They are questions that open-up an area the neutral desires the parties to talk about. Open questions cannot be answered with a simple "yes" or "no."

Examples: What do you hope to accomplish in this mediation?
              In your own words, what happened that brought you to file this complaint?

Advantages of Open Questions
1. They reveal priorities (not necessarily what you assumed).
2. As respondents can structure their answers however they wish, they use their own vocabulary and understanding and may reveal important information you had not considered asking about.
3. Respondents reveal frames of reference (i.e., how they perceive the situation).
4. They reveal how articulate the respondent is.
5. They reveal the respondent's knowledge.
6. They reveal the respondent's emotional state.
7. They permit catharsis.
8. They give recognition to the respondent by simply inviting them to tell the story from their perspective.
9. Open questions are least threatening to the respondent as they appear to have no right or wrong answers.

Disadvantages of Open Questions
1. They are time-consuming.
2. They make conversational control difficult (i.e., controlling who has the floor and when).
3. Recording information is more difficult when presented in free-form fashion (i.e., structuring).
4. Respondents may feel inhibited not knowing how much detail to give.

Closed Questions

Closed questions are a form of direct question that structures in the question itself how the respondent can answer. Multiple-choice questions are an example of closed questions. The most extreme form of closed question are "yes" "no" questions.

Examples: On the average, how many days per week in the last month have you reported late to work?—one or two, three to five, five or more?
Are you familiar with the policies and procedures regarding application for leave?—yes/no?

Advantages of Closed Questions
1. They solicit exactly the information that is required.
2. They are time efficient.
3. They can reduce threat by making an answer an acceptable choice within the question itself.
4. They are most appropriate when it is only necessary that the information be within a range and specific information is not required.

Disadvantages of Closed Questions
1. They assume the respondent understands the categories.
2. They limit answers to exactly what is asked for.
3. They can be threatening because elaboration is not permitted.
4. They have demand characteristics (i.e., they make it appear that the respondent must pick one of the alternatives).
5. Particularly if overused or massed together they can give the respondent the impression of being interrogated.

Direct Questions

Direct questions demand specific information. They assume that the respondent knows the information and is willing to answer the question.

Examples: What time did you take leave for the doctor appointment?
When did Tom become your supervisor?
What was your most recent performance rating?

Advantages of Direct Questions
1. Major way to exercise topic control.
2. They solicit exactly the information that is required.
3. They are time efficient.
4. They can assist a respondent in reconstructing an event.
5. They are most appropriate when the answers do not require elaboration.

Disadvantages of Direct Questions
1. They limit answers to exactly what is asked for.
2. They make it difficult for respondents to elaborate or explain their answers, and respondents may, therefore, become frustrated.
3. They have demand characteristics (e.g., exact times).
4. They can be more threatening than open questions.

Indirect Questions

While many questions asked by mediators are direct, in some situations direct questions may not be effective; **1)** in situations of social desirability (e.g., requiring the socially desired answer), and **2)** in situations of high threat (e.g., requiring sensitive personal information). Hence, we may ask for this information indirectly (e.g., "Do you feel that your supervisor had any reason to assume you are gay?" instead of "Are you gay?").

Indirect questions involve inference—derivation of a probable conclusion from a premise or from evidence. Indirect questions should be followed by direct questions later to verify assumptions.

Examples: How do you feel employees should be disciplined for arriving at work late?
How do you think your supervisor will describe your behavior?

Advantages of Indirect Questions
1. In areas of social desirability, they may yield more complete and accurate information.
2. They may be safe ways of introducing areas of high threat.

Disadvantages of Indirect Questions
1. The inferring inherent in indirect questions may lead us to false assumptions.
2. Respondents may find excessive use of indirect questions to appear to be manipulative.

Leading Questions

Leading questions "lead" the respondent to a desired response. Frequently they contain explicit or implicit references to the desired response.

Examples: How late were you when you arrived at work?

Did you sign the application even though in so doing you knew your statements were untrue?

Advantages of Leading Questions

1. They can help respondents talk about things that are highly threatening to them.
2. They can help respondents acknowledge the facts that they have been resisting.

Disadvantages of Leading Questions

1. They can increase threat, particularly if used in sequence.
2. As they limit the respondent's responses to what is suggested in the question, the answer may be biased.
3. If the respondent doesn't have the information or is unsure, they can be led to assert inaccurate information.

Probing Questions

Probing questions are asked in response to the answer received to a planned question in order to obtain further information. In investigations, it is a general rule to ask one probing question in response to each answer a respondent gives.

Example: Direct question: "About what time did the accident occur?"

Answer: "Seven o'clock."

Probe: "In the morning or evening?"

Advantages of Probing Questions

1. They motivate the respondent to clarify and expand on previous answers.
2. They help insure complete information by directing the respondent to think in detail.
3. They help insure understanding.
4. They help explore reasons, motivations, and feelings.
5. They present a way to repeat a question.
6. They are an important way to maintain topic control.

Disadvantages of Probing Questions

1. They can make it difficult to follow an organizational pattern.
2. They can reach a point of diminishing return (i.e., how much detail is enough?)

So, what's the big deal? Why do question forms really matter? As a mediator, if your question forms make it difficult for participants to have robust dialog, they are far less likely to resolve their problems and reach resolution. I know this seems very technical, and perhaps it is, but mastering question forms will make you a much more effective mediator. The good news is that "technical" doesn't have to be difficult.

Here is some basic guidance for mediators of facilitative processes.

* Generally speaking, favor open questions. Your three smart open question starters are:
  "What . . . ?"
  "How . . . ?"
  "Why . . . ?"
* Open questions require more elaborate answers, and hence, more information to explore. Parties usually reach resolution in mediation because they learn something new. Asking open questions increases the likelihood that participants will disclose new information.
* If you place a pronoun in the second position in a question, it will be closed. If you feel your mouth starting to say "Did you" "Are you" "Have they," etc.—stop. Change your question to a What, How, or Why and you will open it up.
* If a participant is reluctant to talk, ask them a few closed questions to make it easy for them to answer. (Then follow with open questions after they are used to hearing their own voice.)
* If a participant is hogging talk time, ask them very direct and specific closed questions to get them to wrap it up.
* Use closed leading questions as periodic summary to close one topic and shift to another. (So, it is really important to you that . . .)
* Ask open direct questions (specific topic, or to a specific person) to exercise topic control and manage balance of talk time.
* Indirect questions may be open or closed. They can demonstrate cultural sensitivity for people whose cultures favor indirect, high-context communication. They allow participants to think hypothetically, to imagine what they would do if they were the supervisor, etc. Indirect questions are a great tool for facilitating cognitive flexibility.
* The standard for probing questions is one follow-up probe per planned open or closed question. Dig!

In general, open questions are Learner questions and closed questions are Judger questions. Which path do you want to be on? Pay attention to how participants react to your lines of questioning. Do they become increasingly defensive? Do they open up? You, the mediator, are probably responsible for the effect.

THE "SIX THINKING HATS" APPROACH TO QUESTION CONTENT

The "Six Thinking Hats" facilitation tool is excellent for skillfully creating question content that facilitates a variety of types of thinking. Everyone has experienced conversations where you feel like you are speaking a different language from your counterpart. Why can't they understand the perspective you are trying to convey? According to Edward de Bono, author of *Six Thinking Hats* (1985), the main difficulty of thinking is confusion. We try to do too much at once. Emotions, information, logic, hope, and creativity all crowd in on us. It is like juggling too many balls. Some people can juggle six balls at once, and some only one!

The "Six Thinking Hats" approach enables you look at a problem using one way of thinking (e.g., one Hat) at a time. Emotional thinkers are asked to consider ideas wearing another hat—perhaps a rational hat. Rational thinkers are asked to consider an idea wearing perhaps a creative hat, etc. Questions become the primary vehicle for facilitating thinking from any particular perspective or hat.

Once parties are able to consider ideas from a variety of perspectives, they will be able to solve problems in more comprehensive ways. First, we will examine the six types of thinking the hats engage, and then consider how a mediator might use this awareness.

How to Use the "Six Thinking Hats" Approach

Each of the six following "hats" invokes a different style of thinking for the wearer. Each "hat" is characterized by a symbol (e.g., fire), which provides a simple handle for remembering the perspective of that "hat."

White Hat (Paper)
With this thinking hat, you focus on *data*. Look at the information you have and consider what you can learn from it. Look for gaps in your information and knowledge and try to fill them in or account for them. Analyze past trends and try to extrapolate historical data. White Hat thinking looks for facts, figures, and other evidence.

Red Hat (Fire)
With this thinking hat you look at problems using feeling and emotion, intuition, "gut" reactions, etc. Consider how you are affected, and how others are affected and feeling when considering problems and the decisions that are being made.

Black Hat (Night)
With this thinking hat you look at the negatives, barriers, obstacles, and causes for caution. This is important when making decisions because if the dark sides are not considered, you may experience unintended negative consequences that could have been overcome or avoided.

Yellow Hat (Sun)
With this thinking hat you consider the positives. The yellow hat provides the viewpoint of the optimist for whom the glass is always half-full. Yellow hat thinking provides the motivation and hope to keep going even when things are difficult.

Green Hat (Grass)

With this thinking hat you look for the creative and for new ideas. Creative thinking boosts creative problem solving and better quality decisions. It is a way of thinking that encourages freewheeling and suspends evaluation or criticism. Typical tools for Green Hat thinking include brainstorming.

Blue Hat (Sky)

With this thinking hat you organize and facilitate process control. This hat is typically worn when chairing meetings, considering structures, examining how things are organized, etc.

How might a mediator use "Six Thinking Hats" awareness? First, consider what thinking hat(s) you most frequently and least frequently wear. Most of the questions you ask are probably from the perspective of your favored hat(s). This means there is a lot of room for experimenting with different hats. Here is some guidance for using "Six Thinking Hats" awareness in mediation.

* In addition to becoming conscious of the hats you wear and in what circumstances, spot the hats that others are wearing. Wearing different hats is often part of the communication disconnect that has led to the problems between parties in mediation (e.g., the "Red Hat" emotional thinker vs. the "White Hat" logical, sequential thinker).
* Make it easy for a participant to answer your question by framing it in their most favored hat. It is simple for emotional thinkers to answer "Red Hat" emotional questions.
* Eventually switch up the hats! Once a participant is comfortable, change the question/change the hat and engage different thinking.
* Be sure to ask some "Yellow Hat" questions to provide hopeful frames and positive mood.
* Ask "Green Hat" questions to stimulate creative thinking around possible solutions.
* Don't forget "Black Hat" thinking when considering durability of agreement ("What could possibly go wrong?").

Have some fun and switch things up.

SOMETIMES IT'S NOT WHAT YOU ASK, BUT HOW YOU ASK IT

When I was a child my mother used to say, "It's not what you say, but how you say it that gets you in trouble!" This section will focus on the "how" of the message, the nonverbal part. For purposes of this chapter, the nonverbal part of the message is everything other than the words themselves. We will consider three types of nonverbal behavior: vocalics (the sounds that accompany speech), affect displays (facial behavior), and kinesics (body movement). Finally, we will consider some interesting related research on prosocial behavior and consider how mediators can do a better job of aligning the verbal and nonverbal parts of messages to make negotiation tasks easier.

I spend a lot of time in airports. Some months ago my husband was dropping me off at an airport for an extended business trip, but first we stopped for lunch at a nearby Mexican restaurant. Steve finds my food ordering habits amusing, so when I asked the waiter if I could have the special but switch out the burrito for a relleno, he rolled his eyes a little. The waiter shook his head side to side (a "no") but said "yes." Again I asked if the substitution could be made. Again the waiter shook his head and said "yes, of course." We went through several more rounds of this before the waiter started chuckling and I finally got it! The bottom line is, when the nonverbal message contradicts the verbal message, we pretty much discount the words.

If we hope to be persuasive and believable, it is imperative that the nonverbal part of our message support the words we speak. Another example in written form is that of the Stroop Color Word Test (Stroop, 1935). The respondent is asked to read a series of words . . . Red, Blue, Green, etc. The trick is that "Red" is printed in some color other than red, for instance blue, and so on. Try it. You will find it challenging to say the word rather than name the color of the print. Our brains classify "color word" as the typology, and we infer the color of the print instead of reading the word itself.

What are some of the nonverbal behaviors that mediators engage in that undermine the believability of their verbal messages? Behaviors associated with perceptions of trustworthiness, impartiality, empathy, and believability are critical to mediator success. We're finally at Aristotle's third prong of persuasion: ethos (credibility).

Let's explore three categories of nonverbal behavior that are related to ethos: vocalics, affect displays, and kinesics. We don't need to examine studies to know that in primary American culture a mediator must maintain and sustain fairly direct and balanced eye contact, have an open and centered body orientation in relation to the participants, a kind and encouraging facial expression (very slight smile), hands relaxed and on top of the table (not hidden, crossed, or over any part of the face). If I say I am impartial, but I focus most of my gaze on the party who readily returns my gaze, what message am I really sending? If my habit of crossing my legs causes me to inadvertently give one side the cold shoulder, what message am I sending? If I nod encouragingly to one but not the other, what am I communicating? If I ask you a closed question, but my pitch rises at the end, haven't I given you entre to keep talking? We want our nonverbal message to support our fantastic question content.

First, let's consider vocalics in support of effective questioning. Vocalics are the pace (how fast/slow), volume (how loud/soft; decibels), tone (shading), and pitch (musical note of the voice from high to low) of the voice. We want to be able to match these variables to the message. For instance, if someone in your mediation session has just revealed that they have six months to live (cancer), you want to adopt a sensitive, reverential tone and speak at a quiet volume. Conversely, if someone makes an outlandish statement, and you raise your eyebrows in surprise and ask a follow-up probe in a critical tone of disbelief, your behavior will likely be perceived as partial. If one party speaks at a rapid clip, and the other speaks at a snails pace . . . and the mediator matches one or the other, what impact does pace have on perception of the mediator's impartiality and trustworthiness. If a participant asks the mediator to speak louder or slower, and you ignore the request (or do so for only a few words before returning to the pace or volume that feels natural to you), will that participant feel respected and understood?

Tanya Chartrand's recent work in the area of mimicry and prosocial behavior (2012) provides a helpful frame for us to consider further reasons to align the nonverbal parts of our messages with the verbal component. Chartrand and others have studied mimicry extensively, and make a convincing argument that "Chameleons Bake Bigger Pies and Take Bigger Slices" (Maddux, et al, 2007). It turns out that humans perform better on a variety of tasks, including negotiations, when someone with whom they are interacting subtly or subconsciously mimics them . . . smiling (or not), head nodding, hand over mouth, crossed legs, eye behavior, etc. We have greater trust for those who mimic us. In order for mimicry to work when being done deliberately, it must be very subtle (e.g., you cross your legs . . . a few seconds later I cross my legs).

There is also hopeful news for mediators as models of desired behavior. It seems that there are power and status effects associated with mimicry as well. Lower power people are more likely to mimic the behavior of those they perceive to be of higher status. Mediators who persist in demonstrating a particular type of nonverbal behavior, are to some extent likely to see the other eventually emulate that behavior.

One interesting helpful effect of mimicry lies in the area of creative thinking (Mednick & Mednick, 1967). It seems that people who are mimicked engage in more convergent thinking because of the harmonizing effect of mimicry. Conversely, if the mediator wants to stimulate divergent thinking and greater creativity, this is more likely to happen if the mediator is not mimicking the participant.

Mimicry is a pervasive, fundamental human behavior. It is a process that is tied to many phenomena and has significant prosocial consequences in communication between two people. Mimicry creates a more general prosocial orientation towards others, and has an amazing impact on others' cognition, evaluation, motivation, and behavior. In spite of this wide-ranging impact, we remain unaware of mimicry most of the time.

Don't panic. While this business of nonverbal behavior is complex indeed, we can focus on a few key concepts that will help us better align the nonverbal and verbal parts of our questions.

* Develop greater awareness of your nonverbal habits; create a plan to better manage your nonverbal behavior while mediating.
* Mimic behavior you want to encourage (e.g., speaking slower, maintaining eye contact, etc.).
* Watch the way really good actors perform to the verbal message, and practice doing so yourself.
* Always think about how balanced your nonverbal behavior is.
* Make your tone match the content of your question.
* Only raise the end of question pitch when you want someone to treat a question as an open one.
* Think about what prosocial behaviors you want to promote in your session and model them.

CONCLUDING COMMENTS

So, what path do you want to be on? Do you want to promote Judger thinking or Learner thinking? How are you going to engage constructive emotions that provide the hope necessary for disputing parties to collaborate? The question remains the mediator's primary tool to:

* Attend to procedural justice (the parties' sense of having been dealt with fairly).
* Support self-determination, collaboration, and/or exchange among the parties.
* Manage content and the issues discussed in mediation.
* Appropriately deal with personal, emotional and relational issues.

The old is new. Persuasion still rests on the three-part foundation of ethos, pathos, and logos. Effective mediators must master their question forms, their question content, and align the nonverbal parts of the message to support their questions.

Remember that growth is incremental, and you don't need to be a mediator or in a mediation to practice effective questioning techniques.

SUGGESTED ACTIVITIES FOR SKILLS DEVELOPMENT

In addition to trying the tips noted at the end of each section of this chapter, to follow are some additional ways to build your questioning skills.

1. Listen to interviews on the internet, radio, or TV and keep a running list of the types of questions asked of various respondents. Track at least whether the question is open or closed; analyze the sequence. Spot the "Thinking Hats" engaged by the questions, and again spot any patterns. What was the impact of the question structure and sequence on the overall interview?

2. Video or audio tape yourself playing the role of mediator and analyze your question patterns as noted in suggestion one above. Develop an improvement plan for yourself.

Case Study: The High-Level Management Advisor

In Melinda's regular job she is a high-level management advisor. As a new mediator one of her greatest concerns was that she would have difficulty being impartial because she is so used to working with and representing the interests of management. In one of Melinda's early mediations she was perplexed that the management team seemed so resistant and hostile toward her and her efforts as mediator.

Melinda thought it would be helpful to "articulate" management's case through a series of closed leading questions because they weren't doing such a proficient job laying it out for their side. In her eyes, she was just trying to support management's efforts and to help them be more effective in the mediation.

Instead of understanding and appreciating Melinda's efforts, management became less engaged, angrier, and more positional. In response, Melinda found herself trying to convey the initiator's view with the hope of getting some engagement. Now the initiator was acting resistant.

What was happening?

QUESTIONS FOR DISCUSSION

1. What question form was Melinda using most frequently?
2. What unintended impact occurred as a result of Melinda's using that question form?
3. What problem has Melinda created?
4. How can Melinda recover from the problem she has created?
5. What unintended ethical violation has Melinda engaged in?

REFERENCES

Association for Conflict Resolution. (2011). *Model standards for mediator certification.* Available from http://www.acrnet.org/News.aspx?id=842.

Adams, M. (2009). *Change your questions change your life: 10 powerful tools for life and work* (2nd ed.). San Francisco: Berrett-Koehler Publisher.

Ariely, D. (2010). *The upside of irrationality: The unexpected benefits of defying logic at work and at home.* New York: Harper Collins.

Brannon, E., Cabeza, R., Huettel, S., and Purves, D. (2007). *Principles of cognitive neuroscience.* New York: W. H. Freeman & Company.

Chartrand, T. The impact of non-conscious mimicry. *Master Mediator Institute,* Duke University, 5 May 2012.

DeBono, E. (1985). *Six thinking hats.* New York: Little, Brown, and Co.

Forges, J. P. (1998). On feeling good and getting your way: Mood effects on negotiator cognition and bargaining strategies. *Journal of Personality and Social Psychology 74*(3), 565–577.

Jandt, F. (1994). *Effective interviewing for paralegals.* Nantucket: Anderson Publishing Co.

LaBar, K. Affective and social neuroscience. *Master Mediator Institute,* Duke University, 5 May 2012.

Lehrer, J. (2009). *How we decide.* New York: Houghton Mifflin.

Maddux, W. W., et al. (2007). Chameleons bake bigger pies and take bigger pieces: Strategic behavioral mimicry facilitates negotiation outcomes. *Journal of Experimental Social Psychology.* doi:10.1016/j.jesp2007.2.003

Mediator's Institute of Ireland (2007). *MII practitioner mediator core competencies. Practitioner Mediator Core Competencies.*

Mednick, S. A., and Mednick, M. T. (1967). *Examiner's manual: Remote Associates Test.* Boston: Houghton Mifflin.

Mnookin, R. (2010). *Bargaining with the devil: When to negotiate and when to fight.* New York: Simon and Schuster.

Moore, C. W. (2003). *The mediation process: Practical strategies for resolving conflict* (3rd ed). New York: John Wiley and Sons.

Rock, D. (2009). *Your brain at work: Strategies for overcoming distraction, regaining focus, and working smarter all day long.* New York: Harper Collins.

Shapiro, D. L. (2004). Emotion in negotiation: Peril or promise? *Marquette Law Review, 82,* 733.

Stroop, J. R. (1935). Studies of interference in serial verbal reactions. *Journal of Experimental Psychology, 12,* 643–662.

Ubel, P. (2012). *Critical decisions: How you and your doctor can make the right choices together.* New York: HarperOne.

Chapter 4

Mediating Staff Disputes at a Large State University

Jessica Katz Jameson

Academic institutions play an important role in modeling critical thinking, open and active exchange of ideas, and dialogue to achieve the goal of preparing students to become productive employees and engaged citizens. In order to create a culture that values collaborative conflict management, all parts of the university system should practice that behavior. Mediation programs that are available to administrators and staff improve the university's ability to institutionalize alternative dispute resolution practices and provide an important option for addressing staff disputes. Administrative staff members are central to academic institutions and they experience the same kinds of conflicts that are endemic to all organizations.

While campus mediation programs have proliferated since the early 1980's (Warters, 2000), services have often been made available to students and/or faculty, but not necessarily administrative staff. Higgerson (1998) defines support staff as all individuals who are not faculty appointments, generally holding secretarial, administrative, and student work positions (although they may also hold a variety of teaching, research, extension, and/or grant writing appointments). University support staff work with a wide variety of constituents, including students, faculty, department heads, deans, and other staff. Added to the challenge of the diversity of the campus population is the fact that many large, Research I Universities have an ingrained social structure among faculty (according to rank), tenure-versus non-tenure-track instructors, and staff, with support staff often at the bottom of the hierarchy. All of these aspects of the organizational climate create the preconditions for employee dissatisfaction and conflict. Because high staff turnover is frustrating for staff, students, and faculty, it is in the University's best interests to prepare for staff conflicts. There is a strong business case for mediation because universities compete to be the employer of choice for faculty and staff.

WHY MEDIATION FOR ADMINISTRATIVE STAFF?

In the landmark book on campus dispute resolution, *Mediation in the Campus Community,* Warters points out that there is often no appropriate venue for managing staff conflicts (2000). While universities may have a grievance process, staff conflicts over issues such as equal task distribution, work habits, or communication styles are inappropriate for a formal grievance. Higgerson (1998), one of the few authors to write about staff conflict specifically, recommends that department heads and chairs follow a three-step framework for managing staff conflict: minimize conflict potential; set the tone for airing disagreements; and make managing (not resolving) conflict the goal (p. 48). While Higgerson's advice is sound, the assumption that a department head should take on the role of third party can be problematic due to the power imbalances mentioned above. A mediation program that allows staff to speak with a neutral third party provides an option for airing disagreements and may result in the highest likelihood of satisfaction, relational maintenance, and improved working climate. The fact that staff conflicts may include conflict with the department head also supports the need for another conflict management alternative.

Research comparing mediation to other forms of alternative dispute resolution (such as arbitration), consistently finds that mediation leads to greater satisfaction with agreements (Brett, Barsness, & Goldberg, 1996), greater perceptions of fairness of the process and outcome (Blancero & Dyer, 1996; Brett, Barsness, & Goldberg, 1996; Fisher, & Keashly, 1991; Karambayya, & Brett, 1989; Shapiro, & Brett, 1993), and improved relationships with coworkers (Bingham & Pitts, 2002; Bush & Folger, 1994, 2005). Additional potential outcomes of mediation include increased employee empowerment, ability to manage future conflicts more independently, and improved managerial skills, especially listening (Bingham & Pitts, 2002; Bush & Folger, 1994, 2005). Further, research by Friedman, Tidd, Currall, & Tsai (2000) has shown that employees who address conflict directly and use collaborative strategies, such as mediation, have reduced levels of stress and improved perceptions of organizational climate. For all these reasons it makes sense to create or expand campus mediation programs to include conflicts among university staff.

Staff disputes are challenging because they often fall into the category of relationship conflict (Holton, 1998; Jameson, 1999). These conflicts generally present as "task" conflict, such as issues of scheduling (i.e., one employee wants to come in late or leave early), performance (i.e., a staff member accuses another of not meeting expectations), or differences in perceptions of interdependence (i.e., one staff member wants to work more collaboratively than another), which can result in a tendency to treat them as simple problems to be solved. For example, a conflict between two staff members may result when one staff member refuses to help the other. On the surface, this seems like an easy conflict to resolve: the department head simply tells employees they are expected to help each other out and if they cannot they should find employment elsewhere. There are several flaws in this strategy, however. For one, control over the outcome is left in the hands of the department head without participation of the disputants. This has been found to lead to perceptions of dissatisfaction and low procedural justice (i.e., Shapiro & Brett, 1993). Two, one employee may grudgingly agree to help the other, but show his or her displeasure with the employee in other ways, resulting in conflict avoidance rather than open discussion of the conflict. Three, and the key point here, the underlying issue has not been discussed and therefore the conflict itself has not really been managed: the department head has dealt with a symptom, rather than a cause.

Treating only the symptoms of conflict is problematic because it increases the likelihood of conflict reoccurrence. Let's say in the previous example that one employee believes her coworker is a loafer and is not doing her share of the work. This may be the true cause underlying the unwillingness to help out. In this case, the Department Head's solution to remind the staff of the need to work together has not resolved the real problem. The employee is not only likely to become even more frustrated with her coworker, but also to perceive the Department Head as "protecting" or "siding with" her. All these perceptions may only be in the head of the employee, but unless they are discussed, the conflict is more likely to escalate than improve.

TRAINING AND EXPERIENCE HELPFUL FOR STAFF CONFLICTS

In mediation, the attitudes, beliefs, and emotions underlying an employee's behavior are likely to be revealed and create an opportunity for increased understanding and actual transformation of the conflict (Galtung, 1996). Because the majority of mediation requests from staff in our institution are based on relational conflicts, it is important that those who mediate staff conflicts are open to a transformative style of mediation as opposed to a strict "problem-focused" style (Bush & Folger, 1994, 2005). The benefit of the transformative approach for staff conflicts lies in its focus on empowerment and recognition. By allowing parties to fully participate in as many decisions guiding the mediation process as possible, they have a greater stake in the process and are more satisfied with the final agreement. Allowing parties to talk about the issues that are most critical to them also reveals information about the staff members that they probably did not know about each other before, often leading to recognition of the other's situation that did not previously exist (the phrase "I had no idea you were going through that" is often the turning point in a mediation session).

Another important mediator skill for staff conflicts is managing power imbalances. There is an awkward irony on university campuses in that they promote critical thinking and open, participatory models of management, yet academic structures operate within a strict hierarchy. As mentioned above, staff may often perceive themselves to be powerless and as such, can feel intimidated in a mediation session where the other party is their department head, a faculty member, or another staff member with seniority or a higher pay-grade. Mediators need to recognize the power dynamics at play and their potential impact on the mediation, such as a party's willingness to speak openly or the potential to accept agreements that are not in their best interests. Wiseman and Poitras (2002) recommend that mediators address the power imbalance up front by clarifying the unique communication expectations within the mediation session. The mediator can explain that the mediation context requires openness and equal participation, which may be distinct from the procedures in the workplace. This can help reduce the higher-power party's fears of losing their authority, while creating a safe space for the lower-power party to share their concerns. If there is resistance from either of the parties, Wiseman and Poitras recommend an exploration of why the parties agreed to mediation in the first place. This question may help remind the parties of the problem they want to resolve and help steer them toward a more collaborative, trusting, path.

THE EMPLOYEE MEDIATION PROGRAM AT NORTH CAROLINA STATE UNIVERSITY

Our employee mediation program was designed specifically for NC State employees, including EPA (exempt from personnel act, mostly faculty) and SPA (subject to personnel act, mostly administrative staff).[1] The mediators are administrators and faculty from across campus who have participated in mediation training. At the inception of the program mediators were sent to an established mediation consulting firm in another state to complete a 40-hour general mediation training. In 2003, there were 17 trained mediators, (5 SPA employees, and 12 EPA employees, mostly non-faculty). Many of these mediators served in this capacity as part of their administrative work, such as human resources and Office for Equal Opportunity staff). In 2011 we were able to expand the mediator pool by offering an in-house mediation training. Two faculty members with expertise in conflict, relational communication, training, and mediation worked with the Employee Relations Director to develop and implement a 32-hour mediation training for the University context. There were 16 participants in the training, including 10 SPA, 2 EPA non-faculty, 2 EPA faculty, and 2 graduate students. At the time of this chapter we have 31 mediators consisting of 17 SPA and 14 EPA employees.

One benefit of having a variety of mediators is that it allows disputing parties to choose someone in a role that is most comfortable for them. Staff, for example, may want a faculty member to mediate as they may perceive them as neutral and someone they will not have to collaborate with professionally (or they may explicitly NOT want a faculty member to mediate, due to perceptions of power imbalance described above). In cases where faculty members are involved in a conflict with support staff, they may want to have a faculty member mediating as this will increase their comfort. We use a co-mediation model, so often there will be one administrator and one faculty member mediating each dispute, and this allows flexibility based on the situation and party needs. We almost never assign a mediator to a case where they have had any previous interaction with a party or where they are likely to have future interaction. This is, in fact, one of the benefits of having a mediation program in a large institution, as it greatly contributes to confidentiality and the parties' willingness to participate. (Those who are interested in creating a campus mediation program are strongly referred to the Warters book, cited earlier).

Mediators in our program have different attitudes toward preparation for mediating staff disputes. Some prefer to have information about the case and will discuss the parties' concerns with the intake officer (a member of the human resources department). Others prefer to know as little about the case as possible to reduce the chances of bias. The intake process at our institution works as follows: a staff member brings a complaint about a coworker to a department head or has called OEO or human resources. If deemed suitable for mediation (i.e., there is no obvious policy or legal violation that would require formal investigation), the party will be asked if they are interested in mediation. If that party is interested, an HR officer will contact the other party to see if they are also willing to attend a mediation session. Once both parties have agreed, the intake officer locates two mediators who are available. The lead mediator contacts the parties to set a date and time for the mediation, and then HR schedules a room in a neutral location (usually the student center or an administrative building where neither of the disputing parties work). The lead mediator does not communicate with parties individually before the mediation session (except in the event of scheduling changes).

When mediation was first introduced at NC State in 2003 there were 17 requests for mediation, largely coming from SPA employees. Of those 17 requests, 7 were successful (defined as participating to the natural end of the mediation process and either creation of an oral or written agreement or no agreement but parties' expressed satisfaction with the mediation). The other 10 cases ended up not pursuing mediation. In 2004–05 there were 11 requests for mediation, 5 of which were successful. Due to a brief period of transition during which there was no one running the mediation program, there were no requests again until 2008 when a new Employee Relations Director was hired and mediators were brought together to reinvigorate the mediation program. Since then we have received only 2–5 requests for mediation per year. The good news is that there have also been few to no grievances filed, suggesting that perhaps the economic situation of recent years has created an environment in which employees are less likely to report conflicts and risk "rocking the boat."

CHALLENGES OF MEDIATING STAFF CONFLICTS

As described above, campus mediation programs face the obstacles of publicizing the process and encouraging employees to participate. While the university website includes information on the mediation program, it is easily lost among hundreds of pages of protocols and policies. Information provided to all new employees in orientation may also be missed due to information overload at the start of a new job. Like many other organizations, we have found that the best way to publicize the mediation program is through successful cases and word-of-mouth diffusion (Jameson, 1998). The more department heads, deans, and directors are aware of the mediation program and its successes, the more likely they are to refer their staff to the program.

Aside from the challenges of diffusion and staff willingness to participate, there is also the challenge of adoption by managers and higher level administrators. Department heads, like other managers, may not appreciate the benefits of sending their staff to someone else, and may believe that not managing the conflict on their own will be seen by others as a sign of weakness (Jameson, 2001). This is exacerbated by the fact that academic department heads are tenured faculty and not required to attend conflict management training (in fact, while a variety of employee training programs are available to department heads and faculty, most do not take advantage of them as their evaluations and rewards are more directly connected to faculty teaching and research productivity).

Adoption of mediation is also challenging because leaders of all types view problem solving as part of their job, and often frame staff conflicts as problems to be solved (Kolb & Sheppard, 1985). Even when department heads do recommend mediation, support staff may fear taking a problem to human resources out of a belief that it will negatively affect future performance reviews. Human Resources departments face a potential conflict of interests in that they want to be neutral in mediation, yet they are advisory to senior leadership and must revert back to "management" mode in the event mediation is unsuccessful and the conflict becomes a formal grievance (Warters, 2000). Finally, even if a staff member is comfortable with the mediation process, they may perceive it as futile in a conflict with a tenured faculty member or another employee of higher status (Jameson, 2001).

In addition to making information available about a mediation program, there are more proactive ways to spread the word about mediation. Mediators, for example, should be ambassadors for the program and should make sure support staff and faculty they work with are aware of the program and its benefits. Because many employees have never experienced mediation before, it is helpful if someone can spend some time explaining the process to reduce any fears or misconceptions (we have developed a "What to expect during your mediation" brochure to help reduce uncertainty and anxiety). Arguably one of the best ways to improve understanding of the mediation process and encourage participation is to train more employees in mediation. While this may not be economically feasible for large numbers of staff, as mediator attrition occurs, it may be wise to provide mediation training to more department heads and support staff to increase awareness of mediation and institutionalize the process. This not only creates a larger cadre of potential mediators, but empowers more university staff to improve their own conflict management through the internalization of mediation principles. This can obviously have a ripple effect throughout the entire campus community. We are optimistic that we can renew interest in our own mediation program by bringing our newly trained and enthusiastic mediators together to talk about serving as ambassadors for the mediation program in their departments and throughout the University.

Another positive trend is that mediation is becoming more common and accepted as an alternative form of conflict resolution. This may be in part due to the proliferation of peer mediation programs in primary education, as well as increased use of mediation in organizational dispute systems and civil court procedures. Our experience is that when staff experience mediation, they appreciate the opportunity to communicate in a safe space, and often comment that it is the first time they felt heard and understood. While the mediation program here has not seen the level of participation we had hoped, there have been several successes to build upon and the seeds for more productive communication and conflict management have been sown. The following sections include a case study that illustrates how the relationship between two staff members can be transformed through mediation and a role-play that reflects the difficulties of power imbalance in a conflict between an administrative assistant and a Department Head[2]. These examples demonstrate the potential of mediation for managing staff conflicts.

CONCLUDING COMMENTS

Conflict is an inevitable and necessary part of organizational life, and universities are no exception to the rule. In fact, the very nature of universities as complex systems made up of diverse populations suggests that conflict should be anticipated, even welcomed, as members attempt to communicate and coordinate their activities. Numerous studies have demonstrated the effectiveness of mediation as an alternative to rights-based procedures that focus on determining the "right" solution, rather than improving understanding and empowering parties to create the "best" solution for their needs. It is completely consistent with the mission of our universities to develop conflict management practices that encourage communication, dialogue, and understanding. Such processes need to be made available to all members of the campus community, with the ultimate goal of institutionalization of mediation and constructive conflict management practices.

Case Study

Roberta and Margaret work together in facilities management. They share an office that includes a computer and a telephone. There is a table between the two desks for the telephone, but the phone often ends up on one desk or the other depending on who used it last. Because the office space is small, Roberta and Margaret often bump into each other when they are in the office at the same time.

The office situation has created a stressful climate for Roberta and Margaret, who share supervisory duties over the housekeeping staff. While they work different shifts, their schedules overlap so that they can coordinate employee tasks. Roberta and Margaret are constantly bickering, both to each another and about each other, and they undermine each other's authority with the staff. The rest of the department is experiencing the brunt of this conflict and have individually started to complain to the Director of Facilities. Academic departments have also begun to complain about poor service and maintenance standards and the Director recognizes that action must be taken to manage this conflict. The Director has tried to talk to Roberta and Margaret individually, but each one accuses the other of being uncooperative and neither one is willing to admit their role in this situation. For example, Roberta complains that Margaret's chair is always pushed all the way back and that she is unorganized. She also accuses Margaret of not communicating with her. Margaret complains that Roberta is always on the phone and she keeps the phone on her desk rather than returning it to its appropriate place on the table. Margaret is also upset that even though Roberta has been working at this institution for 10 years (8 years longer than her), she refuses to answer any of Margaret's questions and often snaps at her when she asks.

The Director recognizes that both of these employees are valuable—they both come to work on time and, despite their problems with each other, have a good work ethic and loyalty to the organization. She calls the human resources department for advice and learns about the possibility of mediation. She approaches

Roberta and Margaret and strongly recommends that they try mediation because the department can no longer run this way. Roberta and Margaret both agree to give it a shot.

The mediators assigned to this case are a faculty member and a member of the human resources department. Neither mediator has had any previous interaction with Roberta or Margaret. The mediators describe the mediation process, specifically pointing out that the goal of mediation is to help Roberta and Margaret create an agreement that will improve their working relationship. Roberta and Margaret both appear motivated to resolve their conflict so they can improve their comfort and satisfaction in the workplace.

Margaret was the one who originally requested mediation, so she is invited to speak first. She explains that she is very frustrated about their office situation and believes that the small space is the source of their problems. She confides that she has a bad back and must sit a certain distance from the computer keyboard, which means her chair is often pushed back and she knows this is a problem when Roberta is in the office. She also complains that when the phone rings, it is hard for her to get to because it is always on Roberta's desk, and out of her reach, rather than on the table between the desks, where it belongs. Margaret is also offended by the fact that Roberta is very short with her, and she is annoyed that Roberta will not answer her questions. The mediators ask Margaret a few follow-up questions to make sure she feels heard, and then they ask Roberta to share her view of the situation.

Roberta agrees that the office space is a problem. She is very frustrated about the chair, but did not realize there was a medical reason involved. She comments that she is on the phone a lot, and it is just easier to have it on her desk rather than constantly putting it back on the table when she hangs up the phone. She is upset about what she perceives as Margaret's lack of organization, which results in files not being put back where they belong, and post-it notes stuck everywhere. She claims that every time she comes into the office there is a post-it note on her computer with questions or things-to-do, and often she does not get messages accurately. Roberta also cannot understand why Margaret has so many questions when she had the "same exact job" in her previous workplace, where she worked as many years as Roberta has. She perceives Margaret as lazy and a slow-learner, and she does not feel it is her responsibility to get Margaret up-to-speed. Once again, the mediators ask a few clarification questions, and then move on to set the agenda for the mediation by asking both Roberta and Margaret what the key issues are that need to be addressed in order for them to feel better about working together.

With the mediators' help, Roberta and Margaret identify three main issues that need to be worked out: the placement of the telephone and Margaret's chair, communication with each other about what has happened during their shift, and the organization of paperwork and files. They agree to start with the issue of improving their communication with each other. The mediators ask them to come up with specific examples of times they had difficulty communicating. Margaret tells the story of a time they had to coordinate the repair of a leaky roof and she needed to ask Roberta to help her with the task. Roberta just said "you know where the forms are, get them signed and set up the work order." Margaret was hurt by Roberta's unwillingness to help, as she had never done this at a state institution before. Margaret pointed out that while she had held a similar job before this one, it was a private construction firm and their procedures were very different, which has made learning this job very stressful.

When Margaret had finished speaking, the mediators noticed a significant difference in Roberta's physical appearance and tone of voice. Roberta had clearly heard something new, which was confirmed when she said "I really had no idea that things were so different where you worked before. When you got this job, I assumed you knew all the procedures. When you asked me questions, I thought you were just lazy and wanted me to do the work for you, now I understand why you had questions. It must have been really hard for you this past couple of years."

At this point, all eyes were on Margaret, who said "you have no idea how much it means to me just to hear you say that you understand why it was hard for me." Margaret was a bit teary-eyed at this point, so a mediator jumped in and complimented the two for their good work listening to each other and pointed out that they had already made some real progress. At that point, the parties talked some more about specifics regarding how they might improve their day-to day communication with each other and how to organize the office files. After 20 minutes or so of working out those details, a mediator said, "Okay, we have addressed the issues of improving your communication and organizing the office, now we need to talk about the telephone and the chair." Roberta and Margaret both looked at the mediators quizzically and laughed. Roberta said "The telephone? The chair? Who cares about that, that's not important, we've worked out our differences and those things don't even matter now." They agreed that nothing about the telephone or chair needed to be included in the agreement, that those were "little" things that were bothering them because of these larger misunderstandings they had. They both felt that their relationship was different now, and looked forward to returning to the office and a more cooperative, less stressful climate.

QUESTIONS FOR DISCUSSION

1. Should the Facilities Director have intervened in this conflict *before* complaints started coming in? (What signs might there have been that a conflict was brewing?)
2. What assumptions did Roberta and Margaret make about each other's intentions prior to mediation?
3. What aspects of the *situation* may have led to a climate conducive to conflict?

4. What are the underlying interests or issues that helped explain Roberta and Margaret's behavior prior to mediation?

5. What was the role of empowerment and recognition in the transformation of Roberta and Margaret's relationship? What other beneficial outcomes might result from successful mediation?

The Margaret/Roberta scenario illustrates that by paying attention to empowerment and recognition, relationships can be transformed and mediation can lead to effective long-term agreements (Bush & Folger, 1994, 2005). Mediation is more challenging when there are significant power differences between disputing parties because the need for openness and participation stands in contradiction to the hierarchy of the typical academic institutional structure.

NOTES

[1]Readers interested in viewing the NC State University mediation policy are referred to: http://policies.ncsu.edu/regulation/reg-05-35-01.
[2]The case study and role play scenarios are based on a synthesis of actual cases. Details such as names, departments, and titles have been changed to protect any employees who may have been involved in situations like these.

REFERENCES

Bingham, L. B., & Pitts, D. W. (2002). Highlights of mediation at work: Studies of the National REDRESS® Evaluation Project. *Negotiation Journal, 18*(2), 135–146.

Blancero, D., & Dyer, L. (1996). Due process for non-union employees: The influence of system characteristics on fairness perceptions. *Human Resource Management, 35*(3), 343–359.

Brett, J. M., Barsness, Z. I., & Goldberg, S. B. (1996). The effectiveness of mediation: An independent analysis of cases handled by four major service providers. *Negotiation Journal, 12*(3), 259–269.

Bush, R. A. B., & Folger, J. P. (1994). *The Promise of Mediation: Responding to Conflict through Empowerment and Recognition.* San Francisco, CA: Jossey-Bass.

Bush, R. A. B., & Folger, J. P. (2005). *The Promise of Mediation: The Transformative Approach to Conflict* (Revised edition). San Francisco, CA: Jossey-Bass.

Fisher, R. J., & Keashly, L. (1991). The potential complementary of mediation and consultation within a contingency model of third party intervention. *Journal of Peace Research, 28*(1), 29–42.

Friedman, R. A., Tidd, S. A., Currall, S. C., & Tsai, J. C. (2000). What goes around comes around: The impact of personal conflict style on work conflict and stress. *The International Journal of Conflict Management, 11*(1), 32–55.

Galtung, J. (1996). *Peace by Peaceful Means: Peace and Conflict Development and Civilization.* Thousand Oaks, CA: Sage.

Higgerson, M. (1998). Chairs as department managers: Working with support staff. In S. A. Holton (ed.), *Mending the Cracks in the Ivory Tower: Strategies for Conflict Management in Higher Education* (pp 46–59). Boston, MA: Anker Publishing Co.

Holton, S. A. (1998). What's it all about? Conflict in academia. In S. A. Holton (ed.), *Mending the Cracks in the Ivory Tower: Strategies for Conflict Management in Higher Education* (pp 1–11). Boston, MA: Anker Publishing Co.

Jameson, J. K. (1999). Toward a comprehensive model for the assessment and management of intraorganizational conflict. *International Journal of Conflict Management, 10*(3), pp. 268–294.

Jameson, J. K. (1998). Diffusion of a campus innovation: Integration of a new student dispute resolution center into the university culture. *Mediation Quarterly, 16*(2) pp. 129–146.

Jameson, J. K. (2001). Employee perceptions of the availability and use of interests-, rights-, and power-based conflict management strategies. *Conflict Resolution Quarterly, 19*(2), 163–196.

Karambayya, R., & Brett, J. M. (1989). Managers handling disputes: Third party roles and perceptions of fairness. *Academy of Management Journal, 32*(4), 687–704.

Kolb, D. M., & Sheppard, B. H. (1985). Do managers mediate, or even arbitrate? *Negotiation Journal, 1*(4), 379–388.

Shapiro, D. L., & Brett, J. M. (1993). Comparing three processes underlying judgments of procedural justice: A field study of mediation and arbitration. *Journal of Personality and Social Psychology, 65*(6), 1167–1177.

Warters, W. C. (2000). *Mediation in the Campus Community: Designing and Managing Effective Programs.* San Francisco, CA: Jossey-Bass.

Wiseman, V., & Poitras, J. (2002). Mediation within a hierarchical structure: How can it be done successfully? *Conflict Resolution Quarterly, 20*(1) 51–65.

Chapter 5

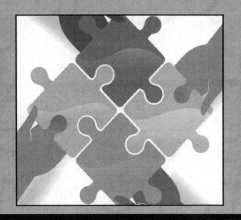

Conflict Coaching in the Federal Workplace: Is It Beginning to Eclipse Mediation?

Cynthia Mazur

"Blessed is the influence of one true human being on another." *George Eliot*

or

"We're here for a reason. I believe a bit of the reason is to throw little torches out to lead people through the dark." *Whoopi Goldberg*

Alternative Dispute Resolution (ADR) formally began in the federal government with the passage of the Administrative Dispute Resolution Act (ADRA) of 1990, Pub. Law 101–552 and Pub. Law 102–354, which was permanently reauthorized and amended by Pub. Law 104–320 in 1996. This was the first ADR legislation enacted by Congress. Thereafter Congress passed the Alternative Dispute

Resolution Act of 1998, 112 Stat. 2993. Collectively, these laws required agencies to adopt policies encouraging the use of ADR in a broad range of activities and required the federal trial courts to make ADR programs available to litigants.

In 1996, President Clinton issued Executive Order 12988 on Civil Justice Reform, directing federal litigation counsel to consult with the referring agency and utilize ADR as appropriate. On May 1, 1998, the President issued a Memorandum directing the Attorney General to lead an Interagency Alternative Dispute Resolution Working Group to promote and facilitate federal use of ADR. This Group, headed by the Department of Justice (DOJ), continues this work up to the present.

During these years, the Attorney General, Janet Reno, became a catalyst and champion of ADR use in the federal government. Mediation was the dispute resolution tool of choice for most agencies and the courts. Accordingly, when an employee approached the agency ADR office requesting services for workplace issues, mediation was generally the recommended course of action. It is important to note, that every agency had an Equal Rights Office (ERO) that is authorized to offer mediation as a step to resolving a discrimination complaint. Equal Employment Opportunity Office Commission (EEOC), Management Directive 110, 1999.

Some agencies have folded their ADR office into their ERO and taken the Equal Employment Opportunity Act as their authority. The EEOC is their partner. Some agencies have set up their ADR Offices independent of and distinct from the ERO, basing their authority on ADRA and partnering with the Department of Justice. These latter ADR offices are charged with a wider scope of conflict management activities by handling all of the other concerns that employees may have regarding the workplace. EEO complaints are not expected to make up the bulk of the agency's workplace issues. Moreover, these offices help with a wide variety of ligation cases, contracts and procurement, regulation and enforcement, and other issues with the public.

Without any organized plan, arbitration and mediation became the two primary tools for the federal ADR office. An arbitration program, however, can only be utilized if authorized by Congress or approved in advance by DOJ. Thus, mediation became the informal dispute resolution technique that was recommended again and again.

Throughout the 90s and most of the first decade of this century, federal ADR offices hired their staff focusing their requirements on professional mediation training and experience. While an extensive mediation background is critical, it is the transferability of these skills that has now become important. Conflict coaching is the fastest growing ADR technique being used in the federal workplace today. Regarding hiring the best candidates for ADR workplace disputes, training and experience in conflict coaching are in great demand. As discussed following, conflict coaching encompasses and expands upon the basic mediation skill set.

Some of the Drawbacks to Widespread Mediation Use

People don't like being associated with a dispute. Bernard Mayer states that when people turn to mediation it is because they are able to admit that there is a problem they cannot solve without the assistance of another (Mayer, 2004). Mediation crystallizes a problem and holds two people accountable for its resolution. By implication these two people are the ones who are responsible for causing it. Employees prefer to keep their disputes private especially from upper management if possible. Participating in mediation might reflect poorly on them. People think that utilizing mediation can be synonymous with broken relationships, failure, admitting weakness, and losing control. Accordingly, avoidance is the number one means of dealing with conflict.

Mediation doesn't address the larger or systemic group issues. Generally when there is an issue ripe for mediation, the whole workplace team is affected. Resolving an issue between two people may not address the larger system that is in play or the back story which will be a major factor in the team functioning. The request for mediation may be a symptom or a sign that interpersonal relations throughout the team or division have deteriorated. In the place of mediation, the ADR office will provide trainings in interpersonal communication, conflict management, negotiation, and problem solving. The office may be asked to conduct team building exercises, conflict coaching, climate assessments, and facilitations designed to look at the larger group issues. It is routine for an ADR office to be asked to undertake group work to enhance productivity, morale, and collaboration.

Mediation is viewed as a way to embarrass the other. One reason that mediation is not seen as the panacea it once was is the fear of retaliation. If an employee requests a mediation with his/her boss, this boss may feel that the employee is trying to humiliate or shame him/her. The boss may feel that the employee is playing "gotcha," and wants to undermine the boss' authority.

Sometimes the request for mediation catches the boss completely by surprise. The power shifts slightly in favor of the person requesting mediation. Even if the manager refuses to participate, he/she is put in an awkward position by turning down this request. And the manager is on notice that there is some type of dispute or problem which is being talked about.

As such, requesting mediation with one's boss can put things in motion that have unintended consequences. It is never clear how another will react to a request for mediation. Even if the other person agrees to mediate, one is never sure if thereafter they will hold a grudge. One employee can undermine another employee in subtle, covert, and disingenuous ways. One expects parties to mediation to come to the table in good faith, but every mediator will admit that one never knows a party's secret agendas. And the mediator cannot protect an employee from retaliation.

Additionally, the requesting party may be branded as a troublemaker and begin to establish a reputation for being confrontational, angry, or divisive in the workplace. To overcome such a risk takes more than courage. It takes an absolute faith in one's boss that he/she will not feel threatened or intimidated. The mediator can help to create a positive atmosphere around these conversations, but to go forward with a request for mediation is fraught with problems in the best of circumstances.

It would behoove all workplaces to attempt to change this culture, and reward people who honestly and openly try to reduce friction and misunderstandings in the workplace. Managers should receive recognition for proactively trying to solve problems and work things out with people. Many problems in the workplace result from poor communication and can be remedied by a ready willingness to address things quickly.

Case versus contact. One final reason for moving from mediation to other forms of ADR is that mediation presupposes a discrete issue that starts on a certain date and ends on a certain date. Often, workplace disputes are not like that. They have ambiguous beginnings, gather steam, grow at an unclear rate, and may or may not end with ongoing ADR support and encouragement.

Most workplace concerns move in a nonlinear fashion. As such, a person could contact the ADR office and over the course of time discuss facets of their workplace performance goals, relationships, aspirations, and setbacks. A relationship of trust and rapport with the ADR professional can deepen. In this context the person can see patterns in their work life and can come to understand themselves, their coping mechanisms, and their options better. This type of ADR does not work on a case model. It lends itself to one-on-one work over time. This is currently called, "Conflict Coaching." Conflict coaching is a powerful tool that can dispense with some of the drawbacks associated with mediation.

CONFLICT COACHING DEFINED

Let's begin with a brief, general definition of mediation. Mediation is "an extension or elaboration of the negotiation process that involves the intervention of an acceptable third party who has limited or no authoritative decision-making power" (Moore, 2003). This third party assists the principal parties in voluntarily reaching a mutually acceptable settlement of the issues in dispute. "Without taking sides or imposing solutions, the mediator's role is to assist the parties in identifying their needs and interests, generating options, and documenting agreements" (Schrock-Shenk, 2000).

Conflict coaching differs from this mediation model in several significant ways. Cinnie Noble (2011), an expert in conflict coaching, believes that conflict coaching is a one-on-one process in which a trained coach helps individuals gain increased competence and to gain confidence to manage their interpersonal conflicts and disputes. It is a goal-oriented and future-focused process and concentrates on assisting clients to reach their specific conflict management objectives. Conflict coaching is a self-conscious process with self-actualization as its main goal.

Another set of scholars, Jones and Brinkert (2004), define conflict coaching as a "face-to-face interaction . . . in which a coach and client communicate one-on-one for the purpose of developing the client's conflict-related understanding, interaction strategies, and interaction skills." Like mediation, conflict coaching is voluntary and can be terminated at any time. It is confidential and carries the same confidentiality exceptions as mediation, such as the mandate to report claims of fraud, waste, and abuse in the federal workplace, sexual harassment, and the threat of harm to self or others. The third party neutral in mediation becomes the second party ally in conflict coaching. And similar to mediation, this coach changes the dynamics and the outcome of the process (Goldberg, Frank, Sander, Rogers, & Cole, 2007).

Generally people are flummoxed, unsettled, and irritated by conflict. The conflict may impact the person's identity and ego. The coach can help the employee make sense of the conflict and capitalize on its challenges. Additionally, the coach can assist with developing leadership abilities, skill building, assessing career tracks, and anger management. Looking at the whole person and the larger workplace dynamics, the coach is meant to be a force multiplier for success.

The coach can inspire the employee around issues that normally might deflate an employee. For instance, the author and philosopher, Emmet Fox stated, "When you are in great difficulties, regard overcoming them as a great adventure." The coach is trained to keep the workplace experiences rich and satisfying. The root meaning of "confrontation" is based on "with strength." So as employees confront their issues they may gain strength. Some scholars correlate conflict resolution skills with interpersonal maturity and strength of character.

Conflict coaching provides a place where a person is able in private to get a handle on their strong emotions and work through them so they are under control. The issues can be addressed without anyone other than the coach knowing anything about it. Conflict coaching can help with emotional intelligence as a person tries to make sense of their reactions. They can practice new and more preferred ways of reacting. With the coach, the employee can talk through possible perspectives and motivations of others in the office.

Bush and Folger (2005) state that a person in conflict is self-absorbed and weak. A conflict coach can help an employee to enlarge his/her perspective and gain a sense of empowerment. The coach can be a teacher. The coach is an expert in problem solving techniques such as interest based analysis from all perspectives, a WATNA/BATNA analysis, brainstorming options, and techniques to access the right brain for intuition, creativity, and imagination. Many times people need the assistance of a second party in fully utilizing these techniques. Levels of creativity are particularly low when a person is stressed or conflicted. A major trait of a conflict coach is good listening skills. A quiet, confidential venue with a professional listener creates a de-stressing space.

A MODEL OF THE CORE STAGES OF CONFLICT COACHING

A student of conflict coaching would take at least a 40-hour training and thereafter have access to mentoring and clients. This person would be a skilled listener and have subject matter expertise in interpersonal relations, conflict management, leadership development, anger management, and emotional intelligence.

Cinnie Noble (2011) offers an advanced training of 40 hours and requires that coaches maintain their skills through skill-based discussion groups and international conference calls where those who have graduated from her classes work to improve skills, discuss issues, address concerns, and generally advance and professionalize the conflict coaching field.

Every coaching relationship is unique, and Noble (2011) and Jones and Brinkert (2008) teach widely different models. Nonetheless, the coaching relationship starts with a discussion of roles and expectations, confidentiality, and an explanation of the process. A generic model for conflict coaching in the federal workplace would also incorporate the following:

1. The employee describes the situation in detail. The coach can then ask the employee to try to summarize the issue in one sentence. The employee, with the help of the coach, sets a goal or series of goals he/she wants to work toward. Then the employee is asked to describe success. How will the employee know if they have succeeded?

2. If the issue involves another person, the coach helps the employee delve into the other person's point of view. What does this other person think, want, need, and assume? What motivates them and how do they view the employee and the situation? If an employee states that they cannot imagine what the other person is thinking, the coach may say, "But if you did know, what might it be?" This is an important step in the process. The coach helps the employee explore seeing the world from the other person's point of view.

3. If the issue involves approaching another person to discuss an issue or problem, the coach helps the employee rehearse the difficult conversation.

4. The coach gives the employee extensive feedback during practice sessions and helps the employee map out the logistics and the myriad twists and turns such a conversation could take.

5. Some models include appreciative inquiry as part of the core steps (Jones and Brinkert, 2008), which as an ADR tool is discussed next.

APPRECIATIVE INQUIRY

Appreciative Inquiry (AI) is a series of questions designed by the coach to direct the employee's attention to his/her highest values and best moments. The inquiry focuses the party on the values that underlie his/her commitment and attraction to his/her work. This often leads to wholly different perspectives. David Cooperrider, who developed the practice of AI, emphasizes the power of "anticipatory images," which he states can guide one's present outlook and behavior (Cooperrider, Whitney, & Starvos, 2003).

AI is based on several assumptions:

* Inquiry creates change,
* Positive questions lead to positive change, and
* Image inspires action.

The seeds of solutions are in the positive images which flow from the AI discussion. Through AI people consider the strengths they bring to the job. An employee can imagine how to build upon successful experiences. The exercise of answering AI questions can strengthen one's capacity to understand, anticipate, and heighten positive potential. AI can be an opportunity for personal and professional transformation.

James Trinka, who has researched "great leaders," rigorously researched managers from the Internal Revenue Service and studied the results of their 26 trait performance evaluation (Wallace & Trinka, 2007). After several years, he found that managers improved their overall score if they worked on their best areas of the evaluation. Statistically, he demonstrated a significant increase in performance scores if the person focused on improving his/her strengths rather than on trying to improve upon on his/her weaknesses. Accordingly, AI directs the imagination away from a discussion of what is wrong. AI does not focus on solving problems or weaknesses.

AI elicits consideration of the elements of the employee's success. The coach might ask the party to consider the following AI questions:

1. What first attracted you to your present work?
2. Relate a time when you were really feeling alive, creative, and excited about your work.
3. Without being humble, describe what you value most about 1) yourself; 2) your work; and 3) your organization.
4. What is the most important thing your work has contributed to your life?
5. Describe how you stay professionally affirmed, renewed, energized, enthusiastic, and inspired.
6. If you were to consider your greatest strengths in the workplace, what would be your top three?
7. What can management do to increase your opportunities to use your strengths?
8. If you were to overhear someone talking enthusiastically about your job performance, what might they be saying?

AI helps people envision how they can create more life-giving moments, and people reflect on how management and family can support and sustain their best experiences at work (Hammond, 1998; Royal, 2001). AI has four cycles.

Discovery: The party explores the life-giving properties in the exceptional moments. The employee uncovers themes and values in the moments when he/she feels most alive on the job.

Dream: The party creates a situation or role where these become the norm. Because these dreams are based in real life past experiences, they create hope.

Design: The party sets forth principles to guide change. As the employee talks about his/her ideal for the future, it becomes clearer.

Destiny: The party can evolve into a preferred future image. A person can shift from "bearing" his/her present situation to fostering the elements that most inspire and support him/her (Watkins, Mohr, & Kelly, 2006).

The AI process elicits a quality of conversation and storytelling that can heighten a person's positive potential. An employee can gain a sense of commitment, confidence, and affirmation. Cooperrider would say, "Inquiry is inseparable from action" (Cooperrider, Whitney, & Stavros, 2003). The coach and employee produce a sense of liberation, creativity, admiration, and connection with an AI conversation. The employee becomes empowered to evoke positive capacity and to articulate vibrant and realizable visions. The images become hopeful and expansive. The employee's imagination can initiate and generate constructive avenues for change.

There is a natural tendency to focus on the "problem." It is human nature to try to spend most of the conversation identifying and describing what is wrong. Using AI the coach changes the normal discourse to a conversation about "What is right." One example involves a coach who was hired to improve communication and productivity as various regional teams were not functioning well together and seemed at cross purposes as they worked as a group on a national project. The coach decided to interview each team and develop a report of best practices of interoperability. The report highlighted the ways the people were working well together and listed ways management could support the practices that were really effective. The report engaged the teams as well as upper management, and best practices were implemented to become standard practices.

The core stages of conflict coaching are setting goals, envisioning the other person's point of view, rehearsing a difficult conversation, and giving detailed and honest feedback. The model can include appreciative inquiry as appropriate. Each session ends with clear next steps, homework, and a check in-check back date. The coach may want to commend the employee's commitment and development.

ROLE OF THE COACH

In the private sector coaches have created a cottage industry. There are nutrition coaches, executive coaches, life balance coaches, values coaches, exercise coaches, even happiness coaches. Many universities offer leadership coaching as an academic program where the institution educates and trains students to coach senior executives. In turn, organizations pay hefty sums to hire people to coach their top level management.

A conflict coach is not an investigator, fact-finder, or decision-maker. The coach doesn't take the information gained to anyone or anywhere else. Instead, the coach listens, and uses appreciative inquiry, ALLURE, as discussed following, and skill building. The coach creates a space for private conversations and self reflection. One of the most important facets that the coach offers is positive regard. At the same time, the coach is expected to give honest feedback about how the employee is managing him/herself through a conflict and reflect on other relevant behavior.

The coach models strategic thinking in preparing a blue print for desired outcomes. The coach is expected to model equanimity, good will, and a desire for excellence. Together the coach and the employee seek out and take advantage of all of the valuable resources that are available.

ALLURE

The coach should always be using the ALLURE process, which stands for:

* **A**sk and be Curious,
* **L**isten for Interests,
* **L**ink the Parties Together,
* **U**nsettle Assumptions,
* **R**e-Position the Parties, and
* **E**ncourage New Narratives (Mazur, 2011).

Ask: the coach models being curious. There is a massive amount of current literature regarding asking powerful and meaningful questions (Adams, 2004; Marquardt, 2005; Strachan, 2006). LeBaron (2003) discusses maintaining a spirit of inquiry for enhancing interpersonal relations and deepening understanding. The foundation of good communication and good conflict management is the spirit of inquiry.

Listen: the coach listens deeply; he/she will hear needs, assumptions, values, emotions, identity issues, interests, and the seeds of solutions. Through listening the coach can hear underlying and related issues, barriers, challenges, and areas for growth. In and of itself, listening is a balm. Samantha Hardy cites Mary and Kenneth Gergen for the proposition that the act of listening can help people cross boundaries of meaning and help establish mutuality (Gergen & Gergen, 2006; Hardy, 2008). When people feel heard they are able to gain greater perspective and take in other points of view.

Link the Parties: the research shows that if disputes or conflicts can be framed as a dual attempt to join forces to solve a problem together, changes of resolution are significantly higher. LeBaron (2003) recommends offering images of connection and of responsible, mutual relationships. The parties are linked through common interests. The participants belong to each other in the conflict narrative. They both want (1) trust and respect in the workplace, (2) to work for a successful organization, (3) to do a good job, (4) to be valued for doing their job well, and (5) to provide excellent customer service. They have shared responsibilities for these things as well. The coach can emphasize interdependence, for example, and that each needs to do his/her part and to recognize that no one can be effective alone. Worlds can be re-narrated through cooperative dialogue and engagement.

The coach emphasizes the individual and collective interest in getting everyone to understand each other despite differences (Drabek, 2003). The workplace brings together numerous diverse backgrounds involving race, gender, age, religion, and politics. There are many tools to help build trust in conflicted relationships (Warfield, 2009). The coach can move the focus from differences to commonalities. If the coach thinks that AI is appropriate, the coach can use it to build connection, affiliation, and concern. The employee could be asked what has worked well in the past between the employee and the other party and what qualities he/she admired in the other (Warfield, 2009).

Unsettle Assumptions: most people have a number of limiting assumptions. Assumptions may make life easier, but they also can undermine the truth. LeBaron (2003) references five cultural traps or lenses: (1) our way of viewing the world is normative, (2) all cultural knowledge can be categorized, (3) true cultural knowledge is beyond our ken, (4) our commonalities are emphasized over against our differences, and (5) our differences are emphasized over against our commonalities. These are false assumptions the coach can help the employee recognize and question. The coach will want to challenge the way the employee understands the world and point out inconsistencies or traps in the person's worldview.

Moreover, many people in conflict engage in negative attribution, which leads to assigning blame and malicious motives to another person; these assumptions are likely to be incorrect and can be unmasked. The coach may teach and ask the employee to apply the principles of the "Ladder of Inference," which is a practical method for dispelling assumptions. This model involves describing to the other party an incident, stating the assumption one is drawing from the story, and asking the other party to share his/her thinking (Schwarz, 2002).

Cobb (2000) suggests that the coach could destabilize the parties' conflict narrative. Hardy (2008) analyzes Cobb's three-step process for destabilizing and unsettling assumptions: (1) recalibrating the legitimacy of the speaker's construction of him/herself, (2) recalibrating the legitimacy of the speaker's construction of the other party, and (3) creating circular logic displaying the interdependence of the parties' actions.

Re-Position the Parties: the coach can help to move the employee from a position as victim, lost, weak, or marginalized to a position of empowerment. Re-positioning is a transformation to a proactive hero with capabilities, strength, and integrity. The hero is fair and admired.

The coach can assist in the reformulation of the position of the other, as well. Mitchell (1981) points out that there is a constant tendency to misperceive and misunderstand an adversary's position even when the employee believes that he/she has a very clear picture of "the other." This misunderstanding of the other party can lead to increased suspicion and hostilities. The coach can guide the employee to become more conscious of the way he/she constructs meanings. A coach can help to remove barriers of communications, including "removal of some of the grosser perceptual distortions and over-simplifications" (Mitchell, 2003). The coach would aim to redefine the view of the other to complexify him/her and dissolve distortions.

LeBaron (2003) promotes the use symbolic relational tools to undercut negative projections, dissimilar meaning making, and different identities, and to deconstruct enemy positioning. Symbolic relational tools include stories, myths, rituals, and metaphors, and they must be used with intention and awareness. These "significantly expand [the coaches'] resources for creating understanding."

Encourage New Narratives: The coach can listen for places where meanings become visible (LeBaron, 2003) and build more expansive stories. The coach can assist the employee to build a new narrative that privileges appreciation, fairness, and reciprocity. The new story line can be populated with roles and images that expand the employee's worldview to include authenticity, collaboration, and triumph. The social rewards for cooperation can be emphasized. Citing Cobb (2000), Hardy (2008) believes that a "coach" could interact with disputants in order to evolve the conflict stories, reformulate relationships, reframe the past, and focus on the future. This new story line positions each human as responsible for increasing cooperation and mutual respect (Hardy, 2008; Picard & Melchin, 2007). The ALLURE system is a simple, effective, and comprehensive coaching tool to work through conflicts, goals, and problems.

The coach works with the employee to set a goal, understand the other person's point of view, rehearse difficult conversations, and give accurate feedback along with the coach's perspective. The coach uses the ALLURE model to bring depth and wisdom to the conversations. LeBaron (2003) states that the coach must embody "collaboration, genuineness, creativity, reflectiveness, sensitivity, humility, and congruence," which she calls "relational adeptness" (LeBaron, 2003). She urges the "coach" to create positive momentum by highlighting compassionate and generous choices. She advises that the "[Coach] live transformation into being," because his/her influence through modeling is a powerful agent.

BASIC TOOLS AND PRINCIPLES CONFLICT COACHES TEACH EMPLOYEES

The conflict coach will have many tools that promote strong conflict management skills. For instance, the coach can discuss span of control. Conflict management presents three choices. When the employee is trying to resolve conflict, he/she has three options: (1) try to change the other person, (2) try to alter the conflict conditions, or (3) try to change one's own communication patterns or perceptions (Wilmot & Hocker, 2010). Changing one's own communication patterns or perceptions takes practice.

To engage a person in non-defensive, non-accusatory dialogue is a key aspiration. Engaging in dialogue in the midst of conflict is an act of commitment to the relationship and to one's own principles. Throughout the dialogue, one tries to stay conscious to adopt an open attitude and frame the other's behavior in the most positive light. The coach can teach the employee the "XYZ Approach." This approach turns one's complaint into a statement or a request and can turn an angry conversation into constructive dialogue (Wilmot and Hocker, 2010). One describes the situation with this phraseology:

When you do X,
In situation Y,
I feel Z.

This breaks the dispute into concrete pieces. Seeking solutions is easiest when solutions are broken down into small steps. The goal is to avoid blame and attribution of ill intent.

A great deal of research is being done on anger management today, particularly regarding violence in the workplace. The following tips are based on the most current thinking. The coach will ask the employee to consider these options if he/she finds him/herself in an angry confrontation:

* Acknowledge the other person's feelings.
* The employee will want to ask him/herself if there is anything he/she can do to reduce the other person's fear.
* The employee can ask him/herself if he/she has the strength to meet the other's aggressiveness with calmness and warmth. Working with the coach on this type of reaction formation is an excellent pursuit.
* Clarify the specific behaviors involved; assume that everyone including the coached employee has blind spots.
* Explore and learn about the conflict and the other person.
* Gauge the intensity and importance of the issues.
* Invite the other to join him/her in working toward solutions.

* Express belief in the goodwill of the other person.
* The employee can be clear to the other person about his/her intention to work out the differences. (Wilmot & Hocker, 2010)

These are just a few examples of the vast array of tools and principles the conflict coaches teach. Coaches use them to increase the employee's ability to successfully negotiate difficult people, emotions, and conflicts in the workplace, motivate the employee in his/her personal and career development, and uncover the employee's habit-energy, themes, and passions.

CONFLICT COACHING CAN PRESENT ETHICAL ISSUES

It is important to note, that conflict coaching as an identifiable, formal ADR tool is relatively new. Conflict coaches do not have model ethical standards of practice like arbitrators, ombuds, and mediators. Ethical issues unique to conflict coaching in the federal workplace, nonetheless, are arising. For instance, mediation as a problem solving tool is never ruled out for the employee just because he/she is working with a conflict coach. If the employee after working with the coach decides that he/she wants to pursue mediation, this raises several concerns. The employee may ask the coach to be the mediator because of the quality of the relationship that they have developed. Some would advise that the coach never be the mediator in such a situation because the coach has established him/herself as an ally for this employee. The coach has formed a bond and alliance with the employee that cannot easily be neutralized. The other employee should question the coach's neutrality. Some suggest that to avoid any appearances of favoritism, the coach should simply remain in the coaching role, coaching the employee throughout the mediation. The coach could help to secure a third party to be the mediator, but maybe not. Some have even suggested that each party to mediation should have their own coach to help them throughout the mediation process (Noble, 2011).

Some assert that conflict coaching is akin to the separate sessions conducted by the mediator in the mediation process. Cobb and Rifkin (1991) would say that no mediator or person can be fully neutral and as such one must be multi-partial, using partiality to advance mutual understanding. This perspective supports the idea that one could be a conflict coach and then, if requested, be the mediator later in the process. Before engaging in such a mediation, the coach would need to disclose to the other party that the coach had been having conversations with the first party and is more than willing to spend time in conversation with the second party before the mediation if wanted. In other words, there must be disclosure and consent. It is difficult to pinpoint how much disclosure is appropriate without violating confidentiality of the first employee. Normally parties do find this type of arrangement acceptable, but on occasion, a second party will feel that the coach has established an "advocacy" relationship with the first party and can no longer be impartial.

Another ethical issue involves record keeping. A coaching relationship may begin with a contract identifying a certain commitment over time and describing the issues and goals of the coaching exchange. The employee may write many things as part of homework assignments. Generally coaches and sometimes mediators strive to avoid creating records that need to be maintained in a system of records subject to Freedom of Information and privacy laws. Some assert that these types of documents and any written homework become the property of the employee and do not become records for the coach to maintain. There are always questions of where these documents will reside and, over time, who has responsibility for keeping them according to federal law.

Advice-giving brings a set of concerns. The coach will tend to be more proactive than a mediator in making suggestions and sharing his/her opinions and perspectives. Conflict coaches are considered subject matter experts on interpersonal relations, conflict management, leadership development, anger management, and emotional intelligence, and are expected to freely share ideas and concepts, give homework, and offer insight and feedback. A disclaimer as to "advice giving" is normally included upfront in a coaching relationship. The coach may have suggestions and propose ideas, but will clarify from the beginning that the employee is a free agent and must take responsibility for his/her own actions. Similar to mentoring, conflict coaching requires that the employee take full responsibility for devising and implementing any action plan.

Concluding Comments

In the past, mediation has been the ADR tool of choice for federal workplace disputes, resulting in an attitude that one size fits all. "Conflict Coaching" is a one-on-one process that provides support and encouragement. The conflict coach tries to discuss problems, impart skills, generate options, and provide opportunities for the employee to role play difficult conversations and new ways of behaving in a risk-free setting. Conflict coaching is edging out mediation as a tool of preference because it provides the client with more control and less exposure. It avoids many of the downsides of mediation and is designed to strengthen and empower employees. The student of mediation will want to consider adding this exciting new skill to his/her toolbox.

Case Study

Jill has come to you, asking for conflict coaching. She has been "acting" in her present job, directing a division, for two years. With an impending change of leadership, she has been promised the position. Thereafter, she heard through the rumor mill that the job she had been promised was given to someone who had no qualifications. Jill will no longer hold the title of "Acting Director," and will now be required to train and advise this new person in directing the division. Jill is furious and feels betrayed. She wants to have a difficult conversation with William, the man who made the promise and then made the subsequent hiring decision. William holds one of the highest positions in the agency.

Jill is emotional, afraid she is going to lose her temper, and will have a hard time keeping her anger out of her voice and manner. Jill has lost all respect for William and feels he has no loyalty or integrity. Additionally, he did not even have the decency to tell her himself. Jill states that William is a blowhard and a coward. The coach and Jill spent the next two hours mapping out this conversation.

Logistics: the coach asks Jill to find the most relaxed time of the work week for William. He has child care constraints so the last appointment of the day may be a time when William would be distracted. Jill determines that mid-afternoon on Friday would be the best time to get William's attention and consideration.

William would no doubt ask the purpose of Jill's visit. He might be reluctant to have this conversation. Jill and the coach want to frame the meeting in a way that would not sound like Jill is demanding an accounting of William's behavior. Jill decides to view William as a valuable source of contacts and knowledge regarding the agency's work. She ultimately tells William that she needs his help and advice regarding her career path and decisions.

Jill's Goals: The coach and Jill discuss her core values and her identity. How does Jill want to define herself throughout this conflict? Jill answers that she wants to be strategic, composed, and one who gives and receives respect. She wants to be successful in this story, not the loser, the victim, or the woman who is out of control.

More specifically, the coach inquires about Jill's goals for this conversation. Jill wants to ask William several questions. What happened? Why did he break his promise to her? Why didn't he give her a chance to weigh in before the job was given to another? Why does she have to learn about this through the rumor mill?

But Jill also wants to retain her relationship with William. She does not want to get mad or be blaming or accusatory. She needs the conversation to stay professional. She wants to leave William's office feeling good about herself and him. She and the coach discuss the steps to make this viable. As Jill enters William's office, she will remind herself that William likes her and can and will want to help her. Keeping a positive attitude toward him is crucial to achieving her goals.

Jill cannot let herself have a meltdown if she wants William to be receptive to her concerns. Jill and the coach decide that there is a real question about how much time William will give her before he will end the conversation. The coach and Jill came up with techniques for Jill to stay absolutely calm and open. Jill wants William to view her as a very rational and competent, loyal agency worker. Jill wants William to see her as one who deserves recognition for sustained, outstanding performance for over 15 years.

Jill wants William to listen to her. She wants him to understand how frustrated she is and how she is feeling at a dead-end in her career. After working things through with the coach, Jill admits William will be anxious and defensive if she does not control her emotion. Emotions are contagious. Jill decides that her top priority is not to seek answers but instead to seek William's advice in deciding what she should do next in her career.

William's Point of View: the coach and Jill discuss William's point of view at great length. How does William want Jill to see him? Jill thinks that he wants her respect and her support. He wants to save face. William doesn't want to be seen as unfair or dishonest. He wants to be given credit for his help to her over the years. He wants recognition for doing his best.

How does William view Jill? Jill thinks that William sees her as an aggressive female who can be quite outspoken and caustic. Nonetheless, Jill thinks William respects her work ethic and recognizes her contributions to the agency over the course of 15 years. What does William want from the meeting? William probably wants Jill to go away happy, but not take up too much time or make things too complicated. If William can be a hero in this story instead of the goat, that would be his preference. Jill thinks that he honestly would like to help her if he could. Jill admits that he cannot give the job to her now; that decision cannot be undone.

Why did William give the job to another? Jill thinks probably he was forced to make that decision for political reasons, or was forced to by someone at a higher level than his. What would William be thinking once Jill entered the room? Jill thinks he would fear that this would be some sort of showdown.

The coach and Jill try to use all of Jill's knowledge of William to find ways that she can speak his language. William wants to be listened to and understood. The coach and Jill discuss the power of listening. William likes things to be quick and to the point. He values the quality and reputation of the agency. He loves sports. He has two small children. He has a background in economics. The coach and Jill work on ways to maximize this knowledge in the conversation. They select concepts, phrases, and words that would capture his interests. Using Jill's tone, pitch, and rhythm of her voice, and her body language, the coach and Jill practice this conversation so William will not be put off.

<u>Practice and Feedback</u>: at the start Jill might mention his children and ask how they are doing. Jill and the coach discuss the power of being appreciative. So Jill decides she will begin the serious part of the conversation by thanking him for his time, she understands how busy he must be. She might want to mention a highly visible accomplishment of his in recent months to emphasize that Jill believes he has contributed to the quality and reputation of the agency. Jill thinks it might be wise to acknowledge that they have had a long relationship and that he has been good to her in the past.

Jill wants to tell William that she has worked very hard over the years with exceptional results. She wants to affirm that she knows that William appreciates her good work. Jill knows that William wants to do the right thing and that he wants what's best for the agency and her. She wants William to know how much she had wanted the job and wondered if things hadn't gone quite the way they had hoped. Jill wants to know if there is anything that William can tell her that might help her to understand.

The coach will want to be very clear with Jill. William may say he had no choice as Jill suggested above, but she also needs to be prepared for a much more negative response, such as, "I did not think in the end that you were the right choice," etc. The coach will work with Jill to establish that she will be open to hearing criticism and preparing her responses. The coach and Jill prepare for potential negative conversation trails. Jill decides that if it appears that they have reached impasse, and she is really devastated or angry, she will ask William for time to consider things, thank him again for his time, and ask if she can come back in a week or so with some fresh ideas for bringing this to a satisfactory conclusion.

Jill will tell William that she is very disappointed that she did not get the job and that she is hoping William can help her devise some next steps in her career. The coach asks Jill to imagine as many ideas as possible that William might help her with regarding her next career move. Jill and the coach brainstorm together and come up with several options that Jill feels are realistic and good for her. She agrees to do some research and make some phone calls about how these options could work. She also wants to be very open to William's ideas and solutions. Jill and the coach consider how to make these options low hanging fruit for William; i.e., that they will present as little burden as possible. Jill will ask what she can do to make this easiest on him; e.g., can she provide her resume or make a list of her major accomplishments over the past year? Is there anything she can do to help him either make a decision or arm him to make a proposal to another?

The coach will work with Jill to imagine both the worst and the best ways that the conversation may go and prepare for all eventualities. They practice responses that will constructively turn the conversation in a productive direction. As the coach and Jill work through this conversation, Jill practices, and the coach gives feedback. Jill surmises how the conversation could unfold. Jill is calm and thoughtful as she practices. She is prepared for almost any response William may give. The coach and Jill work on her attitude, her posture, and her expectations. She will use words like best, right, good, dedicated, and thankful.

Together the coach and Jill design a closure strategy. She will end by thanking William for his time and consideration.

Jill makes her appointment with William according to her plan. She calls the coach the morning before the meeting just to review the major themes. They decide Jill will call the coach as soon after the conversation as possible. When Jill calls back, she is quite happy with the conversation and with her behavior. She says that she lost her cool only once and managed to get things back on track. She says that they discussed options for her future and both came up with an idea that pleased Jill and that William would support. They decided on a one year job-detail to a prestigious institution in the city.

Jill thanks the coach because she believes that this conversation could not have gone as well without the time she spent in conflict coaching. Before she began the coaching, she states, she expected the conversation with William would start with her threatening to quit.

Questions for Discussion

1. As the coach, list the techniques that you might use to build rapport with and provide safety for Jill.
2. Can you think of some sports metaphors that Jill could consider using in her conversation with William?
3. How might Jill work William's background in economics into the conversation to good result? What techniques did the coach use in developing options? What other techniques might work as well?
4. If William were to call you asking for conflict coaching after he had Jill on his appointment calendar but before he met with her, how would you respond?
5. If Jill got angry and William got defensive, and the conversation ended poorly, what would you do next?
6. What do you think would be your biggest barrier to being a good conflict coach, and, conversely, what do you think you would do really well?
7. If you were to contact a conflict coach in the next month, what would be some of your goals?

References

Adams, M. G. (2004). *Change your questions, change your life: 7 powerful tools for life and work.* San Francisco: Berrett-Koehler.

Bush, R. A. B., and J. P. Folger. (2005). *The promise of mediation: The transformative approach to conflict.* Rev. ed. San Francisco: Jossey-Bass.

Cobb, S. (2000). Creating sacred space: Toward a second-generation dispute resolution practice. *Fordham Urban Law Journal, 28,* 1017–31.

Cobb, S., and J. Rifkin. (1991) Practice and paradox: Deconstructing neutrality in mediation. *Law & Social Inquiry, 16*(1), 35–62.

Cooperrider, D. L. (1991). *Appreciative inquiry.* Williston, VT: Berrett Koehler Communications, 1999. Collaborating for Change.

Cooperrider, D. L., Whitney, D., and J. M. Stavros. (2003). *Appreciative inquiry handbook.* 1st ed., premium ed. Bedford Heights, Ohio: Lakeshore Pub. Workshops for Leaders of Change 1.

Drabek, T. E. (2003). *Strategies for coordinating disaster responses.* Boulder, CO: Institute of Behavior Sciences.

Gergen, M. M., and K. J. Gergen. (2006). Narratives in action. *Narrative Inquiry, 16*(1), 112–21.

Goldberg, S. B., Frank, E. A., Sander, N., Rogers, H., and Cole, S. R. (2007). *Dispute resolution: Negotiation, mediation, and other processes* (5th ed.). New York, NY: Aspen Publishers.

Hammond, S. A. (1998). *The thin book of appreciative inquiry* (2nd ed.). London: Thin Book Pub Co.

Hardy, S. (2008). Mediation and genre. *Negotiation Journal,* 2008: 247–68.

Jones, T., and R. Brinkert. (2007). *Conflict coaching: Conflict management strategies and skills for the individual.* Thousand Oaks, CA: Sage Publications, Inc.

LeBaron, M. (2003). *Bridging cultural conflicts: A new approach for a changing world.* San Francisco: Jossey-Bass.

Marquardt, M. J. (2005). *Leading with questions: How leaders find the right solutions by knowing what to ask.* 1st ed. San Francisco: Jossey-Bass.

Mayer, B. (2004). *Beyond neutrality: Confronting the crisis in conflict resolution.* 1st ed. San Francisco: Jossey-Bass.

Mazur, C. S. (2011). *Seven days in the crescent city: Katrina's handlers, crisis discourse, and story lines.* ProQuest Dissertations and Theses, George Mason University, Fairfax, VA.

Mitchell, C. R. (2003). *Conflict as a resolvable problem.* Fairfax, VA: ICAR George Mason University.

Mitchell, C. R. (1981). *The structure of international conflict.* New York: St. Martin's Press.

Moore, C. W. (2003). *The Mediation process: Practical strategies for resolving conflict* (3rd ed.). Revised. San Francisco: Jossey-Bass.

Noble, C. (2011). *Conflict management coaching: The CINERGY™ model.* Toronto, Ontario, Canada: CINERGY™ Coaching.

Picard, C., and K. Melchin. (2007). Insight mediation: A learning-centered mediation model. *Negotiation Journal, 23*(1), 35–53.

Royal, C., and S. A. Hammond. (Eds.). (2001). *Lessons from the field: Applying appreciative inquiry* (Rev. ed.). Plano, TX: Thin Book Pub. Co.

Schrock-Shenk, C. (2000). *Mediation and facilitation training manual: Foundations and skills for constructive conflict transformation* (4th ed.). Akron: Mennonite Conciliation Service.

Schwarz, R. M. (2002). *The skilled facilitator: A comprehensive resource for consultants, facilitators, managers, trainers, and coaches* (2nd ed.). San Francisco: Jossey-Bass.

Strachan, D. (2006). *Making questions work: A guide to how and what to ask for facilitators, consultants, managers, coaches, and educators* (1st ed.). San Francisco: Jossey-Bass.

Wallace, L., and J. Trinka. (2007). *A legacy of 21st century leadership: A guide for creating a climate of leadership throughout your organization* (0 ed.). Bloomington, IN: iUniverse, Inc.

Warfield, W. (2009). Race narratives in dispute resolution. *Dispute Resolution Magazine,* Spring: 10–13.

Watkins, J. M., Mohr, B. J., and Kelly, R. (2011). *Appreciative inquiry: Change at the speed of imagination* (2nd ed.). San Francisco: Pfeiffer.

Wilmot, W., and J. Hocker. (2010). *Interpersonal conflict* (8th ed.). New York: McGraw-Hill Humanities/Social Sciences/Languages.

Chapter 6

Divorce Mediation: Resolving Issues of Parents' Property and the Custody of Their Children

Jerry Bagnell

Most couples who choose mediation do so because they want to avoid litigation, either because they realize it will exacerbate any anger they are feeling or because the adversarial process always concludes with a winner and a loser. For individuals who want to uncouple but not destroy the other party, mediation is an ideal solution.

Divorce mediation can be conducted in several settings. Court referred cases are a good place for new mediators to begin their practice. Because cases are referred to the mediator, there is no need to do any marketing. Cases are normally held in the courthouse so an outside office is not required. Screening to determine if the case is appropriate for mediation is often done by court personnel. Some courts have an individual who manages their mediation cases, does the screening, prepares agreements from mediators' notes, and keeps records.

Cases normally involve disputes about custody, visitation, and child support. Couples may be unmarried. Often the disputes involve post divorce or other noncompliance matters. Parties are usually unrepresented by attorneys and most have not consulted with attorneys to obtain any legal advice.

Another setting for divorce mediators is as an independent contractor for an agency or organization. Again, this is a good place for new mediators to start. Cases are referred by the agency and meeting facilities are provided. Screening to determine if the case is appropriate for mediation is done by the mediators. Mediators will be expected to provide all the necessary forms needed. Since the mediators are independent contractors, they will need to have their own malpractice insurance. Parties pay an hourly fee to the agency and the agency pays the mediators a portion of that fee. The scope of cases can be as simple as court referred cases or as complex as a comprehensive divorce with issues ranging from custody, visitation, child and spousal support, to distribution of property and sharing of debts. Most parties are represented by attorneys or have consulted with attorneys before or during mediation.

A third setting is private practice. It may be a solo practice or a corporation. My practice in Virginia was a corporation with a full time office manager. Our mediators, other than me, were independent contractors referred to as "mediation associates." They represented a number of professions: attorneys, psychologists, nurses, educators, realtors, financial planners, and social workers. We routinely used teams of co-mediators, some of whom were fully qualified mediators. Some teams consisted of a mediation associate and a mediator in training referred to as a "mediation intern."

WHY IS THIS TYPE OF DISPUTE SUITABLE FOR MEDIATION?

The adversarial court system works well when a judge can determine guilt or innocence, or the liability of an individual based upon a presentation and evaluation of factual evidence. While there is some consideration of evidence in divorce proceedings, such as whether or not adultery has occurred, there are no specific criteria for determining the best interests of children. State laws vary about the distribution of property and sharing of debts.

Although divorcing couples come to court expecting a judge to render a fair decision, they frequently discover that the judge must only render a decision that is legal. Neither party may perceive that decision as fair. Even though judges have the authority to make decisions about custody and visitation, the best they can do may not satisfy either parent. Mediation gives the parents an opportunity to use their personal knowledge of their children to determine what is truly in the children's best interest.

An issue for all married couples regardless of gender is the division of their property. Some individuals live together without the benefit of marriage. Laws applicable to divorcing couples do not apply to them. An exception is a civil union. The issues of whether marriage is the union of a man and a woman, whether a marriage can be between persons of the same gender, or whether partners in a civil union should have the same legal rights as married persons varies from state to state and, in some cases, even within states. I'll keep it simple and define the ways property is commonly characterized and subsequently divided in cases where there is applicable law.

The first step in determining who will keep or receive property in a couple's possession is to determine if it is marital property or separate property. One factor considered is when the couple separated but since that is a subject unto itself, I'll not include that in this explanation.

Separate Property (SP) is property owned by one spouse prior to marriage, and in most states, not subject to distribution in a divorce. It includes gifts to the spouse or property inherited by the spouse either before or during the marriage. Frequently disputes occur during a divorce when the parties argue that a gift such as the down payment for the marital home made by the parents of one spouse was a gift to that spouse or a gift to the marriage. Separate Property can also be established in a prenuptial agreement.

Marital Property (MP) is property acquired by spouses during marriage. It includes wages and other earnings of both parties, items purchased during the marriage regardless of which spouse paid for the property or, in most cases, regardless of how that property is titled. The marital home, unless owned by one party prior to the marriage, is generally considered marital property even if one spouse made all the payments. Pension or retirement plans are generally considered marital property because they are the result of contributions from wages. Spouses should be advised to consult an attorney for a legal determination of the characterization of their property, although parties can choose to divide property in any manner that is mutually agreeable after receiving legal advice from separate and independent attorneys.

A concept called commingling that means mixing separate property of one spouse with that of the other or placing it in a joint account may cause that property to then be considered marital property. The increase in value or appreciation of separate property such as a business or an investment may change the characterization of that property if the spouse who did not first own the property exerted any effort to assist the other spouse in managing the property or providing advice about how to manage it. Some states consider the appreciation of separate property to transmute it into marital property even when there is passive effort on the part of the other spouse. Whether or not commingling, transmutation, or recharacterization has occurred is a legal matter that requires a decision by a court and should not be a matter determined by a mediator. This is a matter parties should discuss with separate and independent attorneys before or between mediation sessions.

Courts divide property and debts in accordance with the laws of the various states. There are three basic methods:

COMMUNITY PROPERTY (CP)

In states shown in the chart, all property of married persons is classified as either community property (owned equally by both spouses) or the separate property of one spouse or the other. At divorce, community property is generally divided equally between the spouses, while each spouse keeps his or her separate property.

EQUITABLE DISTRIBUTION (ED)

Assets and earnings accumulated during the marriage are divided equitably ("fairly"—a term not defined in the law), but not necessarily equally. Courts exercise judicial discretion to determine what is equitable. Decisions vary widely between courts and may be based upon age, experience, gender, or other characteristics of the presiding judges. In some of those states, the judge may order one party to use separate property to make the settlement fair to both spouses. The "crap shoot" here is that the discretion of judges varies and, in some cases, has become so obvious to attorneys that they strive to have a particular judge hear a case for a party they are representing because of the history of decisions made by that judge.

KITCHEN SINK (KS)

The so-called Kitchen Sink states include separate property in the marital estate subject to distribution.

Whether a court considers community property or equitable distribution for the majority of cases, some courts make an exception in situations when the spouse who has little or no property titled in his or her name would have a demonstrated need for support that would not be accomplished by a strict application of CP or ED. This chart shows the property distribution law for states, Puerto Rico, and the District of Columbia.

State	Community Property	Equitable Distribution	Kitchen Sink	Exception
AL	*			Include SP if spouse without title has demonstrated need
AK	*			Include SP if spouse without title has demonstrated need
AZ	*			
AR		*		Include SP if spouse without title has demonstrated need
CA	*			
CO		*		
CT			*	
DC		*		
DE		*		
FL		*		
GA		*		
HI		*		Include SP if spouse without title has demonstrated need
ID	*			
IL		*		
IN			*	
IA			*	
KS			*	
KY		*		
LA	*			
ME		*		
MD		*		
MA			*	
MI			*	
MN		*		Include SP if spouse without title has demonstrated need
MS		*		
MO		*		
MT			*	
ND			*	
NE		*		
NV	*			
NH			*	
NJ		*		
NM	*			
NY		*		

Continued.

NC		*		
ND			*	
OH		*		Include SP if spouse without title has demonstrated need
OK		*		
OR			*	
PA		*		
PR	*			
RI		*		
SC		*		
SD			*	
TN		*		
TX	*			
UT		*		
VT			*	
VA		*		
WA			*	
WV		*		
WI	*			Include SP if spouse without title has demonstrated need
WY			*	

When some couples in mediation argue about the value of the marital home, one party may comment that she made all the drapes in the home while the other states that he planted every rose bush in the back yard. A court doesn't consider these subjective criteria, but for some parties they are more important than whether the home is appraised for one dollar amount or another.

Mediation allows parties to consider the subjective value of their assets while a court considers only the objective value. A myth or presumption about the distribution of marital property in divorce is that only attorneys can facilitate such a negotiation because of the need to apply the law to the facts of the case. Although laws vary from state to state, only the couple knows how they personally and individually value their assets. A husband digging up prize rose bushes at 2:00 A.M. and escaping with them in his pickup truck illustrates that the dollar value of the shrubs was not the husband's criterion for their value.

In mediation, the parties themselves decide how to divide their assets using standards that they define. Division of property does not necessarily mean an actual physical division of the assets. For example, you can't receive an actual half of the marital home, a car, or a boat. The court may simply award each spouse a percentage of the total value of any marital property. Each spouse may be awarded personal property, assets, and debts the value of which adds up to a particular percentage of the total value of the marital property. At that point, each spouse can negotiate with the other, ideally facilitated by a mediator, to determine how the dollar value will be apportioned. As mentioned previously, the "value" as perceived by either spouse will influence what final distribution may be agreed to.

WHAT DOES THE CURRENT MATERIAL SAY ABOUT MEDIATING THIS TYPE OF DISPUTE?

Some explanations of the divorce mediation process have been so well written that they have become classics. The following summarizes portions of an article by Joan B. Kelly, a past-president of the Academy of Family Mediators (now ACR), that appeared in the first edition of *Mediation Quarterly* in 1983.

> The explicit goal of divorce mediation is negotiating a settlement of issues identified by clients and the mediator as germane to the dispute. Central to this goal is the principle that the settlement should be mutually beneficial and agreeable to both parties. Mediation promises its clients a specific end product—a negotiated settlement. If this end product can not be obtained, the mediation terminates. If the mediation is successful, the visible result is a written agreement (Memorandum of Understanding).
>
> Mediation begins with an initial contracting session, which has clear content and a structure that causes the expectations of both mediator and clients to be verbalized. Mediators explain the nature of the process, the desired end results, and the expectation for full disclosure, confidentiality—except mandated reporting of child abuse, and independent lawyer review at the end of the process. Clients sign a Contract for Mediation covering these points, fees, and an agreement not to subpoena the mediator to testify on the behalf of either client if the mediation breaks down. Clients understand what they are contracting for and the procedure and intent. Clients and mediators have also agreed on their participation in the process and on the desired end result.
>
> The role of divorce mediators is very active. They educate clients regarding information needed for settlement, clarify and organize data, facilitate discussion and cooperative communications, structure sessions so tasks can proceed, manage conflict, refer clients out for expert information or advice, help clients weigh the consequences, conduct negotiations, and produce a Memorandum of Understanding. Mediators do not make decisions for the couple but facilitate the client's own decision-making process. The relationship to the clients is one of impartiality and balance, working actively with each client throughout the process to develop a fair and equitable agreement.
>
> Competent mediators possess knowledge of budgetary needs, spousal and child support considerations, various types of assets and methods of valuing them, and common monetary practices.

For years I have shared the concern of many practitioners for divorces or separations that involve children. That concern is explained by Bob Emery (1994) as follows:

> Mediation is a useful tool for helping parents to renegotiate their relationship. Mediation is of value because it encourages parents to cooperate—a distinct contrast to the traditional method of adversary settlement. Perhaps the greatest benefit of mediation, however, it that it helps parents to redefine new boundaries in their relationships. These boundaries are defined explicitly by the specific and detailed terms of a mediated agreement and implicitly through the process of negotiation that occurs in mediation.

Of course, divorce mediation is not always a workable way for two spouses to uncouple. If there is an imminent danger of abuse, whether physical or psychological, a person can not be a willing participant. Since one of the principles underlying mediation is voluntariness, a person who feels intimidated or coerced or who is in fear of bodily harm, cannot give their informed consent to participate. It is important to recognize that how the person feels subjectively is more significant than how the situation appears objectively to the mediator. Since there can be a history of violence, how a person feels about that when they are deciding to participate in mediation is what is relevant.

Some organizations and individuals believe that mediation is not appropriate if there has been violence in a relationship. Many of the clients I've had over the years have acknowledged that they were victims of psychological or physical violence in the past, but still wanted to use mediation to divorce rather than litigation. In fact, a process such as mediation, which is based upon self-determination, can do more to empower a victim of domestic violence than protracted litigation in which an overzealous advocate might decide to make strong suggestions about how the person should proceed thus controlling his or her decision-making at a time when he or she is trying to rebuild self esteem.

Because domestic violence is a possibility in every marriage or parenting relationship, I always screened for the presence of domestic violence with the goal of either ruling it out or determining what effect it would have on the voluntary and uncoerced participation of either or both parties. Mediation is appropriate when the parties volunteer to participate and their individual decisions to participate are not based upon intimidation or coercion. It is also important to determine if the parties are able to participate. Arguments abound about whether it is the mediator's role to determine if the parties are competent, if there is a balance of power and knowledge, and so on.

A mediator's primary consideration in determining the suitability of parties to participate in the process is governed by the maxim, do no harm. Of course that is the mantra of any professional service provider, but assessing the probability of the parties being harmed during or after mediation is not something that can be learned in a training session. A mediator must be realistic about his or her ability to handle the myriad of situations that can occur during divorce mediation, whether they are in session or between sessions. A mediator can not learn at the expense, financial, psychological or physical, of the parties to the mediation.

A realistic assessment of whether or not mediation is appropriate for a couple should include a consideration of the following principles underlying the mediation process: voluntariness, informed consent, confidentiality, and self-determination. All of these considerations are subjective and depend upon how the parties perceive their ability, not just how the mediator perceives that ability. A mediator must also consider if either party might not be acting in good faith. No checklist can assure the mediator that the process is appropriate for the parties so it is important to be vigilant throughout.

TRAINING AND EXPERIENCE NEEDED TO MEDIATE DIVORCE, POST DIVORCE, OR PARENTING DISPUTES

Most divorce mediators have at least an undergraduate education. Some have graduate and postgraduate degrees in law, psychotherapy, education, business administration, and other professional areas. Many transition into divorce mediation from other professions rather than become divorce mediators as their initial professional endeavor.

Some colleges and universities as well as law schools offer courses in mediation. These courses usually are general in nature and do not address all of the specific skills required to become a competent divorce mediator.

Most divorce mediators take a forty-hour course in family mediation. The majority of these courses are presented by nationally known trainers who are members of organizations such as the Association for Conflict Resolution (ACR) or the Association of Family and Conciliation Courts (AFCC). Some courses may be sponsored by state mediation organizations. In either case, these courses by themselves do not qualify individuals to become divorce mediators. The trainers who present these courses routinely make that point to persons attending the courses. They also tell them that completing the course does not provide any guarantee that clients will flock to the offices of those who complete the course.

Most states require that divorce mediators take a course in that portion of state law that applies to mediation, the judicial system, and divorce. Topics may also include grounds for divorce, custody and visitation, child and spousal support, and distribution of property. There is usually a requirement that divorce mediators attend an annual update of this training. Some states require training in screening for and dealing with domestic violence in the context of mediation as well as a course on ethical issues in mediation.

Following training, divorce mediators should obtain supervised experience to be able to receive referrals from a court or to acquire a professional designation. The labels for such designations vary by state and may be called certification, accreditation, or some similar term. However, in most states mediators are not required to be licensed as other professionals such as attorneys or therapists are.

Interns in my practice from 1999 to 2001 in Virginia had the following requirements for certification as a Juvenile and Domestic Relations District Court Mediator: Observation of at least two complete domestic relations family mediation cases with a certified mediator and supervised co-mediation of at least five complete domestic relations family mediation cases with a certified mediator.

If they wanted to increase their certification to Circuit Court-Family Mediator so they could receive referrals for cases involving spousal support and distribution of property, there were additional requirements: Observation of at least two (one if already certified as a Juvenile and Domestic Relations District Court Mediator) complete Circuit Court-Family mediation cases with a certified mediator and supervised co-mediation of at least ten hours of family mediation including five (two if already certified as a Juvenile and Domestic Relations District Court Mediator) Circuit Court-Family mediation cases with a certified mediator.

Many of our interns recognized that these requirements were only entry level experience and continued to co-mediate with our associates to prepare themselves for independent practice and also obtained training in a variety of divorce related subjects such as:

Managing Angry Parties
Recognizing and Reporting Child Abuse and Neglect
Basic Crisis Negotiation Skills
Calculating Child Support
The Effects of Domestic Violence on Children
Spousal Support
Bankruptcy
Estates, Trusts and Taxes
Developmental and Psychological Impact of Divorce on Children
Identifying and Preventing Violence in Separation and Divorce
Pension Benefits in Divorce
Property Classification Issues
Estates, Wills, and Implications for Mediation
Active Listening
Agreement writing

Most national and state organizations provide their members with a title or designation in addition to those obtained from the state in which mediators practice.

For example, mediators who meet the requirements for certification or similar state regulated status as a divorce mediator and have a sufficient numbers of hours of practice can be designated as an "Advanced Practitioner Member" by the Association for Conflict Resolution (ACR). The Academy of Professional Family Mediators (APFM), founded in 2006, comprised of family mediation practitioners, is the largest and most focused professional family mediation organization. Members who were previously designated as Advanced Practitioners by ACR are designated as "Professional Mediators" by APFM.

Mediators certified or who have a similar designation from the state in which they practice usually have requirements for continuing education and must obtain a certain number of hours annually. Mediation organizations often have similar requirements for their members.

How Does a Mediator Prepare for This Type of Mediation?

There is so much more to preparation than training, certification and additional continuing education classes. In order to be successful, you have to be known—and be known for your skill, not just be a familiar face in the community.

Membership in national and state mediation organizations provides opportunities for additional training both as a student and a presenter. Presenting training to your peers is one way to establish your credibility.

Ironically, I found that even though I was a psychotherapist by profession of origin and a member of organizations with other therapists, I received very few referrals from therapists. Attorneys that worked in our practice reported the same cross professional situation. They received very few referrals from other attorneys. One experienced attorney in our practice theorized that professionals don't like to admit to their peers that they can't handle a case they are working on and have to refer it to someone else. Whatever the reason for this enigma, I accepted the fact that I had to look at a variety of professionals to obtain referrals.

Consider networking with financial advisors especially if you do divorces that involve property and financial assets. It can provide you with opportunities to learn about the financial aspects of divorce and can also produce referrals.

Consider joining the bar association both at the local, state, and national level. Most of my referrals came from judges and attorneys. It is important to network with your referral sources and establish credibility by presenting training about mediation. It is also very helpful to establish relationships with one or more attorneys who can advise you on the legal aspects of divorce. You can ask them to review memoranda for you and even refer clients to separate and independent attorneys to create whatever legal documents might be necessary to implement the terms of an agreement reached by the parties to a separation or divorce.

When establishing credibility with judges, it is important to have an identity and a role that is clear. Market yourself as a divorce mediator, not a mediator of every possible type of dispute. Attorneys specialize in particular types of cases. Judges want to refer cases to experts in those areas. A judge told me once that some mediators confused him. He explained that a mediator might appear in his court on a Monday as an expert witness or a custody evaluator testifying that "Mrs. Jones" was a better parent than "Mr. Jones." Then, on Tuesday that same mediator would expect the judge to refer a case to him because he was fair and impartial. The judge said it was also difficult to determine what services someone actually offered. Were they a therapist or a mediator? Lesson learned. If you want to be a divorce mediator, don't offer other services that blur the boundaries of your practice. If mediation is an additional aspect of your menu of professional services, you may be perceived as a part time mediator. Most potential clients, as well as referral sources, look for full time professionals assuming they are more qualified that someone that does mediation as a sideline.

An exception to offering other services is parent education. Most states mandate that parties filing an action involving custody, visitation, or support of children attend classes on the effects of separation and divorce on children. Mediators who present these classes have an opportunity to demonstrate their knowledge and credibility for groups of as many as 30 or 40 parents in one session. This can result in referrals and also promotes the use of mediation.

When establishing a practice, if you want to be more than a solo practitioner, have a number of mediators from a variety of professions as independent contractors. That gives you the ability to assemble mediation teams with complimentary skills such as law and therapy or financial planning and education. As your practice grows, hire an administrative assistant or office manager. You want to be available to mediate and network, not be tied up doing routine paperwork.

Accept the fact that it may take a year or more before you have a sufficient number of cases to pay the bills. If you have adequately prepared and are known for your expertise, ethical, and professional behavior, you can be successful as a divorce mediator.

WHAT ARE SOME TYPICAL AND UNIQUE PROBLEMS ASSOCIATED WITH THIS TYPE OF MEDIATION?

Problems or typical areas of difficulty unique to divorce mediation occur with mediators themselves and also with the parties to mediation that are separating or divorcing.

A history of, or the potential for, domestic violence is a factor in every case when parties are separating or divorcing. Some protocol or procedure for screening is essential. The screening should be ongoing throughout the mediation. An example of such a process is discussed in the case study that follows.

Since divorce mediation is not an entry level profession, many mediators can blur their role as a mediator with that of their profession of origin. Therapist mediators may become too concerned with the social functioning of their clients or employ strategies to improve their relationship with regard to parenting.

Attorney mediators may tend to be more directive and may make suggestions that border on giving legal advice. Their knowledge of the law can enable them to answer clients' questions about legal issues rather than referring the clients to separate and independent attorneys. There is a tendency for clients to perceive attorney mediators as somehow more qualified than those with backgrounds in other professions. While they may know more about the law than non-attorneys, their skills as a mediator are not necessarily related to their legal expertise. One of our mediation associates who was an attorney used to say that the only guarantee you have when you hire an attorney is that he or she is licensed to practice law, not that he or she is competent. Of course the same situation applies to many other professionals.

Whether the divorce mediator is an attorney or not, giving legal advice is never appropriate. Attorney mediators can be sanctioned for dual representation. Non attorney mediators can be accused of and may be sanctioned or even prosecuted for the unauthorized practice of law.

Regardless of their profession of origin, divorce mediators must maintain their focus on encouraging client self-determination, avoid making suggestions and giving advice, and make appropriate referrals even when they know the answers or possible solutions to situations separating and divorcing parties may encounter.

Divorce mediators are often mandated reporters of child abuse and neglect. Frequently parents will accuse each other of behaviors that constitute abuse or neglect. Mediators may be faced with the dilemma of differentiating between what may be accusations that are unfounded and those that they suspect are accurate and place children in jeopardy. Most mediators advise their clients of the mediator's responsibility to report suspicion of child abuse or neglect, or suspicion of bodily harm or violence to another person. Such language usually appears in the contract for mediation signed by the mediator and the clients. For example, "protect the confidentiality of the mediation except for mandatory reporting of suspicion of child abuse or neglect, or a suspicion of bodily harm or violence to another person."

Mediators also have ethical considerations that may not be readily apparent. For example, they may not unnecessarily prolong mediation if the parties are not making progress. While there is no magic number of sessions that it will take to mediate a separation or divorce, when the process goes on for more than five or six two-hour sessions, mediators must consider whether to continue trying to facilitate a resolution or possibly terminate the mediation and make appropriate referrals.

One strategy for enhancing the efficiency of divorce mediation is to accept the fact that parties are dealing with highly emotional issues and need time to think about their options and gather information. As a rule, I scheduled sessions at least two weeks apart so that the parties could have enough time to gather information needed to make informed decisions. Also as a practical matter, few couples have the financial ability to pay for sessions that are scheduled too close together. Spacing sessions out over a period of weeks enables the parties to deal with financial as well as emotional considerations.

Another consideration for divorce mediators is referred to in most states as "substantial full disclosure." In Virginia, the parties agree in their contract for mediation to "provide substantial full disclosure of all relevant property and financial information necessary to reach a just agreement." They acknowledge in their contract that, "failure to do so may result in the agreement or any order incorporating or resulting from such agreement being vacated by the court."

A challenge for the divorce mediator is to ask questions that will not only encourage substantial full disclosure, but also provide a level of confidence that such disclosure has occurred. In cases involving self-employed clients or those in which one party handles all financial matters, it is essential to make sure that all relevant information has been disclosed.

Typical and unique problems from the clients' perspective are also quite common in divorce mediation. One of the most pervasive is Parental Alienation Syndrome (PAS), defined by Richard Gardner (1989) as, "a disturbance in which children are preoccupied with condemnation and criticism of a parent that is unjustified and/or exaggerated." Gardner posits that indications of PAS are seen in about 90% of children that are involved in lengthy custody litigation.

Some problems experienced with clients are a normal part of the stress of separation and divorce. Anger is quite common. If you are uncomfortable dealing with angry parties who can berate each other with a litany of profanity, you don't want to be a divorce mediator. Besides having clear ground rules that are explained in your contract with the parties, there are several ways to control their behavior.

Interruptions can be handled by using a technique I call "Telling, Telling, and Retelling." It works like this: The mediator specifies a short time, e.g., no more than two minutes, for one party, let's say "John," to explain some specific aspect of the problem to be resolved. The second party, "Mary," is told to listen carefully because at the end of that two minute period, she will have the opportunity to summarize what "John" said by providing a verbal summary to him. "Mary" is not permitted to take notes because the statement will be a short one with limited content.

"John" is told to listen carefully to "Mary's" paraphrased summary. The mediator then asks John, "Did she get it right?" If "John's" answer is, "No," the mediator tells "John" to tell "Mary" again. "Mary" paraphrases for "John" and he "retells" what he originally said until he is able to agree that "Mary" can tell him what he said. This doesn't mean she understands or agrees with "John." It merely means that she can restate what "John" said.

The mediator then reverses the roles of the parties and continues the process.

The purpose of this intervention is to teach parties, by means of an imposed consequence, to listen to what another party is saying rather than prepare an answer, interrupt, or present an argument to the contrary. Each time a party has to re-peat the telling and retelling, they will probably change their statement somewhat based on what has been retold to them by the other party. Each restatement should be clearer than the previous one. "Telling, Telling, and Retelling" can be effective when parties are angry or are not paying attention to what the other party is saying.

I also used a continuum of interventions for managing angry parties:

Mild:
    a. Carefully empathize with parties and normalize feelings
    b. Interrupt with questions
    c. Remind them of the ground rules they agreed to accept; e.g., not interrupting
    d. Explain how disruptive behavior distracts you from listening

Moderate:
    a. "The Anger Two-Step": 1. Acknowledge their anger and 2. Move on
    b. Pause and summarize facts while acknowledging feelings
    c. Take a short break or use a caucus to explore interests and clarify concerns
    d. Impose an agreed to consequence such as "Telling, Telling, and Retelling"

Serious:
    a. Give short, specific commands to interrupt the parties
    b. Take a long break; e.g., over lunch
    c. Postpone the session and reschedule
    d. Terminate mediation and make appropriate reports or referrals

Lack of knowledge about the legal and financial aspects of divorce is common. Sometimes parties may say that they have been told something by their attorneys that the mediator knows is not correct. It is often impossible to determine if the parties misunderstood what they were told or if they are merely saying the infor-mation came from their attorneys. Since the mediator can not advise, referrals to attorneys, financial advisors, or other professionals are appropriate to resolve any such issues.

Controlling power imbalances and differences in knowledge can also be a prob-lem. Using questions effectively, establishing ground rules about the length of time each party may speak, and referrals to other professionals to balance knowl-edge are common interventions.

Many separating and divorcing couples have preconceived ideas about the process that are simply not correct. These ideas may come from the media or from others who have separated or divorced. Emphasize that everyone's experience is dif-ferent and what is important is that the parties you are working with should consider what they want and need for their particular circumstances. The influence of family members, friends, or a new significant other can encourage parties to make decisions in a session or change their minds about agreements reached in prior sessions.

Frequently parents will refer to their children as "my son" or "my daughter." An effective intervention is to suggest using the children's names since when a parent calls a child, they don't say, "Come here, my daughter." They would say, "Come here, Sally."

One of the most problematic situations in a separation or divorce is either party's new significant other. Often that person may be blamed for the break up of the relationship. One party may have established a relationship with someone new following the separation. In either case, when there are children involved, one parent may want to establish a parenting plan that precludes any contact between the new partner and the other parent. While judges vary in their opinions about exposing children to new partners, the situation can be handled by the mediator by explaining that children whose parents are separating are often confused about the situation and expecting them to accept a new adult in the life of either parent is not realistic.

When facilitating the construction of parenting plans, safety of the parents and children must be considered. Sometimes the mediator may be able to ask questions so that parents become aware of safety considerations. In other cases, attorneys reviewing memoranda or preparing orders for the court may recommend the inclusion of some of the constraints that follow. When divorce mediators and attorneys have a good working relationship, judges expect that parenting plans will contain provisions regarding the safety of parents and their children.

Detailed and specific plans are in the best interest of children and their parents. Courts prefer them, because just like Activity-based Parenting Plans, they are easy to interpret and enforce. Vague terms such as "reasonable visitation," "by mutual agreement," and "shared time or responsibility" are not specific enough to be clearly enforced. They afford an abused parent and children little or no protection from an abuser who may interpret the terms in a manner that permits the abuser to gain access to the abused parent by means of contact with the children. Parenting plans when necessary, may minimize any physical contact between parents.

Joint legal custody requires a balance of decision-making power and is usually not appropriate in cases in which threats, intimidation, and coercion are present. Plans calling for picking up and dropping off the children at the home of either parent should be avoided. Transition activities such as one parent dropping the children off at school or at an extracurricular activity and the other parent picking them up should be considered.

Plans calling for the payment of child or spousal support in cash or by direct contact should be avoided. Joint meetings of the parents such as school conferences, children's sports, and social events should also be avoided. Teachers and counselors can meet with parents separately. Parents do not need to sit together at sporting events. The abuser should be required to contact the school, not the other parent, to obtain report cards or any information regarding school activities.

The abused parent should have all necessary ID cards and forms to obtain medical coverage or treatment for the children without having to contact the abuser.

Any co-payments, if they are to be paid by the abuser, should be paid directly to the doctor, dentist, or medical facility.

Parenting plans should include a provision that requires the abuser to notify the other parent and the school or daycare in writing in advance of any planned visit. Children should not be permitted to take keys for the abused parent's home with them when visiting the abuser. Requirements for therapy involving both parents and the children or both parents should be carefully considered and scheduled only when no other alternative is available.

While divorce mediators are limited in how much they can influence their clients, safety must be the primary consideration when preparing any parenting plan. The skillful use of questions to call parents' attention to provisions that affect safety is essential.

Concluding Comments

Divorce mediation can be a very different process depending upon the setting in which it is conducted. Court cases can be short and relatively simple. Private practice cases can be lengthy and quite complicated. In either setting, challenges include dealing with a possible intense level of anger and behavior that is anything but civil.

The intricacies of separation and divorce call for skills on the part of the mediator that are much greater than knowledge of just the mediation process. Divorce mediators must know the law that applies to such cases, not so they can advise, but so they will not unknowingly facilitate an agreement that would not be acceptable to the court. It also goes without saying that if separate and independent attorneys review memoranda prepared by mediators that are replete with errors, the credibility of the mediators will certainly be suspect. Mediators without credibility will not get referrals from attorneys whose clients can not expect competence during the process of mediation.

The amount of training and experience required to be a competent divorce mediator means that choosing this field involves quite some time to develop professionally between initial training and succeeding as a practitioner. Divorce mediation cases produce outcomes that have long range implications for parents and children. Even when children are not involved, issues resolved hastily by mediators whose goal is agreement between the parties can result in less than pleasant consequences for the mediators. Mediators can not afford, literally, to learn at the expense of clients. Malpractice insurance is a must since parties who may be appreciative at the time an agreement is reached can become very angry at mediators when the parties realize the long term implications of agreements facilitated by the mediators. Of course, divorce attorneys are no less likely to have disgruntled clients, but not all mediation clients sing the praises of their mediators in the months following the conclusion of mediation.

If you believe that you can make a difference in people's lives by helping them reach a greater understanding and appreciation for each other's points of view, mediation may be a way for you to achieve that goal. Success in mediation means that the parties know and appreciate each other's interests. This doesn't mean that they will agree. They have the opportunity to do so, but the choice is theirs. Mediators who advertise success based on the percentage of cases where agreements are reached are missing the point. When mediation is a success, that success is defined by the parties.

Especially when working with separating or divorcing couples, it is important to recognize that they came to mediation because they were not able to resolve issues themselves. That doesn't mean they want someone to resolve the issues for them, although they may ask mediators to do that. Divorce mediators must respect the right of their clients to make decisions that may be quite different than what the mediator might decide. If you want to make decisions for others, mediation is not the profession you should choose. If you want to help others reach mutually agreeable decisions by facilitating discussions without attempting to influence the outcome, mediation may be a way to do that. If you want to do that at a time in people's lives when their decision making is impaired by the emotional aspects of separation or divorce, divorce mediation is a profession you might consider.

Case Study

Prior to meeting with a couple, they were screened individually by phone to determine any history of domestic violence, the potential for domestic violence to recur, and the effect any history or recent incidents might have on either party's ability to participate voluntarily, in an informed manner, and without coercion or intimidation. Routinely women were screened first and then the men were screened usually at a different time and/or on a different day. If the telephone screening indicated that a more in-depth screening would be necessary, our protocol was to schedule separate and individual face-to-face sessions. That rarely occurred.

A letter confirming the appointment was sent to each client explaining that sessions would be two hours in length, the fee structure, the name of the co-mediator, and that a mediation intern might be present to take notes. Some practitioners believe that the parties have to agree for anyone to be present other than the mediator. We routinely used a co-mediator team and a recorder. Whether the case was in the court or private practice setting, we never had an instance of the parties objecting to the presence of a mediation team. Our rationale was similar to that of doctors scheduled to perform surgery. Patients don't get to decide how many people doctors choose to assist them.

Prior to the arrival of the parties, the mediation team spent 30 minutes or so discussing information about the parties, such as whether or not they had children or if they did, their gender and ages. We also decided who would be responsible for taking the lead during various portions of the mediation session.

John Doe, 35, and Mary Doe, 28, were married in 2004. They separated on June 15, 2011, and are now living separate and apart from each other, but have not yet filed for divorce. Mary acknowledged that the reason for their separation is she had an affair with her boss that the boss' wife discovered. The boss fired Mary in an attempt to repair the relationship with his wife.

John is now living in an apartment near the school where he is employed as a sixth grade teacher. Mary still lives in the marital home. Mary is now unemployed. John and Mary have two children: Steven, seven, and Diane, five.

Mary's parents gave the couple $10,000 for the down payment on their current home just after Diane was born.

Mary inherited $4,000 from her mother's estate when her mother died in 2009 as well as her mother's time share condominium in the Bahamas. Mary deposited the money in the couple's joint checking account and used the money to pay for a family vacation at the condominium in 2010.

Although divorces can include a consideration of child and spousal support as well as distribution of property and allocation of debts during a number of sessions, this case study will only consider the initial mediation session. Questions for Discussion will address issues about property distribution.

We began the session by reading the Contract for Co-mediation aloud interjecting explanations of terms when appropriate and pausing to answer questions. Clients seemed to appreciate our taking time to explain what they could expect in detail rather than just rushing into something that they had never experienced.

Occasionally, parties brought attorneys to sessions. When the parties told us that in advance, we sent an information packet to each attorney that also included our protocol for attorney participation in mediation. The protocol was prepared by several of the attorneys that worked as mediators for our practice. Attorneys that attended mediation sessions seemed to appreciate that we had explained our expectations for them. They were used to following rules for the courts in which they appeared and none objected to the protocol we had established.

Essentially, that protocol was: "Each party may have their attorney present or consult with their attorney at any time during mediation and is encouraged to do so. Mediation is most effective when all parties involved work within certain guidelines. During mediation, attorneys do not actively participate, but may confer with their clients at any time. Attorneys should encourage their clients to accept responsibility and speak for themselves by stating what they want and need including their intent, reasons, and feelings."

When we had finished reading the contract and answering questions, copies were circulated so that each party present had a copy with the signatures of all present for their records. The balance of advanced fees was collected and we continued with the session.

Our goal for the initial session was to focus on those issues relating to the custody of children. Some mediators prefer to begin by discussing property and then move to issues involving children. Since the focus of our practice was families with children and was advertised as such, parties expected that children would be the priority subject to be discussed.

Frequently parents had preconceived ideas about custody and visitation. Many of these ideas were incorrect. Some parents began by saying they wanted "full custody," meaning that they wanted total control over the children. Others wanted "50/50." Rather than confront either parent and tell them their information was not correct, we explained custody in simple language and answered as many questions as necessary before moving on to what options each parent wanted. It proved to be more effective to determine their underlying interests before asking for their positions.

Legal custody was explained as "decision making." Decisions might include education, medical treatment, religious training and manner of discipline. We explained that these decisions could be made by one parent or by both after discussing the situations. If one parent were to consider the other's thoughts and feelings concerning important decisions for the children, but then have complete and final authority to make decisions in any of these matters, that was "sole legal custody" as defined by law in Virginia. Another option that we referred to as the decision-making aspect of "shared parenting," was that decisions would be made jointly by both parents. This was called "joint legal custody" in Virginia. Different states may have different labels. Our point was to explain that custody was about decision making and that it was not a total package that included visitation and child support.

We then explained visitation by using the term "parenting." Since raising children has to do with so many considerations other than who they will be with at any given time, parenting was a far more inclusive and appropriate label. The process we used we called "Activity-based Parenting."

An Activity-based Parenting Plan is a detailed and specific plan prepared by parents for supervising the activities of their children. It includes more than the traditional visitation schedule and explains how the parents will share responsibility for maintaining the children's daily routine. It focuses on the best interests of the children despite any inconvenience to either or both parents. It does not consider which parent has legal or physical custody because those factors deal with how significant decisions are made for the children and where the children have their primary residence. Those factors are parents' business. An Activity-based Parenting Plan makes the children the priority and does not make one parent more "powerful" than the other because of legal or physical custody.

One concept upon which the Activity-based Parenting Plan is based is called "social capital." It consists of all those factors that have an influence on the best interests of children that are not directly related to their parents. Those factors include: extended family, peer groups, familiar neighborhood surroundings, living arrangements, sports and extracurricular activities, etc.—in short any positive aspect of the children's lives other than parents that affects the children's best interests.

The Activity-based Parenting Plan is a logical outgrowth of "social capital" and is constructed by using the child's activities and routine as the basis. The underlying philosophy is that as a child grows older, except for time spent sleeping, he or she usually spends more time away from home than at home. The assumption is that the best interests of the child are served by following a plan or schedule that is least disruptive for the child and changes his or her daily routine as little as possible.

We asked the parents to tell us what the children did each day from the time they got up in the morning until they went to bed at night. Obviously, this varies from child to child and even within families based on the age of the children. Research has shown that age is the most significant factor to consider when determining a child's best interests with respect to activities and contact with parents.

It becomes obvious that children have to be treated as individuals and that the Activity-based Parenting Plan for one child in a family could be very different from that of his or her brother or sister. Hopefully, this will give a thump on the head to all those attorneys, mediators, and judges that treat the children as a unit and lump their visitation together based on the parents' schedules. We also hope this will bring an end to standardized visitation schedules characterized by such parent-oriented concepts as "alternating weekends and major holidays." Parenting is not supposed to be an easy task for the parents and a difficult experience for the children. Let's stop and consider what each child is doing on the weekend!

Another concept in Activity-based Parenting is "parental availability," a period of time each parent is available to supervise the activities of the children. It is the basis for determining "periods of responsibility." The amount of time the children spend with either parent is not the primary consideration. If the Activity-based Parenting Plan is truly in the children's best interest, the time spent with either parent does not have to be equal and the "periods of responsibility" for each parent could be reversed with little or no impact on the children.

Children benefit from the supervision and active participation of both parents. Schedules that provide one parent with 26 days of supervision per month and the other with four when that parent is only responsible for alternate weekends are not in a child's best interest. They are an example of one parent trying to exercise more control over the children and limit the children's time with the other parent.

Simply stated, once we know what the children's schedules are, we ask parents how they plan to share the responsibility for providing supervision. Rather than a particular weekend being "Dad's weekend," when using an Activity-based Parenting Plan, it means that Dad is responsible for the children on a particular weekend. He can discharge that responsibility in three ways: personally, use a sitter or a family member, or ask the other parent to assume responsibility. The other parent has the option of saying, "Yes" or "No." Because the other parent is "off-duty," he or she is not required to provide supervision since it is the first parent's "period of responsibility." Parents tend to look at the Activity-based Parenting Plan as the schedule for the children and "periods of responsibility" as a schedule that tells them who is on duty and what their rotating shifts look like. This makes the parents equally responsible for the shift when they are on duty and avoids the labels of custodial and non-custodial parent.

This helps parents look at caring for children in a different way than who would "have the minor children" for what period of time or what day or weekend. We wanted parents to place the best interests of their children ahead of any considerations of control by either parent. Activity-based Parenting is a very different concept than alternating weekends.

Another concept in Activity-based Parenting is "transition activities"—events such as school, sports, scouts, lessons, etc. that provide a child with the opportunity to transition from one parent to another by participating in an activity that enhances or reinforces the child's "social capital." The idea is that one parent would drop the child off for the activity and the other parent would pick the child up. This also permits parents to spend time with children during the school week, but still have the child sleep in the same home throughout the school week if that will assure a better focus on schoolwork. In situations where direct contact between parents has exposed the children to parental conflict, "transition activities" provide a way for the children to escape being caught in a crossfire between feuding parents.

Activity-based Parenting considers parental responsibilities as opposed to parental rights. When there is harmony in a relationship between parents, there may still be disagreements between them as to who will be responsible for taking a child to ballet or soccer or who will be available to care for them on any given evening. Our goal was to encourage parents to accept that children have a routine that is not defined in terms such as "mom's weekend" or dad's weekend." Rather, for example, we focused on who would be responsible for caring for the children on a given weekend. Our emphasis was on the reality that the children have two homes, the concepts of which are explained by Isolina Ricci (1997) in "Mom's House, Dad's House."

Using the Activity-based Parenting concepts of "periods of responsibility," "social capital" and "transition activities," parents were able to prepare a parenting plan very different than the stereotypical visitation schedule where children might be treated as objects passed back and forth between parents. Parents agreed that Activity-based Parenting was much more like what they had been doing to supervise the daily lives of their children. Judges in the courts we worked with also liked the concept because it clearly defined which parent was responsible for which children at any given time. Many judges told us that post divorce compliance issues with respect to parenting were reduced and fewer parents returned to court with disputes about what was "reasonable" or "mutually agreeable."

The ultimate outcome of considering the children's "social capital" instead of the "parent's rights," basing a parenting plan of the activities and routine of the children instead of the parent's schedules, and describing the time each parent has with the children as a "period of responsibility" rather than a visitation schedule, is that the emphasis shifts to the children and the relationship between the parents becomes far more business-like. They can truly make the best interests of their children "job one" and conduct business with each other in a civil and respectful manner taking turns supervising the children in accordance with the daily routine the children recognize as the world they live in.

John and Mary told us that the children were living with Mary in the marital home and that they wanted that arrangement to continue. Despite the feelings each had because of the affair and Mary being fired, neither parent wanted to disrupt the children's routine. They also agreed that they would continue to make any decisions about the children jointly as they always had.

Steven played soccer for his school team. They had practice on Tuesday afternoon after school and played games against other school teams on Saturday mornings. Diane had piano lessons on Wednesday afternoon after school and had ballet class on Thursday from 6:00 until 7:00 P.M.

John and Mary liked the concept of Activity-based Parenting because it was very similar to how they had been parenting before they separated. They agreed that John would be responsible for taking Steven to soccer practice and that he would remain overnight with John who would be responsible for taking him to school the following morning. Whenever Steven had a game on Saturday, John would be responsible for taking him. If the game occurred on a weekend that was John's period of responsibility, Steven and Diane would live with John beginning when school was dismissed on Friday and spend the remainder of the weekend with their father. John would be responsible for taking both children to school on Monday morning.

Mary accepted responsibility for taking Diane to piano lessons and ballet classes. The parents agreed that, with the exception of Steven on Tuesday, the children would live with their mother during each week school was in session.

Despite the initial tone of agreement between parents, an argument began when we discussed the Thanksgiving holiday. The tradition had been that Steven's mother would come to spend that entire period with the children and their parents at the marital home. Mary told us that since the time that grandma became aware of the affair and Mary's being fired from her job; she became very hostile toward Mary and had encouraged John to divorce her.

Mary made it quite clear that she did not want to continue the Thanksgiving tradition since she knew that John's mother might cause a scene in front of the children that would spoil the entire holiday. Since this would be the first Thanksgiving since the separation, both parents agreed that John would be responsible for the children and take them to their Grandmother's. Mary acknowledged that she would get a break since she wouldn't have to prepare the meal. She said she would have dinner with a woman from the choir at church with whom she had a close friendship.

John agreed that the family would spend Christmas together acknowledging that his mother was also included in that tradition, but stating that he and Mary would think about that holiday and make a decision during the next mediation session.

Essentially parenting for the remainder of the year would be based upon alternating responsibility for weekends and major holidays. The traditional for the children's birthdays was to have a party at Chuck E. Cheese or a similar location and invite all the children's friends. Both parents would attend as they always had.

Since John's schedule was based on the school year, he had summers free and could be responsible for the children when Mary began a new job. The parents agreed that would be the plan unless Mary's work schedule made it possible for her to spend more time with the children. The unique aspect of this plan was that the children would live in the marital home at night and John would be responsible for them during the days of summer.

John and Mary agreed to return in two weeks to complete their parenting plan and to discuss financial and property issues. Until then, they agreed each would continue to drive the car they had routinely used and that John would pay the credit card account both used for purchasing gas.

When John and Mary departed, the mediation team spent approximately 30 minutes processing what had occurred during the two-hour session. The senior mediator would begin by asking the recorder, usually a mediation intern, what was different than what he or she expected. The intern then queried both mediators to determine, for example, why certain questions were asked and what the mediators expected when the parties responded. The goal of a processing session was for all members of the mediation team to discuss the progress and substance of mediation while it was still fresh in their minds. The final aspect of processing was to prepare a brief written plan for the next session to be discussed when the team met prior to beginning that session.

Questions for Discussion

1. What are the pros and cons of using a mediation team rather than a single mediator?
2. How did the parent's focus on their children facilitate preparing a parenting plan?
3. How might unresolved issues or issues not discussed affect the next mediation session?
4. Suppose Mary thought the down payment for the marital home was a gift from her parents to her?
5. How might Mary's depositing the money she inherited affect how it would be characterized as an asset?
6. Should the condominium be considered as marital property?
7. Suppose after the mediation session, John discussed with his mother what he and Mary agreed to?

8. Things seemed to be fairly amicable for a couple where an extramarital affair occurred. Should the mediators have asked about that?

REFERENCES

Emery, R. E. (1994). *Renegotiating family relationships: Divorce, child custody and mediation.* New York: Guilford.

Gardner, R. A. (1989). *Family evaluation in child custody mediation, arbitration, and litigation.* New Jersey: Creative Therapeutics.

Kelly, J. B. (1983). Mediation and psychotherapy: Distinguishing the differences. *Mediation Quarterly, 1,* 33–44.

Ricci, I. (1997). *Mom's house, dad's house.* New York: Simon & Schuster.

Chapter 7

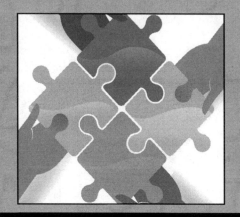

Victim Offender Mediation

Lawrie Parker

Once considered an emerging field in mediation, victim offender mediation is now recognized as an integral part of many communities throughout the United States. With the assistance of a trained mediator, usually a community volunteer, victim offender mediation is a *restorative justice* approach that brings offenders face-to-face with the victims of their crimes. Crime is personalized as offenders learn the human consequences of their actions, and victims (who may be ignored by the criminal justice system) have the opportunity to speak their minds and their feelings to the ones who most ought to hear them, contributing to the healing process (Price, 2001). The practice is also called victim offender dialogue, victim offender conferencing, victim offender reconciliation, or victim offender meetings. In some practices, the victim and the offender are joined by family and community members or others. The victim, in a safe and secure setting and in the presence of a trained mediator, is able to let the offender know how the crime affected him or her, to receive answers to questions, and to be directly involved in developing a restitution plan for the offender to be accountable for the losses they caused. The offenders are able to humanize their crime, to take direct responsibility for their behavior, to learn the full impact of what they did, and to develop a plan for making amends to the person(s) they violated.

Victim offender mediation is one of the clearest expressions of restorative justice, a movement that has received significant attention throughout North America and Europe. The idea of bringing together a victim of a crime and the person who committed that crime is based on age-old values of justice, accountability, and restoration. The practice is used more widely for juvenile property offenses but has been implemented successfully in adult crimes and in violent crimes. The first victim offender reconciliation program was started in Kitchener, Ontario, Canada in 1976. The first program in the United States was started in Elkhart, Indiana in 1978. In 1990, there were approximately 150 such programs and by 2000 there were more than 1,200 world-wide.[1] Yet, the essence of what now is being called restorative justice is deeply rooted in the traditional practices of many indigenous people throughout the world, such as Native Americans, Pacific Islanders, Maori in New Zealand, and First Nation people in Canada (Umbreit, 1998). In many ways, restorative justice and approaches such as victim offender mediation are Western ways of implementing what many indigenous and traditional cultures have been practicing for generations.

WHY VICTIM OFFENDER MEDIATION?

The current juvenile and criminal justice systems in the United States are primarily offender-centered, placing the emphasis on guilt, punishment, and the rights of the accused (Price, 1995). Crime is viewed as an offense against the state and little help is offered to crime victims. Moving beyond the offender driven focus, restorative justice identifies three clients: individual victims, victimized communities, and offenders. Crime is seen primarily as an offense against people within communities, as opposed to the more abstract definition of crime as a violation against the state. Those most directly affected by crime play an active role in restoring peace between individuals and within communities. Restoration of the emotional and material losses resulting from crime is far more important than imposing ever increasing levels of punishment on the offender (Umbreit, 1998).

 ## Two Different Views[2]

Criminal (Retributive) Justice	Restorative Justice
• Crime is a violation of the law and the state.	• Crime is a violation of people and relationships.
• Violations create guilt.	• Violations create obligations.
• Justice requires the state to determine blame (guilt) and impose pain (punishment).	• Justice involves victims, offenders, and community members in an effort to put things right.
• *Central focus: offenders getting what they deserve.*	• *Central focus: victim needs and offender responsibility for repairing harm.*

Three Different Questions[3]

Criminal (Retributive) Justice	Restorative Justice
• What laws have been broken?	• Who has been hurt?
• Who did it?	• What are their needs?
• What do they deserve?	• Whose obligations are these?

Statistics from a cross-section of the North American programs show that about two-thirds of the cases referred resulted in a face-to-face mediation meeting; over 95% of the cases mediated resulted in a written restitution agreement; over 90% of those restitution agreements are completed within one year. On the other hand, the actual rate of payment of court-ordered restitution (nationally) is typically only from 20–30% (Price, 2001).

Why such a huge difference in restitution compliance? Offenders seldom view court-ordered restitution as a moral obligation. It seems like just one more fine being levied against them by an impersonal court system. When the restitution obligation is reached voluntarily and face-to-face, offenders experience it in a very different way. Perhaps most important, after facing the victims of their crimes, offenders commit fewer and less serious offenses than similar offenders who are processed by the traditional juvenile or criminal justice system (Price, 2001).

Umbreit's (1994) research indicates:

* About two-thirds of the crime victims who are invited to participate in mediation choose to do so,
* About two-thirds of the cases referred to mediation result in a face-to-face mediation session,
* Over 90% of the cases actually mediated face-to-face result in a written agreement,
* Over 90% of the written agreements are satisfactorily completed,
* Victims and offenders who participate in mediation are very likely to experience satisfaction and a perception of fairness and justice,
* Victims who participate in mediation report a reduction in their fear of being re-victimized by the same offender, and
* Offenders commit fewer and less serious offenses after participating in mediation.

TRAINING AND EXPERIENCE NEEDED FOR VICTIM OFFENDER MEDIATION

How Victim Offender Mediation Differs from Other Types of Mediation

Mediation is commonly used in a number of conflict situations such as divorce and custody disputes, community disputes, commercial disputes, and other civil court related conflicts. In these settings, the parties are referred to as "disputants," with an assumption being made that they both are contributing to the conflict and therefore need to collaborate and compromise in order to reach a mutually satisfactory settlement. Often, mediation in these settings is focused heavily upon reaching a settlement with a lesser emphasis upon discussing the impact of the conflict upon their lives.

In victim offender mediation, the involved parties are not "disputants." Generally, one has clearly committed a criminal offense and has admitted doing so, while the other has clearly been victimized. The issue of guilt or innocence is not mediated. Nor is there an expectation that crime victims compromise and request less than what they need to address their losses. While many other types of mediation are largely settlement driven, victim offender mediation is primarily dialogue driven, with the emphasis on helping the victim heal, offender accountability, and restoration of losses. Most victim offender mediation sessions do result in a signed restitution agreement. The agreement, however, is secondary to the importance of the dialogue between the parties. The dialogue addresses emotional and informational needs of victims that are central both to their healing and to development of victim empathy in the offender, which can lead to less criminal behavior in the future. Research has consistently found that the restitution agreement is less important to crime victims than the opportunity to talk directly with the offender about how they felt about the crime. A restorative impact is strongly correlated to the creation of a safe place for dialogue between the crime victim and offender (Umbreit, 1998).

Another significant difference is the voluntariness of victim offender mediation. In other types of mediation as it is practiced in civil or commercial disputes, courts mandate that both "disputants" attend at least one mediation session. By contrast, voluntary participation is a basic tenet of victim offender mediation and victims are never coerced into participating. The offender's participation is usually characterized as voluntary as well, although it should be recognized that offenders may "volunteer" in order to avoid more onerous outcomes that would otherwise be imposed (Umbreit, 1994).

TRAINING AND EXPERIENCE NEEDED

There is ongoing discussion in the field about what should be included in the training of victim offender mediators, how long the training should be, and which training model is best. While there is no standardized training for certification within the victim offender field, the international Victim Offender Mediation Association (VOMA) has in the past provided a 24-hour basic victim offender mediation training at its annual conferences (Amstutz, 2009). Most victim offender mediation programs provide an average of 12 to 40 hours of training. The trainings include an introduction to a restorative justice framework and philosophy, victim and offender awareness and sensitivity issues, risks and benefits of victim offender mediation, communication skills, conflict resolution and negotiation skills, the role of the mediator, an introduction to the dialogue process between victims and offenders, and conducting the various elements of the process, including calling the victim/offender, meeting with the victim/offender separately, and then conducting the joint mediation session. Some states have certification requirements for mediators, which may dictate the number of training hours needed (Amstutz, 2009). Mentoring under the tutelage of an experienced victim offender mediator is highly recommended and in some programs, required.

A major emphasis in victim offender training is the dialogue driven mediation model often referred to as transformative mediation. In their widely acclaimed book *The Promise of Mediation,* authors Robert A. Baruch Bush and Joseph P. Folger emphasize the importance of genuine empowerment and mutual recognition of each other's humanity, in addition to the value of compassionate strength among parties in conflict. A particular application of transformative mediation, which is well-suited for victim offender mediation, is the humanistic model of mediation introduced by restorative justice researcher and pioneer Mark Umbreit (1994). A humanistic mediation model is grounded in underlying values and beliefs about the nature of human existence, conflict, and the search for healing. They are: (1) belief in the connectedness of all things and our common humanity, (2) belief in the importance of the mediator's presence and connectedness with the involved parties in facilitating effective conflict resolution, (3) belief in the healing power of mediation through a process of the involved parties helping each other through the sharing of feelings (dialogue/mutual aid), (4) belief in the desire of most people to live peacefully, (5) belief in the desire of most people to grow through life experiences, and (6) belief in the capacity of all people to draw upon inner reservoirs of strength to overcome adversity, to grow, and to help others in similar circumstances (Umbreit, 1998).

Victim offender mediation training also emphasizes that a number of significant changes in the dominant Western/European model of mediation need to change in order for the transformative, humanistic mediation model to flourish.

These mediation practice changes include: (1) centering of the mediator (clearing the mind of clutter and focusing on the important peacemaking task at hand), (2) reframing the mediator's role (from directing a settlement driven process to facilitating a process of dialogue and mutual aid), (3) pre-mediation sessions with each party (listening to their story, providing information, obtaining voluntary participation, assessing the case, clarifying expectations, preparing for the mediation), (4) connecting with the parties through building of rapport and trust (beginning in the pre-mediation phase), (5) identifying and tapping into parties' strengths (beginning in the pre-mediation phase), (6) coaching on communication, if required (during the pre-mediation sessions), (7) non-directive style of mediation, (8) face-to-face seating of victim and offender (unless inappropriate because of the culture of parties or individual request), (9) recognition and use of power of silence, and (10) follow-up sessions (Umbreit, 1998).

It is important to note that a non-directive style of mediation should not to be confused with a passive style in which the mediator provides little direction, leadership, or assistance. The mediator remains in control of the process and, although saying little, is actively involved nonverbally and able to respond or intervene at various times as required, particularly when people get stuck and indicate a need for assistance.

HOW DOES A MEDIATOR PREPARE FOR VICTIM OFFENDER MEDIATION?

Preparing the Clients

Preparing for victim offender mediation is quite different than the approach a mediator takes for a traditional mediation. First, pre-mediation separate meetings with the involved parties are standard. Collection of information, assessment of the conflict, description of the mediation process, and clarification of expectations are important tasks. The most important task is developing trust and rapport that enhances the dialogue process. Often, offenders and victims of their crimes are unable to even imagine talking with each other (or wanting to) until a victim offender mediator offers such an opportunity in a way that makes the prospect seem desirable and safe. Listening to the victim's and offender's stories of the crime and encouraging the expression of feelings are critical. With all parties trusting that the mediator will insure that they are honored and respected in the mediation process, both victim and offender are more likely to be honest and open with each other. Their trust in the mediator is essential to a meeting in which they may be able to let go of their fear and defensiveness, become vulnerable and real and open the way to understanding, empathy and healing (Price, 1995). As clients consider participating, the mediator may encourage them to reflect on the following questions, if appropriate: (1) What would it be like to sit across the table from the other party and hear her or his story? (2) How do you think the other party might feel, meeting with you face-to-face? (3) To the offender: have you ever experienced being a victim? What was that like? (4) What might you like to say to the victim or offender, (5) What are the risks and benefits of mediation to you? (Umbreit, 1998).

The mediator must also determine whether the crime and the parties are appropriate for mediation. The physical and emotional safety of the victim must be the overriding concern. The mediator learns what happened from the people who were involved, whose stories may differ greatly from the police report or other referral information. During the pre-mediation meeting, the mediator can assess the parties' motivations and their ability to communicate verbally. A victim who is too intimidated to speak to the offender is probably not a good candidate for mediation; neither is a victim who seeks only to "bash" the offender (Price, 1995).

An offender who does not acknowledge involvement or responsibility in the offense (or at least partially on some level) is not suitable for victim offender mediation. Such a person is an "accused" or "defendant" but not an "offender" (Price, 1995). If guilt has not been admitted or adjudicated and a defense is anticipated, then an accused is ill-advised to mediate, out of concern for avoiding self-incrimination. From a victim's standpoint, a confrontation with an accused who denies the offense and/or blames the victim is often experienced as a "re-victimization." Equally re-victimizing is an offender who shows no expression of remorse or regret. To protect the victim, mediation should not take place. At a minimum, a victim should be advised of the offender's stance and be given a choice to participate or not. Obviously, mediation should not take place with an offender who seems predisposed to threaten, assault, or retaliate. Best practices dictate that the offender should be approached first, regarding participation. A victim who wants to participate only to find out the offender does not, might feel re-victimized.

Another purpose of pre-mediation meetings is to discuss other support people the parties may want in attendance (a family member, friend, neighbor, community leader, minister, teacher, probation officer) and various options they may want to include in an agreement. Mediators may wish to describe the kinds of solutions other victims and offenders have found helpful, such as: (1) monetary restitution, amount not to exceed victim's out-of-pocket loss, (2) community service, site and hours to be determined by both parties (a value may be established for the unpaid work as a way of partially or completely fulfilling what would have been a monetary obligation), (3) personal service such as mowing the lawn or painting a fence, (4) charitable contribution, amount not to exceed victim's out-of-pocket loss; (5) apology, verbal or written, (6) creative restitution designed by the victim and offender, building on the interests of the victims and the abilities and/or interests of the offender, such as creating a work of art, writing an essay, etc., (7) classes, training, counseling, treatment program for the offender, (8) combinations of the aforementioned that are mutually agreed upon as fair, safe, and reasonable (Umbreit, 1998).

Victim offender mediation programs that conduct individual pre-mediation meetings typically mediate two-thirds to three-quarters of the cases referred; participants rarely fail to appear for a mediation session after having individual meeting with the mediator. On the other hand, programs that do not conduct preliminary meetings with victims and offenders typically experience a 50% no-show rate for scheduled mediations. Thus, a number of people who show up, ready and willing to mediate, are inconvenienced and leave with feelings of anger and disappointment. For victims, it may be a re-victimization but this time by the program. Without adequate screening and case assessment, there is a substantial risk that a mediator will conduct a victim offender confrontation that should not take place at all, or one that the mediator will not be prepared to handle (Price, 1995).

Preparing the Room

On the day of the mediation, the mediator needs to arrive early to arrange the room in a manner most conducive to mediation. The space needs to be quiet and private, small enough to create a sense of intimacy and facilitate ease of hearing, yet large enough to avoid a sense of confinement. Seating is also important and can impact the session. Generally, seating is arranged so that the offender and victim have the opportunity to face each other directly across a table or circle. Some victim offender mediation programs offer refreshments after the mediation as a symbolic "breaking of the bread" together. Mediators should also equip the room with Kleenex, anticipating that these visceral meetings may become emotional for the parties.

Preparing Oneself

Prior to the mediation, the mediator should arrive early and review the case briefly. He or she should consider strategies that came to mind during the pre-mediation interviews, tailoring the mediation to the unique factors of the case. The mediator should also take a few moments of silence to clear the mind and prepare to give full attention to the parties (Umbreit, 1998).

TYPICAL AND UNIQUE PROBLEMS ASSOCIATED WITH VICTIM OFFENDER MEDIATION

Reluctance of Parties to Participate

There is little practical value in forcing someone to participate in victim offender mediation. If participants do not have some level of commitment to the dialogue process, it is likely to be an unpleasant experience for everyone, including the mediator, and an exercise in futility. This is true for offenders too. Offenders must see potential benefit for them to participate meaningfully. Mediators must be knowledgeable about issues important to offenders and connect those issues to a dialogue-driven mediation. Restorative justice practitioner Eric Gilman suggests that a normative, but often unarticulated, goal for offenders is to be accountable in ways that make sense to them. Gilman expands this self focus so that the offender's obligation is to be accountable in ways that also make sense to the victim and the community. He explains to offenders that the community is interested in finding a resolution that will enable them to deal responsibly with their offense, that will enable them to put the offense behind them and that will enable them to move forward with their lives in a positive way. These outcomes relate directly to important issues for offenders (Gilman, 2006).

The restorative value of victim offender mediation to crime victims is directly related to how the mediator understands the function and value of restorative justice. Gilman proffers that the primary purpose of making contact with the victim should not be to suggest or encourage their participation in a dialogue process. Rather, using a holistic approach, the purpose of the contact should be primarily focused on the community pro-actively responding to individuals who have been harmed by crime in ways that meaningfully address their needs. The purpose of the initial contact is to: (1) acknowledge the harm done to the victim, express the community's concern about that harm and its commitment to the victim, (2) express the community's commitment to hold the offender accountable, hopefully in ways that are meaningful to the victim, (3) acknowledge the victims' feelings and concerns, and (4) to provide options for addressing victims' needs. This approach often segues to participation in victim offender mediation, but the distinction is important. If the initial contact offers some restorative value, then contact with a victim that does not result in a mediation that is not considered a failure or wasted effort. In other words, the goal of the contact is to serve the crime victim well, not to get them to participate in any specific program or process.

Criminal Justice System Buy-In

Traditional wisdom says crime should be dealt with by criminal justice professionals but restorative justice expands stakeholders to include victims, offenders, support persons, and the community. Its emphasis on people and broken relationships causes discomfort among some professionals who see restorative justice as usurping their authority and being soft on crime. But restorative justice is not a replacement for the legal system, nor is it an "either/or" issue. Crime has both a public dimension and a private, or social, dimension. The legal system focuses on the public dimension, on society's interest and obligations as represented by the state. By putting a spotlight on and elevating the private dimensions of crime, restorative justice seeks to provide a balance on how justice is experienced (Zehr, 2002).

Cultural Bias

As noted previously, victim offender mediation was developed primarily within the context of a Western, Eurocentric framework. The facilitation styles may reflect this bias and thus may not be appropriate for people from other traditions. Some have argued that the basic assumptions underlying victim offender mediation and the theory of restorative justice contain these unconscious biases (Amstutz, 2009). One example of culturally-specific modifications made to programs is Morris Jenkins' work on Afrocentric restorative justice. He states that Afrocentric and Eurocentric theory differ in four fundamental principles: cosmology (worldview); axiology (values); ontology (nature of people), and; epistemology (source of knowledge). He provides a "cultural justice model" that practitioners could use in the African American community (Jenkins, 2005). Fundamentally, victim offender mediators need to be aware of their own biases and must include and listen carefully to the perspectives of those from other traditions.

Confidentiality

Mediators often promise to keep everything that is said during mediation confidential. This promise is straightforward but presents a trap for the unwary, especially in victim offender mediation. Repeating the promise of confidentiality during mediation gives mediators and parties a sense of security about their conversations, but unfortunately the promise does not yield an impermeable shield of confidentiality. Victim offender mediation programs rely on the assurance of confidentiality as a vital part of providing a safe space for dialogue. A trend is emerging, however, to put some limits on confidentiality, particularly disclosures that are of "significant" or "compelling" public interest (Bird & Reimund, 2001). There is interest in addressing the community's concern that justice may require the disclosure not only of offenders' self-incriminating statements, but also of exculpatory statements as well.

Another issue for mediators is jurisdictional reporting requirements that limit confidentiality. Some states require mediators to report instances of child and elder abuse or threats of serious bodily harm. Pre-meeting disclosure of any confidentiality limitations can be helpful, such as anything the offender says about crimes other than the current offense are not offered protection from disclosure. The Victim Offender Mediation Association (VOMA) offers the following guidelines for evaluating confidentiality: (1) Does your state have a statute or rule covering confidentiality in mediation? (2) If so, does it specifically include victim offender mediation or has there been an interpretation of that statute that makes it inclusive or exclusive? (3) Are there specific statutory exceptions to confidentiality protections? (4) Who does the statute protect (mediator as well as the parties) and what protections are afforded? (5) Are there other professional standards that may govern how to deal with confidentiality, such as for attorneys, mental health professionals, social workers, police, or probation officers? (Bird & Reimund, 2001). In addition, VOMA has issued ethical guidelines for mediators, which include handling issues of confidentiality.

CONCLUDING COMMENTS

Restorative justice programs have been implemented in almost every state and are composed of a variety of methods, including victim offender mediation. They offer a different framework in which to view and respond to crime, in addition to the traditional criminal justice system. To be effective, mediators must be carefully recruited, trained and managed. Victim-offender mediation, with its focus on *restorative justice,* cannot provide all of the answers to our crime problem, but it is an essential part of the solution.

Case Study: The Softball Celebration (from Piedmont Dispute Resolution Center; Warrenton, Virginia)

The high school girls' softball team had just won the regional championship game. Giddy with excitement, three of the players piled into a friend's car and went on a joyride. As they drove through a nearby subdivision, group mentality set in and they began using their bats as weapons in a frenzy of gleeful mailbox bashing. By the time the police were notified and their foray halted, ten mailboxes were damaged. The juvenile intake officer referred the case to the local victim offender mediation program.

The two mediators assigned to the case met individually with each girl and her parent(s) and made contact first by letter, followed by a phone call and individual meetings with each of the residents of the houses affected. Two of the girls were genuinely remorseful during the pre-mediation meetings, but two were flippant and scoffed at the idea of victim offender mediation. "What's the big deal," they said. "It's just mailboxes. Get over it." In the end, however, all four girls and their parents agreed to participate. Five residents also agreed to participate. They were informed that some of the girls didn't seem remorseful but decided they still wanted to confront them. The mediators offered alternatives to the five that did not participate; two wrote letters which the mediators said would be read during the mediation.

The mediation was held in the corner of a local church's social hall, to accommodate the large crowd of 15 people and two mediators. The mediators arranged the seating so that the girls were sitting directly across from their victims in the circle. During the pre-mediation meetings, the victims were asked if they wanted to speak first or if they wanted the girls to speak first. They decided that the girls should speak first and sure enough, while two were apologetic, two were recalcitrant, shrugging their shoulders and staring at their shoes. The mediators then asked the parents of these two girls to read the letters from the victims who chose not to participate in the mediation. Both letters described the anger and hurt caused by the girls' vandalism. One letter came from a senior citizen with disabilities who said she had no one to help her put up a new mailbox and must now drive to the post office to pick up her mail. These victims wanted a letter of apology and an explanation.

Then it was the remaining victims' turn. One by one, as the mediator called upon each of them, they expressed their disappointment and shock. They wanted to know if they were singled out or was it a random act of destruction. They were concerned for the girls' future. Some had children the same age as the girls and said they felt sorry for the parents. Finally it was a young mother's turn to speak. A loner in the neighborhood, she was expressionless during much of the mediation. Slowly, deliberately and in a quiet, sad voice she shared her story with the girls and her neighbors.

Prior to moving into the neighborhood, she was a victim of domestic violence. In fact, she didn't have the courage to flee until her husband started turning on the children. They lived in a domestic violence shelter for a while and a homeless shelter. At last she was able to get on her feet, taking a job as a cashier at a local supermarket and renting a little house in the neighborhood. To celebrate their new life and freedom, the young mother and her children planted flowers at the base of their mailbox. "When I came home from work, turned the corner and saw the mailbox and the flowers smashed," she said, looking directly into the eyes of the girls, "the first thing I thought was, 'he's found us.'" Terrified, she called the police on her cell phone. It was the officer who responded to what he thought was a domestic violence call who caught the girls. "You didn't just smash my mailbox," the young mother continued through tears. "You took away my sense of security. You took away my sense of community. You robbed me of my joy."

The two nonchalant girls were visibly moved and their countenances changed dramatically. The mediators had to suspend the session briefly so that the girls, all of whom were sobbing, could regain their composure. Everyone agreed that the offenders would each write and hand-deliver letters of apology and replace the damaged mailboxes. The neighbors reached out to the young mother. Everyone agreed that they all—the girls and the neighbors—would meet the following Saturday and plant new flowers around her family's mailbox.

QUESTIONS FOR DISCUSSION

1. How did the mediators use what they learned in the pre-mediation meetings during the actual mediation? What strategies did they use?
2. Given that some of the girls were not remorseful, should the mediation have taken place? Why or why not? In what ways did the mediators deal with this situation?
3. How does victim offender mediation compare and contrast with traditional (retributive) justice in this case?
4. What were some of the challenges of this victim offender mediation involving multiple offenders and multiple victims? How were these challenges addressed?
5. Who was restored and how?

NOTES

[1] See Victim Offender Mediation Association website, *Where did the idea of RJ come from?*
[2] Howard Zehr, *The little book of restorative justice,* Intercourse, PA: Good Books, 2002, p. 21.
[3] Ibid.

RERERENCES

Amstutz, L. S. (2009). *The little book of victim offender conferencing.* Intercourse, PA: Good Books.

Bird, K. and Reimund, M. E. (2001). RJ dialogue processes are they confidential? *Victim Offender Mediation Association Connections,* Autumn: 9.

Bush, R. A. B., and Folger, J. (2005). *The promise of mediation: The Transformative Approach to conflict,* Revised Edition, San Francisco: Jossey-Bass

Gilman, E. (2006). *Engaging offenders in restorative dialogue processes.* Clark County, Washington Juvenile Court, September.

Jenkins, M. (2005). Ph.D., Afrocentric restorative justice. *Victim Offender Mediation Association Connections,* Summer: 5.

Price, M. (1995). Comparing victim-offender mediation program models. *Victim Offender Mediation Association Quarterly,* Summer: 6(1).

Price, M. (2001). Personalizing crime: Mediation produced restorative justice for victims and offenders. *Dispute Resolution Magazine,* American Bar Association, Fall.

Umbreit, M. S. (1994). *Victim meets offender: The impact of restorative justice and mediation.* Monsey, NY: Criminal Justice Press.

Umbreit, M. S. (1998). *Victim sensitive victim offender mediation training manual.* Center for Restorative Justice & Peacemaking, School of Social Work, College of Human Ecology, University of Minnesota.

Zehr, H. (2002). *The little book of restorative justice.* Intercourse, PA: Good Books.

Chapter 8

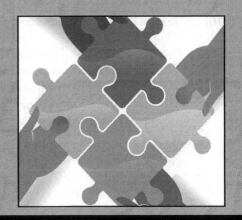

Mediation for the Department of Social Services: Facilitated Child and Family Team Meeting

Amanda Jordan-Brainard

You are Mary. You have a 10th grade education. You are 22 years old and wait tables at Waffle House (when you can pick up shifts). You have two children by two different dads. You walk through a metal detector at Department of Social Services (DSS) and meet with the case worker who will determine if you are a "fit" mother for your children. There will be many people there, with fancy titles and name badges. Most will wear fancy clothes and use big words like appropriate, suitable, mental health, developmental, IOP, SAIOP, DVOP, etc. This is all scary, so you nod and agree to what ever they want you to do—you want your kids!

This was the process that the New Hanover County Department of Social Services (DSS) previously used to work with families in their system. Since 2004, The Alternative Dispute Resolution Center, Inc. in conjunction with New Hanover County DSS has been using a new model: the Facilitated Child and Family Team Meeting (CFTM). Ideally, the facilitator is an employee of an outside agency, like a mediation center, as opposed to being an employee of DSS.

The facilitated CFTM has many strengths. We will examine those as we walk through a meeting. Oftentimes, the meetings are held at a neutral location and scheduled (via phone calls) by the neutral party. So from the very beginning, someone other than "the system" is interacting with the participants. When parties arrive for the meeting they all wait in the same waiting room—the family members, the case workers, the attorneys, the people with the big titles are in the same position as the family. The facilitator brings the parties to the room together.

Who is at the table? The family (one or more children and the parents) are asked who they would like to invite to the meeting to ensure they have their "supports" present. Participants may include mom, dad 1, dad 2, step-parents, grandparents, great-grandparents, extended family members, clergy, AA sponsor, neighbor/friend, parent's boyfriend/girlfriend, probation officer, mental health professionals (for parent and/or child), school representative(s), speech therapist, occupational therapist, development professional, Neonatal Intensive Care Unit (NICU) nurse, parent's attorney, foster parents, pre-adoptive parents, Guardian ad Litem (GAL) for child, GAL for parent, GAL's attorney, DSS case worker, DSS case worker's supervisor, DSS attorney—meetings range from 4–22 participants! You NEVER know what to expect!

It should also be noted that whenever appropriate, the child or children involved in the case should be invited to the meeting. This is a process where everyone works together in developing and achieving a plan, and instead of having a plan happen to them, it is beneficial for the child's voice to be heard and have them assist in developing a plan that will work for them also.

Where does the meeting take place? Ideally the meeting takes place at the neutral location of the mediation center, although sometimes meetings take place at other locations. To allow multiple participants from a school, sometimes meetings are held at the child's school. Other locations mediators have been known to go to include a therapist's office, the hospital, jail, a family home (inside or even on the porch). As you can see, there is a trend developing in this—always be flexible!

What kind of DSS cases are appropriate for facilitation? All DSS cases are appropriate for facilitation of this matter. There is no topic too "taboo" to be discussed at the table (abuse, incest, substance abuse) and no conflict too extreme for this setting. If the parents (or other relevant participants) have restraining orders against each other, one of two things can happen: two separate meetings are held, or the judge grants an exemption allowing the parties to jointly attend and participate in the meeting. If there is concern regarding extremely explosive behavior or violence (due to mental health or substance abuse issues and past behaviors), the meeting is best held at DSS where all participants must first go through a metal detector and where sheriff's deputies are on hand in case things get out of hand.

Mediator vs. facilitator: Although there are various models mediators use (facilitative, transformative, evaluative) the goal is always for each party to come to their agreement free of duress. When DSS is involved, they automatically have the upper hand and control so much regarding the children that the process is tilted in their favor. It is our job as facilitators to use the same techniques we use as mediators to help guide the process and ensure the families at least understand what is being asked of them, have the opportunity to ask meaningful questions and have control over aspects of their case that are appropriate.

During an opening statement, as the facilitator, you explain the neutral third-party role you serve, provide an overview of the structure of the meeting and, if you choose, review ground rules. Also important to point out in the opening statement is that the meeting is a good time to ask questions, get information, and gain a better understanding of what is expected. The Alternative Dispute Resolution Center, Inc. utilizes a strength-based, future-focused approach that is explained in the introduction.

Then you begin participant introductions, when as facilitator I like to try to help neutralize the situation by using common words and language wherever possible (the facilitator should *not* show off their knowledge to the "title people"/ professionals, but needs to be accessible to the family) and first names (to avoid the Mrs. Jones, Dr. Webb, and Mary).

Ground rules: Some mediators prefer to utilize ground rules to help ensure the meeting moves forward in a constructive manner. Typical ground rules include talking one at a time, no name-calling, not speaking for another person, remaining future focused, no cell-phones, and no physical aggression.

Strength-based approach: A focus of the New Hanover County DSS, as well as our approach to facilitated CFTMs, is to remain strength-based when possible. After introductions, the facilitator asks participants to share strengths they see for the children, for each parent, and/or the family as a whole. This starts the meeting off in a more positive tone as well as reminding everyone there are strengths that can be used to build on. The group is challenged to find ways to build on the strengths when developing a case plan and utilize the positives that are already in place (i.e., family supports).

It can be so powerful when a mother comes into a meeting because she "screwed up really bad" and is waiting for everyone at the table to tell her what a horrible mother she is and how she has done everything wrong and ruined her children (what she fears the meeting will be like) and the meeting starts with these professionals saying things like: "Mom clearly loves her children and they clearly love her; Mom advocates well for her child's needs and has ensured they are met; Children are bright, well mannered and nicely dressed which is a clear reflection on what mom has done; Mom has transportation and appropriate housing." Sometimes after hearing these types of strengths a mother will start crying. She had forgotten she had done something right and is moved that others have noticed; the meeting participants will not overlook the problems that brought the family to the attention of DSS, but they also do not overlook the areas that are going or have previously gone well.

The above examples of strengths tell the other participants at the table important information too: areas that do not need to be addressed, that mom will have transportation to get to necessary services (a frequent barrier), and although children may need services, they should be able to benefit from common services and will not need more extreme help.

At this point, hopefully everyone has softened somewhat, mom is more prepared to hear the concerns (not problems/offenses), and will be willing to work with the group instead of against the group. Note that I used the word "concerns." It is important to remember that labels and descriptors matter. When asking what the "problems" are, it is better to ask what "issues" or "concerns" will be addressed. These words sound less accusatory and are softer. By using non-judgment language it is easier for the family to listen without being focused on being offended.

Future-focused approach: As a facilitator it is helpful during the introduction to ask participants to remain as future-focused as possible. There clearly is a need to discuss some of the behaviors and concerns that led to DSS involvement, but the goal of these meetings is for everyone to work together to determine what can and should be done to move toward a mutually acceptable goal. This is a concept that the facilitator uses as a tool throughout the meeting.

During the "meat" of the meeting, parties discuss what their concerns are, how to address them, what DSS expects, what the parties need and the plan for how the concerns will be addressed. This is when DSS may discuss the issues that resulted in DSS involvement, laying out the case plan elements, and stating the objectives that the parent(s) must achieve to work towards case closure. This is also an opportunity for the family to share concerns they have and barriers they may need assistance with. The family can ask about help with transportation to attend counseling or they can share a concern they have that DSS had not planned to address in the case but can assist with. For example, the father may have called the school with a concern regarding possible bullying of his child and had trouble getting a satisfactory response. The DSS case worker could offer to help in coordinating communication with the school to help the dad with this process. Another example could be that a care provider shares they had a recent expense (new tires for their car) and are now having trouble with their water bill. The DSS case worker may help them in applying for some additional emergency funds to ensure there is no disruption in service. A phrase we often use to encourage parents and other participants is "get as much out of DSS as you can while you are working with them!"

Below is an example of a possible case plan that might be discussed: it does not start off looking so simple. The discussion might start with the mom sharing that she has been feeling very overwhelmed and stressed and that is why she started drinking and using marijuana again. The discussion might continue with mom, maternal grandmother and the case worker who might discuss the mom's past substance abuse and their concerns that maybe the substance use is the mom's way of self medicating. Maybe there is an underlying mental health cause for most of the problems. Then, the group starts focusing on how to identify the needs and address them. During this time, the facilitator may be encouraging mom to share some of this information and share what has worked for her in the past when she felt things were going well or what may be keeping step-granddad from focusing on and bringing up the mom's short comings. The facilitator may also ask questions regarding who will pay for services (insurance, mom, DSS); if transportation is in place, and try to identify other barriers that may prevent the plan from being successful.

Goal—Develop Case Plan

Case plan elements and objectives:

1. Emotional/Mental Health
   a. Parent agrees to participate in psychological assessment and follow recommendations
      i. DSS agrees to set up and pay for the assessment
      ii. Parent agrees to attend an assessment on May 4, 2–5 P.M., at 123 C Street
      iii. DSS will provide bus vouchers for transportation
2. Substance Abuse
   a. Parent agrees to participate in a Substance Abuse Intensive Outpatient Program (SAIOP) at New Horizons; New Horizons provides transportation
   b. DSS agrees to pay for SAIOP
   c. Parent agrees to sign a Release of Information so case worker can confirm participation in the program
   d. Parents agrees to submit to random drug screens; all understand that the drug screen must be done the same day case worker requests it; case worker will provide transportation if the parent does not have another means of transportation that day
3. Visitation plan
   a. Parent will have supervised visits with children at DSS on Tuesdays 2–4 P.M.; parent will provide activities to engage in with the children; parent understands no food or drink is allowed at visitation
   b. DSS & GAL agree to revisit the visitation plan as progress is documented/achieved

While case plan development meetings can be time consuming and involved, sometimes meetings that are addressing only one issue can be much more difficult. One example: DSS has not taken custody of the children, but is involved in a "treatment" case. This means the parents retain legal custody of the children while they work a case plan with a case worker. Sometimes the children remain with the parent(s) and there are no supervision requirements.

But, for this discussion let's assume that the family is a mom and a step dad who have had the children living with them; and the biological father who typically has the kids on alternating weekends. DSS got a call regarding supervision of the youngest child and upon investigating found mom to have a substance abuse issue. The kids lived with biological father full time while mom was in inpatient rehabilitation. Mom is now out and wants the kids back home with her per the custody agreement. Biological father wants to keep the kids, but has not yet filed anything with the courts. DSS has the position that they do not get involved between parents in custody battles. They accept that the children are at home with mom, but they want mom to be supervised with the children at all times for a certain period of duration. Mom and step-dad have a plan in place for him to supervise, but that would allow the kids to be home with mom and step-dad and start working back towards "life as normal." YIKES, right? Pretty complicated and no simple answer!

Kids are safe with the biological father. Kids are safe with step-dad. No need to continue to punish mom when she has voluntarily completed an inpatient rehab program and is continuing to participate in an intensive outpatient program. AND DSS really isn't going to tell them what the plan will be, just that they need to have a plan in place. This is a great situation for a facilitator to come in and work with the families to identify what their priorities are (the children's safety and emotional well being) and what their personal desires are.

The case filled up the entire two hour time slot just figuring out a temporary custody/visitation plan. There was no discussion of DSS's case plan at all. The case worker primarily stayed silent for the entire meeting. The solution involved a graduated plan and slow transition. It also included repeat facilitated meetings along the way to evaluate how things were going. The parties had a lot of trouble communicating at the beginning and were very emotional. They benefited greatly from the structured setting of facilitated meetings. Over time, they got better at working on things on their own, and were able to make changes without a facilitator involved, ergo a success story!

During this part of the meeting, the facilitator has the responsibility to control the flow of information, ask questions to ensure everyone understands and is hearing the same message, and uses techniques to keep people calm and focused. Facilitators employ a variety of special skills during this part of the meeting. Some of these skills are the types of skills one can be taught through mediation trainings and classes. An experienced mediator acting in the role of a facilitator knows how to "go with the flow" and employ the necessary tools and skills as needed.

Poker face: it is important for a good facilitator to maintain a neutral or poker face, especially while sometimes hearing "jaw dropping" information. Information may suggest that the clients reality may seem very "wrong or different" to the facilitator. The facilitator must not let that show (i.e., the parents are first cousins). It is not our job as facilitators to pass judgment on the situation that is being discussed (i.e., drug use, physical abuse of a child, molestation). We use appropriate terminology and speak calmly and "normally" about these issues. And, when someone makes a declaration that may catch other people off guard, we must not let it show if we were also surprised; e.g., a mother declares, in front of her own father, that the bruises on her neck and arms are not due to domestic violence but are because "I like it rough, ok?"

No-judgment zone: To assist with the above poker face, it helps to just "decide" that you will not judge the participants for the choices they have made and behaviors that they are/were engaged in. It is also important in remaining neutral that you do not judge DSS or the other professionals for the decisions they make. Clearly, the parents have made poor choices that resulted in DSS involvement (substance use, domestic violence, criminal acts, etc.); but sometimes DSS makes decisions that are hard for us as mediators to understand. It is crucial to remember that we do not have all of the information that DSS has, and that DSS personnel are well trained and responsible for making the decisions. It is not our place to question them.

An example of a DSS decision that may not be clear at the outset may be placing a child with a parent with criminal record of Indecent Liberties with a Minor. What we may not know is that these "indecent liberties" were the relationship between dad (18 years old) and mom (16 years old) that produced this child. That sounds a little different than what we may have initially imagined; i.e., a 26 year old in a relationship with a 14 year old.

Leave your formal education at the door: Depending on whom the "audience" members are, it is important for mediators when serving as facilitators of a Child and Family Team Meeting to be comfortable leaving their formal education, big obscure words, and all their fancy degrees at the door. This is not a time to show off all your knowledge. This is a great opportunity to ask questions (although you probably already know the answers) to allow the participants at the table to hear the answers. Good mediators when facilitating a CFTM run the show without seeming as if they are in charge. You use a quiet, behind the scenes, type of control. This is not the place to be the center of attention. You are not often praised for your fancy footwork, but you also are not blamed for everything that goes wrong!

Cultural sensitivity: Different cultures have different comfort levels with conflict and have different ways to communicate in general. When referring to "culture" it could be the country a person is from, it could refer to race, or just the type of people they surround themselves with. Some groups of people are very conflict averse and are uncomfortable expressing an opposing view or idea. When working with such people facilitators must help them find their own voice in a safe setting. Other people may speak very loudly and argue about everything, although this does not necessarily mean they are mad or upset. As facilitators, you must be comfortable with these variations and not impose your own conflict style on others. This also must be done with a semblance of following some general ground rules (i.e., no name calling, taking turns speaking, showing of respect to each other).

Difficult people: There likely could be an entire book devoted to tools and language to use to deal with difficult people, and while all of those would be useful, it is often hard to remember that many. It takes experience to really help you fine tune how to identify a "difficult" person and which "tool" to use with them "when." When facilitating CFTMs, it is safe to assume that the parents are not happy DSS is involved in their life. They have a dislike for the system and/or their case worker to varying degrees. Some of these parents love their children and strongly believe they did nothing wrong. Some love their children, know they screwed up, but would rather fix the problem themselves than having the system make them jump through hoops. Some frankly don't really care so much about their children, but they still want the system out of their lives and would like to deal with the problems within their family. Regardless of where the family fits into this, they would rather be left alone. So from the start people are NOT happy to be at this meeting. How they show this unhappiness also varies. Some people try to just do everything they are told, agree to everything that is asked of them, and play nice. They believe this is the way to make DSS go away. Others feel it is important to fight and argue about everything. Others fall somewhere in between.

Obstinate people: A common personality trait one encounters in these cases is the determined person (typically a parent) who has one view of what has happened, what should be happening currently, and what should happen in the future. They can be very defensive about what has been charged (which can be softened by starting with strengths) and be very angry about the course of events that they have been through. Sometimes they are very calm in their approach but unwilling to listen, other times they are very loud, they yell, they storm out of the room.

"Yes-ers": A goal of the impartial facilitator in a neutral location is to allow more of a voice to the parents; however, some parents are still intimidated by the professionals and the system. These parents are scared of disagreeing or questioning DSS and automatically agree to anything said or asked of them. While this may seem like it would make the facilitator's job easier, it is a barrier to a successful meeting. The problem is that the parent is not asking for clarification when they need it. They may agree to go to meetings and services when they may have no way of getting there or paying for it. The facilitator should try to probe these issues as much as possible. Often times asking open-ended questions, such as, "how will you pay for therapy?" as opposed to "can you pay for therapy" may help them be honest, and then in turn the group can brainstorm ways to help them achieve success. The facilitator can also ask clarifying questions themselves of the professionals (even if they already know the answer) so the yes-er parent can hear the answers. If the facilitator asks enough of these questions the parent may start feeling more comfortable to follow suit.

Overly emotional: Let me start by saying I use the term "overly" with caution, because regardless of what I may have done, if DSS had my children or I had made a poor enough decision to get DSS involved in my life, I would likely be emotional and with good reason. Showing emotion is better than being cold and emotionless. However, there is some expectation that the parents and family should get it together enough to sit through a meeting without completely losing all semblance of composure. This may be the grandmother, who, every time she is asked a question she pauses, starts to talk, then cries and shakes her head. It may be the father who is so heartbroken about what has happened in his children's lives and too embarrassed to cry in front of people that he repeatedly leaves the room. It may be the mother who sobs uncontrollably the entire meeting. For starters, we all have a BIG box of Kleenex in the middle of the table. But other than that, it is not the facilitator's job to tell parents and family members that things are going to be ok (they may not be), or to help them get through this therapeutically. It is important for the facilitator to be unmoved or affected by any emotional behavior from participants.

Persons at the meeting other than parents and family members may also display emotions. If an emotional display by any participant is completely hindering the process, you may ask if the person needs to take a break to splash water on their face or use some other technique to recover his or her composure. Otherwise, if the person declines to take a break, keep the meeting moving. It is okay for them to cry, this is an emotional time. The tears and the way they deal with the meeting may provide important information to the other professionals at the table.

Difficult professionals: Although when discussing "difficult people" one might automatically think that this would refer the parents/families involved, there are plenty of times when it is the professionals that are the hardest to manage. They provide a different type of challenge since oftentimes we focus our style around maximizing a positive experience for the family with less regard for the professionals. They shouldn't be taking this meeting personally. This is their job. But if they can not, you have even more personalities to juggle.

One type of difficult professional may be the DSS case worker. The behavior of case workers we encounter is usually appropriate. Most are well trained for the methods we use in our CFTM facilitations, but there is always that one that sneaks by. This case worker could have a certain knack for pushing the buttons of the parent. Every time you get everyone all calmed downed and focused, the case worker riles everyone up again. When this happens, it is the job of the facilitator to shut that cycle down and refocus that person, even if it is a "professional."

The fabulous benefit from this is that the parents witness it also, seeing that the facilitator really is neutral and expects ALL parties to be respectful of one another and work towards a future focused goal. The downside to this is the case worker may not like you after this; but that is okay, because we, as facilitators, are professionals also and do not take people not liking us in our professional lives personally. I must also add that the case workers usually get over it, because in a future case when the facilitator is blocking the parent from cussing the case worker out, they appreciate the facilitator once again.

Another rut some professionals get into is trying to run the meeting themselves. It may be a school principal, a therapist, or some professional who typically is in the role of authority and main "speaker." They sometimes try to take over the meeting and determine what should be talked about, when, how, and next steps. As the facilitator of the meeting, it is important to reclaim your role. Again, it is not so you will be "in charge" but it is so the participants will be able to recognize that they all have a voice and say so in what happens. Usually what you can do as a facilitator is speak up and ask a question, or recap something you have heard so the speaker will calm down and let you take back over. Sometimes you must interrupt numerous times to get control back. There may even be a time when you have to put it bluntly: "I understand that you have some valuable questions and information Sarah, but I would really need to hear from Jane. I will be happy to come back to you for input soon."

When we set up for meetings, we have a long rectangular conference table, the facilitator sits at the head of the table (which can often remind people to let that person "be in charge") and we place a piece of paper and pencil at each seat around the table. If people have trouble interrupting or speaking out of turn, they can be encouraged to write down their thoughts so they will not be forgotten and the group can come back to them later.

This is different than how we do other types of mediations. For example, in our district court mediation we like to sit on one side of the table (not the head) and have the defendant and complainant sit across from us, so we can see both faces at the same time. Other times we prefer a round table. Each mediation and situation benefits from a different formula of approaches!

Here I will also talk about the Guardian Ad Litem (GAL) volunteers. In North Carolina a GAL does not have to be an attorney. These are trained volunteers who have the responsibility to represent the child or children involved in the case. They attend meetings, meet with the children, and make recommendations to the court separate from DSS's recommendations. Most of the time, these volunteers are very helpful to the process. Occasionally, they, much like professionals, can speak out of turn. This is a different type of sensitive situation in that this is not their "job," however, it is an important role and they are supervised by GAL staff members. It is important to be sensitive to the fact that they are "volunteers" but not so sensitive that you let them get out of control. They should be held to the same standards as the other parties.

Another factor that often plays a role here is that many of the GAL volunteers in our county are senior citizens. Many are sharp, well trained, and up to date on current societal norms; but occasionally they are not. An example that comes to mind is when during one mediation someone mentioned a Blackberry. The volunteer was confused and thought they meant the fruit.

No "ONE SIZE FITS ALL": All mediators, even when serving as a facilitator, typically have a script and a style that they use. Experienced mediators know when to adjust this to the situation and the participants. It is important to be able and willing to go with the flow and alter your approach as needed to fit the case and the various personalities in the room.

Now, here comes the hard part. While you are juggling everything above, the mediator is also typing a Memorandum of Understanding (MOU) that outlines the strengths of the family, services that are currently in place, and summarizes the main points of the meeting. This is not to be a transcript of the meeting, but the highlights of an agreement. If there is a lengthy discussion regarding what day and time visitations should occur, the only thing necessary to type is the agreed upon day and time of visitations. Sometimes, there is not an agreement and both parties agree to research issues further. Possibly DSS has requested the mother submit to a hair sample drug test and the mother is uncomfortable with this. The mother may agree to go and consult with her attorney about this and report back to the case worker. This is information you would document. Or, maybe the facilitator would explore more about why the mother is uncomfortable with this. Is it because she has a past history she doesn't want to document? Is it because her hair is short and she is concerned that they will remove a patch and that would look ugly? The discussion could include the difference between mom's perspective and what will actually be done, or maybe they could explore using pubic hair instead of head hair to maintain the aesthetics of the hair cut.

Language use: As the meeting is moving forward, the facilitator is also typing into the MOU. The language should be simple and easy to understand. It is important that the facilitator continue to use the language that the parents use and understand. The agreement should be specific in regards to expected future tasks: "Mom will call Dr. Smith at 656–2812 by Monday, March 12 to set up an appointment."

The agreement should be general in terms of alleged abuse that may be argued in court. Instead of stating "Because of mom's drug use she must participate in random drug screens," either just go straight to "Mom agrees to participate in random drug screens" or if it must be addressed, state "Due to a concern regarding substance abuse. . . ." The facts and allegations must be addressed and argued in court not in the CFTM and it is important not to state things in the MOU in a way that appears one-sided.

This is also an effective practice to use in delicate situations. If the case involves a child that molested his sister, for instance, as opposed to stating that specifically it may be appropriate to use wording such as: "Due to a concern regarding past sexual behaviors, it is important that Tom and Mary are not allowed left alone without supervision." This way you have addressed in a general manner the reason that the very specific behavior is expected.

Now, after you print out the MOU and everyone reviews their copy guess what comes next?

NOTHING!   This is one of the special parts of a Child and Family Team Meeting. You have a short-lived relationship with the clients as opposed to other parties, who have on-going work with the clients. As a mediator serving in the role of a facilitator, you may never see the client again, or not until they come for a follow up meeting. The DSS case worker will continue to work with the client and other parties, as will therapists, school personnel, etc. But as a facilitator, you are done. When you leave work that day, you don't have to think about what you will do to help this person accomplish their goals. You have done your part. This is one of the things that drew me to the profession of mediation. It is more "touchy feely" than the law, but you become "less enmeshed" than you do with clinical therapy. In mediation I have found my perfect professional balance.

Who can be a DSS CFTM facilitator?   As you have probably learned by now in your studies, mediation is a very young profession and has yet to develop consistent qualifications and certifications for mediators across the country. Qualifications and appropriate trainings also vary depending on the type of mediation one wants to practice. For the CFTM facilitations, this center uses college educated, basic mediation trained individuals that are then required to observe experienced facilitators facilitate meetings, then co-facilitate, then facilitate while observed. Our current mediators have varying backgrounds, experience, and credentials including a Master's degree in Conflict Resolution, a retired police detective, a Master's degree in psychology, a Juris Doctor (JD), and several retired professional mediators.

Why facilitated CFTMs?   As mentioned previously, New Hanover County, North Carolina has utilized an outside agency to facilitate their CFTMs since 2004. Throughout the state of North Carolina this process has proven to be very successful whether or not an outside agency provides the service (but we are biased towards an outside agency!). Duke University has studied this process and has found increased family satisfaction with both child welfare services and the relationship between the family and the case worker (Duke University, 2006). This format ensures that the family's culture is considered when creating and documenting a plan (Thomas, Berzin, & Cohen, 2005) and ensures the families are involved in a meaningful process in which their voices are not just heard but considered (Pennell, 2006). We expect to see this process grow in popularity in North Carolina and throughout the country!

Case Study: A Heartbreaking Story

The Department of Social Services sends you a referral for a Child and Family Team Meeting. This is a follow up to a case that you have done in the past. A glance at your last MOU reminds you that the three male children were still in mom's legal custody, but were currently in a voluntary kinship placement with their maternal grandmother.

The issue that resulted in DSS involvement was alleged domestic violence between mom and her boyfriend. DSS was asking mom to keep the boyfriend away from the children and was asking the boyfriend to participate in a Domestic Violence Offender program prior to being in the home with the family again.

The current meeting starts off friendly. All three children are present, along with mom, grandmother, and the DSS case worker. Everyone exchanges pleasantries and the facilitator gets some updates from the family and the children on how the children are doing (the boys are between the ages of 9 and 16).

The case worker then brings up concern regarding two incidents where the safety plan was broken and the children were in the presence of the boyfriend. Since grandmother cannot adhere to the safety plan, the children cannot remain in her care.

The mother is then asked what her plan is regarding the future of her relationship with the boyfriend. The mother shares she loves him and he really does mean well.

Each child then shares his/her individual feelings regarding the boyfriend. They each tearfully recount stories of times they were fearful for their own safety around him and then worried about their mom's safety without them there to protect her. They beg her to break things off with the boyfriend so they can return home to her. She cries, she apologizes, and then hugs them goodbye.

The DSS case worker then has to take the boys to two foster homes (one in one home, the other two in another home). They will not see their mom or grandmother again until the next week for a one hour supervised visit at DSS.

QUESTIONS FOR DISCUSSION

1. What are your first thoughts regarding the mother? How do you keep these from coloring the way you treat her?
2. What role can or should the facilitator play in this meeting?
3. What are some important questions the facilitator can ask or issues to consider?
4. How does having the children participate in the meeting change the dynamics?
5. Who else do you think should have participated in the meeting?

REFERENCES

Duke University, Center for Child and Family Policy, Terry Sanford Institute of Public Policy. (2006, June 30). *Multiple Response System (MRS) evaluation report to the North Carolina Division of Social Services (NCDSS).* Durham, NC.

NC Division of Social Services. (2012). *Family support and child welfare services manual, Chapter VII: Child and family team meetings.* Raleigh, NC. Available from http://info.dhhs.state.nc.us/olm/manuals/dss.

Pennell, J. (2006). Restorative practices and child welfare: Toward an inclusive civil society. In B. Morrison & E. Ahmed (Eds.), Restorative justice and civil society, special issue of *Journal of Social Issues, 62*(2), 257–277.

Thomas, K. L., Berzin, S. C., and Cohen, E. (2005). Fidelity of family group decision making: A content analysis of family conference and case plans in a randomized treatment study. *Protecting Children, 19*(4), 4–15.

Chapter 9

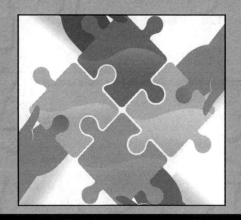

Mediating Student Disputes in Higher Education

Catherine S. Powell

Mediation is rapidly emerging as a preferred vehicle for resolving dispute among students on American college and university campuses. Mediation is a centuries old process that was successfully used in various forms and environments before it was introduced in higher education Because of the exponential rates at which higher education institutions have implemented mediation programs, the total number of such programs in existence today is unknown (Hayes & Balogh, 1990; Rule, 1994; Warters, 2000). However, over the last three decades, there has been a growing trend toward increasing student participation in mediation.

This chapter is written from a mediation practitioner's perspective within the context of higher education. The primary focus is mediation's suitability and applicability for resolving disputes among students. Toward that end, the chapter also includes brief historical accountings of formal student judicial processes as well as the emergence of mediation in higher education. The pros and cons of both mediation and formal student judicial processes are explored to give insight into mediation as both an alternative and as a supplemental tool for resolving student disputes. To provide enhanced experiential learning opportunities, a case study and practical exercise are also included.

TERMINOLOGY

Most terminology is contextually defined. The term, higher education students, for example, refers to students who are enrolled in formal education curricula beyond the high school level. References to colleges and universities are limited to American institutions, only.

Disputes, as discussed in this chapter, are differentiated from conflicts. Conflicts are generally viewed as deeply entrenched, systemic disagreements involving issues such as human values, needs, and fears. Conversely, disputes are more narrowly defined as articulations that result from conflicts (Moffitt & Bordone, 2005; Powell, 2009). In essence, disputes are less entrenched and generally more amenable to resolution than conflicts.

Mediation is a structured problem-solving process that is facilitated by a third party or mediator. Unlike judges or hearing officers, mediators do not make decisions. Instead, mediators are neutral individuals who are trained to assist disputants to resolve their own disputes in mutually satisfying ways (Beeler, 1986; Hayes & Balogh, 1990; Powell, 2009; Serr & Tabor, 1987; Warters, 1998; 2000; Wing, 2002).

Mediation differs from other dispute resolution processes in several ways, including the fact that it requires voluntary participation by disputants. Disputants can opt to stop participating at any time. Mediation can also be described as a structured, informal, and confidential process. These attributes interact with the mediator's facilitation to create a "safe environment" of trust, openness and empowerment wherein disputants voluntarily participate in establishing the mediation framework, identifying the issues surrounding their dispute, negotiating resolution options, and reaching consensus on how to resolve their dispute (Beeler, 1986; Hayes & Balogh, 1990; Powell, 2009; Serr & Tabor, 1987; Warters, 1998; 2000).

Another unique characteristic of mediation is its ability to give "voice" and empowerment to participants. *Voice* refers to the fact that mediation gives each disputant the opportunity to tell their own story about the dispute and its effects. Also, disputants are treated as equals during mediation. They are empowered to resolve their disputes in mutually satisfying ways instead of having a hearing officer or other administrative authority make decisions for them.

A common misunderstanding about mediation is the notion that it comprises only one structured process that mediators should apply in all cases. In fact, several different mediation models exist. It is a common mediator practice to decide, on a case by case basis, which model is most appropriate for resolving specific disputes (Powell, 2009; Van Hoorebeek, Gale, & Walker, 2011; Warters, 1998; 2000). Decisions about which mediation model(s) to use in a particular case are contingent upon such factors as the nature of the dispute, the parties involved, the setting, and so forth. More detailed information about pertinent mediation models is discussed later.

STUDENT CONFLICTS AND DISPUTES IN HIGHER EDUCATION

Reflective of American society as a whole, the pervasiveness of conflict and disputes on college and university campuses is well known. Faculty, staff, administrators, students, and all campus constituencies are affected. However, some conflicts and disputes are unique to the experiences of students.

Disputes among higher education students usually stem from competing interests related to life styles or personal preferences. Study and sleep schedules, social activities and privacy needs are often underlying causes of student disputes. In general, such disputes do not involve policy or rule violations. Left unresolved, however, serious conflicts can evolve and escalate to levels requiring formal institutional intervention (Beeler, 1986; Hayes & Balogh, 990; Powell, 2009; Serr & Tabor, 1987; Warters, 1998; 2000).

Students' success with dispute resolutions in higher education hinges, to a great degree, on institutional dispute resolution systems. When higher education institutions view conflicts and disputes as naturally occurring phenomena and take appropriate actions to address them, many positive outcomes can be created. Dispute resolutions in these circumstances foster and encourage collegiality, healthy intellectual debates, respect for individual differences, inclusion, diversity, and many other positive environmental factors.

Likewise, the use of ineffective methods to manage conflict and resolve disputes can create dire consequences, not only for the students directly involved, but for institutions as a whole (Beeler, 1986; Rule, 1994; Todaro, Brattle, & Stafford, 2002). Until recent years, formal student judicial processes were the only methods available for institutional interventions (Beeler, 1986; Hayes & Balogh, 1990; Powell, 2009; Serr & Tabor, 1987). Mediation is a much newer approach to dispute resolutions in higher education.

DISPUTE RESOLUTION PROCESSES: AN HISTORICAL OVERVIEW

Early Student Judicial Processes

Formal judicial procedures for higher education students in America originated prior to the1800s. The earliest processes were quite simple and highly punitive. Designated officials within colleges and universities were responsible for resolving student disputes. These officials made unilateral decisions about how disputes would be resolved. The same individuals were also likely to administer punishment if they deemed it to be appropriate (Beeler, 1986; Hayes & Balogh, 1990; Warters, 1998).

Over the years, the procedures became more formalized. Premised upon the notion that someone was right and someone was wrong, the formal judicial procedures continued to be punitive in nature. However, they were formalized to encompass strict student conduct codes that were enforced through legalistic frameworks for disciplinary actions. Adversarial relationships were inherent byproducts. In essence, campus judicial proceedings reflective of our nation's formalized, antagonistic justice system, including court-room like proceedings, were the norm for America's colleges and universities (Beeler 1986; Hayes & Balogh, 1990; Warters, 1998).

The adversarial court-like proceedings proved to be inadequate and, in many cases, detrimental to the ability of colleges and universities to achieve their goals and missions. Legalistic procedures, such as investigations and formal hearings that culminated in findings of guilt or innocence and created "win-lose" situations proved to be costly and time consuming impediments to positive interpersonal relationships and collegiality. The procedures were also more likely to suppress conflict than to effectively resolve either conflict or disputes (Beeler 1986; Hayes & Balogh, 1990; Warters, 1998).

Motivated by desires to overcome the many disadvantages of formal judicial proceedings and prompted by great social unrest and legal challenges during the 1960s and 1970s, higher education institutions began to seek new ways to manage conflict and resolve disputes. Student demands for equality, inclusion, and respect for diversity created greater impetus for institutional changes. Consequently, new student conduct codes (with more student input) were adopted (Beeler 1986; Hayes & Balogh, 1990; Serr & Tabor, 1987; Warters, 1998).

Contemporary Student Judicial Processes

Contemporary student judicial processes began to emerge during the period of 1964 through 1971. This was a period of unprecedented unrest, pervasive distrust and opposition between students and campus authorities (Beeler, 1986; Hayes & Balogh, 1990; Warters, 1998). Although the trend toward legalism continued, newer process evolved with greater emphasis and attention to "due process," equal rights, and student involvement (Beeler, 1986; Hayes & Balogh, 1990; Warters, 1998). Despite the positive changes, formal judicial processes still have serious shortcomings that suggest these processes should be used only in cases where suspected rule or policy violations warrant their use.

As has been the case historically, contemporary student judicial processes are still enforced legalistically through investigations, hearings, and so forth that culminate in findings of guilt or innocence. Punishment of guilty parties is a normal expectation (Beeler, 1986; Hayes & Balogh, 1990; Powell, 2009; Warters, 1998; 2000). Many negative consequences are identifiable. These include: (a) the fact that "winners" in these processes are often determined by students' ability to influence decision makers by the way in which they present their version of the issues or incidents involved in the dispute, (b) the processes are adversarial, time-consuming, and often delayed by backlogs, and (c) the underlying causes of conflicts leading to the disputes may never be divulged.

Mediation

Formal Student Judicial processes left serious gaps in higher education governance and educational goals. Mediation was first introduced in America as an effective dispute resolution process with other populations, including church groups and America's workforce. The major thrust of mediation as a dispute resolution process on college and university campuses began in the late 1970s (Beeler, 1986; Hayes & Balogh, 1990; Serr & Tabor, 1987; Warters, 1998; 2000).

Mediation has proven to be a flexible, highly effective dispute resolution option with few minimum requirements. The minimum requirements are the following conditions: (a) disputants can participate as equals, with no significant power imbalances between them, (b) underlying issues in the dispute can be defined, (c) all parties to the dispute are willing to work toward consensus, and (d) the disputants are willing to implement terms of their negotiated agreements (Beeler, 1986; Bush & Folger, 1994).

Although other models exist, four mediation models are most often employed by mediation practitioners in higher education settings. The models are known as: (a) facilitative, (b) transformative, (c) restorative, and (d) evaluative. These same models also predominate as choices for mediating cases involving workforce participants, including faculty, staff, and administrators (Powell, 2009).

All four models focus on engaging disputants in joint problem-solving activities, such as problem identification, interest based negotiations, and consensus building to resolve their disputes (Powell, 2009). Unlike judges or hearing officers, mediators do not make decisions. The mediator assists the disputants to make their own decisions. The degree and methods by which mediators engage directly with disputants is contingent upon the mediation model employed.

For example, facilitative and transformative mediation model protocols require mediators to steer disputing parties away from discussions of guilt or innocence regarding their dispute. Instead, the disputants are encouraged to focus on identifying the issues involved and resolving the dispute. "Win-win" decisions are encouraged (Powell, 2009).

Transformative protocols, however, are less structured than facilitative. Transformative protocols also encourage disputants to go beyond problem-solving to effect positive personal transformations or growth experiences during mediation to improve future relationship skills (Bush & Folger, 1994).

Evaluative Mediation is more legalistic than either facilitative or transformative mediation. This model more closely mirrors traditional judicial processes than facilitative and transformative mediation models. Under an evaluative mediation protocol, the mediator intervenes more directly. Among other actions, the evaluative mediator assesses the strengths of each disputant's case and advises them on the strengths and weaknesses of their positions to "nudge" them toward agreements.

As implied by its name, restorative protocols can be used to help students move past dispute resolutions to focus on relationship issues. Through this model, disputants are encouraged to work toward mutual agreement on what needs to be done to restore effective future relationships between them. Acknowledging deeper understanding of the other party's feelings about an incident, agreeing that unfairness may have occurred, or apologizing for offenses (even when unintentional) are examples of ways disputing parties may agree to "move forward."

Although clear delineations between the different mediation models are identifiable, mediators generally do not strictly adhere exclusively to the protocols of any one mediation model. As inferred earlier, and for the reasons previously stated, blending of the models is considered most appropriate. Practitioners are wise to view the models as continuums rather than isolated frameworks from which to choose (Powell, 2009; Warters, 2000). However, knowledge of the different protocols and their intended uses helps mediators and disputants determine, on a case by case basis, which model or "blend" is most effective for the needs of the disputants and the issues to be resolved.

MEDIATION'S SUITABILITY FOR RESOLVING STUDENT DISPUTES

Mediation is well-known for its flexibility and usefulness as an effective tool for resolving disputes. However, it benefits campuses and students in many other ways. One benefit often overlooked is mediation's value as an educational tool. Consistent with the mission statements of most higher education institutions, mediation assists students to develop skills supportive of maximum personal development and effective interpersonal relationships (Hayes & Balogh, 1990).

Collaboration, problem-solving, and compromise are some of the invaluable skills that mediation imparts. Mediation also minimizes the negative consequences of unresolved conflict by enabling students to informally and confidentially resolve their disputes while also averting the possibility of escalating anger and hostility as well as the need for formal judicial proceedings (Beeler, 1986; Hayes & Balogh, 1990; Powell, 2009; Serr & Tabor, 1987). As a consequence, mediation fosters fraternal and collegial relationships essential for successful higher education experiences while also teaching responsible adult behavior and attitudes for responsibly dealing with future conflict and disputes (Hayes & Balogh, 1990; Warters, 1998).

The goal of mediation is to actively engage disputants in communicating and listening to each other, to understand the dispute from their individual perspectives in order to generate feasible alternatives, and ultimately to create resolutions whereby both parties believe they have gained (win-win solutions). Also, as a result of this process, disputants can identify underlying reasons for the conflict, recognize and appreciate the feelings and emotions experienced by the other disputant(s) as well as their own, and learn valuable lessons about how to avoid or resolve disputes in the future, while also building greater capacity to engage in positive interpersonal relationships in the future.

Certain assumptions about human values and behavior are essential prerequisites for establishing credible mediation services for students. These include: (a) beliefs that desires to cooperate are common to most students, (b) that disputants are capable and most knowledgeable about how their disputes should be resolved, and (c) that the disputants will, given the appropriate forum and environment, negotiate fairly and honestly (Hayes & Balogh, 1990).

Despite its many benefits to students and higher education institutions, mediation cannot replace formal student judicial processes (Beeler, 1986; Hayes & Balogh, 1990; Serr & Taber, 1987; Van Hoorebeck, Gale, & Walker, 2011). Some disputes require formal judicial action. From the perspective of rules and policies, mediation may be appropriately used to resolve student disputes in the following ways: (a) as a supplemental process to the formal judicial process, and (b) as an alternative dispute resolution process. In cases where clear violations of rules or policies are indicated, appropriate formal processes must be applied to protect the rights of students and all involved. Where no rule or policy violations exist, mediation may be a first and final service for resolving students' disputes.

Mediation as an Alternative Dispute Resolution Process

As discussed earlier in this chapter, most student disputes do not involve policy or rule violations (Beeler, 1986; Hayes & Balogh, 1990; Serr & Taber, 1987; Van Hoorebeck, Gale, & Walker, 2011). Competing interests, life styles, and personal behavioral standards are more likely to be underlying causes of conflict and disputes among students. Because formal judicial processes are designed to address specific policy or rule violations, mediation serves as an alternative vehicle for students to address their concerns or disputes before they become major conflicts to be addressed formally. If mediation in these cases results in a negotiated agreement between the disputants, mediation services should be the first and only step for dispute resolution. Of course, the mediator should follow up with disputants to ensure that agreements are working. If agreements are not working, the disputants should be brought back to mediation to either amend the agreements or to negotiate new agreements as appropriate.

Mediation as a Supplemental Dispute Resolution Process

Mediation is viewed as a supplemental dispute resolution process when it is used in addition to formal student judicial processes. Disputes arising from legal or institutional policy or rule violations require formal judicial action. However, such cases may be initially reported to mediation services. Therefore, strong collaborative processes between mediation services and other campus dispute resolution processes are essential to the need for expeditious case referral and processing.

Investigations, formal hearings and other fact-finding functions leading to determinations of guilt or innocence are not mediation functions (Beeler, 1986; Hayes & Balogh, 1990; Powell, 2009; Serr & Tabor, 1987; Van Hoorebeck, Gale, & Walker, 2011). Cases of this nature are usually handled by Judicial Affairs or designated institutional entities for formal dispute resolution proceedings. It is imperative that mediation services screen each new case to determine whether such a referral is appropriate. Again, the need for strong collaborative relationships is underscored as all parties are best served when mediation services and the receiving entities confer prior to effecting such referrals.

Although collaboration is strongly encouraged, mediation services' credibility demands limited informational exchanges. It is essential that mediation's core values: voluntariness, impartiality, and confidentiality remain guiding principles in communications with other professionals (Inlow, 2006). Hence, only basic information should be shared, such as the type of case involved. In general, no confidential information should be included in communications with other organizational entities. Informal and formal dispute resolution processes should operate separately.

If laws or policies exist to require that certain information should be reported (such as criminal acts, bullying, or threats of violence), students should be duly informed. Divulging confidentially shared information otherwise threatens the credibility and ultimately, the effectiveness of mediation services. This dichotomous relationship between the need for strong collaborative relationships with other organizational entities and the need to strictly adhere to mediation's core values can be problematic. Open communication (lateral and vertical) and mutual respect across organizational entities are essential.

Even in cases where punitive action is justified, mediation may still be used. In this case, it would be used as a *supplemental dispute resolution process*. Rationale for determining whether the use of mediation is appropriate, as a supplement to formal judicial processes, varies as much as the types of disputes students may present. Examples of appropriate cases are those where disputants indicate interest or demonstrate a need to mend relationships between them. Also, cases where there are needs or desires for students to learn how to interact more effectively in the future with others who are different than them (Powell, 2009; Wing, 2002).

Diversity among disputants may also be a factor in determining when mediation may be appropriately used as a supplemental process. While increasing diversity among college students is a positive phenomenon, new conflicts and challenges to dispute resolution practices can be expected to arise with the changing demographics (Powell, 2009; Warters, 2000; Wing, 2002). How people view conflict as well as the way they respond to conflict strongly correlates with their diversity (Powell, 2009; Wing, 2002).

Assessing diversity among student disputants in conjunction with the issues involved in a dispute may lead to inferences of diversity-related disputes that are best resolved through mediation. Assisted by a trained mediator, student disputants can identify deficits in intercultural communications and relationships, discuss options for overcoming the deficits, and negotiate agreements that govern future interactions between them (Beeler, 1986; Hayes & Balogh, 1990; Powell, 2009; Serr & Tabor, 1987; Van Hoorebeck, Gale, & Walker, 2011; Wing, 2002). Essentially, as college and university admission offices engage more aggressively in recruiting students from minority races and cultures, they must also give greater attention to dispute resolution services.

Also, mediation as a supplemental service may be quite appropriate for cases where retribution beyond traditional punitive penalties may be justified. For example, roommate issues between two students may result in punitive action against one student. There is no reason to assume that the punitive action will result in improved relationships between the two. In fact, the process and subsequent penalty may exacerbate the situation. Since additional rooms for separate living arrangements are often not unavailable, and disputants may still have regular contacts through classes and other campus activities, special attention should be given to help the students find ways to interact positively in the future.

Left to resolve on its own, disputes of the type just described can seriously affect the disputants in many ways, including interruptions in their academic performance. Mediation can be especially helpful in cases of this nature. Mediators can assist the students to fully explore the issues surrounding their dispute and to negotiate their own agreements regarding behavioral expectations. When used as a supplemental process, mediation can help students capitalize on opportunities for creating meaningful learning experiences that not only improve relationships between them, but also position them for successful relationships and problem-solving skills for the future.

Mediation can be an effective vehicle for early intervention and dispute resolution. If the mediation results in consensus between the disputing students, and the students agree on how to resolve their dispute, no further intervention is likely to be necessary. The mediator, of course, should follow up to ensure that the agreements are working. If the original agreement does not work, the disputing students can be brought back to mediation until they arrive at "workable agreements." This approach is much more likely than formal student judicial processes to preserve, and possibly improve future interactions and relationships between the disputants.

SPECIAL CHALLENGES TO MEDIATION SERVICES

Mediation's success as a dispute resolution processes in higher education is rooted in its ability to respond to contemporary student values and behaviors that mirror our society in general (Beeler, 1986; Powell, 2009; Warters, 2000). Despite mediation's many positive attributes, some special challenges or typical problems should be examined as the future of mediation services for higher education students is considered (McCarthy, 1980; Serr & Tabor, 1987; Rule, 1994). The discussion will now focus on a few such challenges along with suggested ways to overcome them.

Strong collaboration and communication processes are essential to the successful implementation and operation of mediation services in higher education. Mutual respect and appreciation for the special skills and abilities that all staff, including mediators, bring to dispute resolution systems for students are equally important. A mandatory need for respect and appreciation across organizational lines driven by the fact many of mediation's most appealing qualities are antithetical to those of traditional student judicial and legalistic processes. Those variances are highlighted in Table 9–1.

Some of mediation service's greatest challenges arise because of the environments in which higher education institutions operate. Marske and Vago (1980) noted that "As the university becomes more of a bureaucracy than a community, its members are turning to the courts to resolve disputes they once settled informally." The same tendencies toward litigation exist today. Students, like other campus community members and our society as a whole, often turn to legal proceedings first. Our court system and many human rights organizations, such as the Equal Employment Opportunity Commission and Department of Justice, upon receipt of such cases, are more likely today to refer them to mediation before determining whether any legal action may be justified. One positive note here is the fact that disputants are introduced to mediation although it would not have been their initial choice for dispute resolution. To overcome barriers in this regard, a strong need for aggressive education and awareness about mediation services and benefits is indicated.

Although not always obvious, organizational structures can create major impediments to the implementation of mediation services. Structural impediments can cause students to become entangled in organizational conflicts that undermine all efforts to resolve disputes effectively and efficiently. Consequently, the promises of mediation are aborted and greater stresses and frustrations are created along with serious threats to the institution and academic progression of students. Additionally, students are denied learning opportunities and new skill sets inherent in mediation.

Organizational silos are prime examples of structural impediments. The term, *silo,* refers to highly vertical hierarchal organization structures that minimize or exclude lateral communications and collaborations. These organizational structures generally advocate strict adherence (for students and staff) to vertical communications. When silos exist within organizational entities responsible for dispute resolution, full integration of dispute resolution services is aborted, and

Table 9.1   A Comparison: Mediation and Traditional Judicial Processes

Mediation	Traditional Judicial Processes
Confidentiality	**Documentation**
No records are created in mediation. Only the agreements that disputants develop are reduced to writing. Copies are provided to the disputants and the mediator retains a copy for follow-up.	Records must be created and maintained from the beginning of contact throughout the dispute resolution process. In some cases, the records become a part of official student records to be maintained perpetually.
Empowerment	**Disempowerment**
Disputants are given an opportunity to develop guidelines for the mediation, and to participate in determining how to resolve their disputes. Mediators do not make decisions. Impartiality on the part of the mediator is required.	Disputants do not make decisions. Third parties, such as hearing officers or other designated authorities decide how disputes will be resolved as well as what penalties may apply.
Reduced Stress	**Stress**
No determinations of guilt or innocence are involved. Each disputant can "tell their story" without interruption and participate fully in all decisions.	The processes are stress-provoking. Investigations, hearings, and courtroom-like settings are created.
Voluntary	**Mandatory**
Disputants can opt not to participate at all. Or, they can choose to leave mediation at any time.	Participation is required. Disputants cannot leave until instructed to do so.
Creativity	**Pre-Determination**
Disputants, using interest based negotiations creatively develop their own solutions (provided no institutional policy or rule violations are involved).	Institutional policies and procedures, including past practices determine how the dispute resolution process will operate as well as how each dispute will be resolved.
Voice	**Voice**
Each disputant is heard without judgment.	Disputants' narratives about the dispute are controlled by the decision-making authority. The primary goal is to decide guilt or innocence.

students are denied the full range of services, including mediation, that could and should be available to them.

By their very nature, silos are barriers to open communication, creativity and innovation. *Functional silos* are created as only the learning that occurs within the *silo* is used. As such staff within these organizational structures are more likely to operate from frameworks of distrust toward mediation and notions that disputants, whether students or employees, should be allowed to determine the terms and conditions for resolving their disputes, whether institutional issues are involved or not.

Silos can also lead to "turf-guarding" that can be a detriment to efforts to integrate mediation with other dispute resolution processes. Turf guarding can result in refusals to refer students for mediation and actions to discredit mediation services. Without clear lateral communications and agreements, some staff may feel threatened by the fact a mediator is engaged to help resolve student disputes. The mediator's involvement may be perceived as an indication that other staff's competencies are underappreciated.

In summary, organizational structures should be thoroughly assessed for potential impediments. Open communications and understandings about mediation as an "added value" to the formal dispute resolution processes should be a top priority. Full integration of mediation services is a bonus to all campus constituencies!

The following are additional challenges and suggestions for overcoming some of the most pervasive impediments to campus mediation services:

1. Students, like faculty and staff, may hesitate to admit they are engaged in a dispute. Given the voluntary nature of mediation, some students may decide not to participate unless and until the dispute evolves into major conflict. Also, students may refuse to participate in mediation because they fear records will be created, or that they may be perceived to have done something wrong. Mediation services can encourage participation through campus wide education programs and by thoroughly discussing the mediation process with students prior to mediation.

2. The need for open communication cannot be overstressed. However, mediation services must establish and maintain ethical boundaries for communicating with other organizational entities. Student confidentialities must be maintained at all costs.

3. The need for strong collaborative processes also cannot be overstressed. Yet, it is critically important that mediation remain a separate process from formal judicial proceedings. Students should never be involved simultaneously with formal judicial proceedings and mediation. Mediated agreements must be adhered to if the process is to benefit students by resolving their disputes.

4. Confidentiality is a core value that mediators must embrace. In some cases, colleagues engaged in legalistic dispute resolution processes may question the me-

diator's "team spirit" when confidential information is withheld or documentation is not provided to bolster legalistic defenses.

5. Mediation records should be maintained for program administration and evaluation purposes, only. Therefore no personally identifying information should be included. Instead, data such as status of disputants (students, faculty, staff, and so forth), the organizational entity from which the dispute arose, the nature of the dispute, and the mediation outcomes should be recorded. Again, these practices, in general, conflict with recordkeeping practices that prevail in formal dispute resolution processes. The degree to which this may be problematic for mediation services is contingent upon the campus environment and leadership support.

6. Neutrality, another one of mediation's core values, can conflict with traditional judicial processes. While the mediator is often a loyal employee, paid by the institution, bias or partiality that compromises mediation's neutrality is unethical. The mediator should have no vested interest in the outcome of mediation. Because of mediation's neutrality promises, individuals who serve as judicial hearing officers or as part of judicial hearing processes should not serve as mediators. Disputants, who are aware of the other roles, are not likely to perceive such individuals as unbiased. Also, should the case move from mediation to a formal judicial process, none of the information from mediation should be included. Therefore, any judicial officer who mediates a case should be disqualified from participating in the formal process.

7. A major criticism of mediation is its propensity to encourage disputants to focus so narrowly on the issues involved in their dispute in order to identify the problems. The possibility that the full scope of the issues may be missed is a genuine concern. To avoid this outcome, mediators should closely observe their personal mediation styles to ensure that disputants are empowered to create holistic views of the issues from both their own and the other party's perspectives. A review of this chapter's discussion of the mediation models can also help in this regard.

8. Developing and maintaining adequate resources for campus mediation programs can also be challenging. For many reasons, including the need for objectivity and neutrality, a pool of well-trained mediators is recommended. Peer mediators can be strong attractions for students to use mediation services. For consistency and credibility, one person should supervise mediators.

MEDIATOR TRAINING REQUIREMENTS

Unlike court systems, mediators in higher education from various states, including Florida, have no specific certification or standard requirements. Many higher education institutions and professional organizations offer training for mediation practitioners. In most cases, basic mediator training involves a minimum of 40 instructional hours that include role plays, mentorships, and other experiential learning activities. Such programs can be located through basic computer searches.

Many higher education institutions now offer academic credit and degrees in conflict resolution. Mediation theory and practice are usually integral curriculum components. Academic coursework, combined with special institutes or training programs, such as those previously referenced, can be effective for developing competencies for mediating in higher education.

Practitioners can also benefit from memberships in professional organizations that provide regular literature and training updates. These organizations include The Association for Conflict Resolution (ACR), American Bar Association's Dispute Resolution Section, International Organization of Ombudsmen (IOA), and University and College Ombudsman Association. Again, basic computer searches can lead to identifying these resources.

Concluding Comments

Mediation services for higher education students are still emerging (Beeler, 1986; Hayes & Balogh, 1990; McCarthy, 1980; Van Hoorebeek, Gale, & Walker, 2011; Warters, 1998; 2000). The services benefit higher education institutions, students, and other campus constituencies. A strong need for close collaborations between mediation services and other campus entities, especially judicial affairs and other staff responsible for conflict/dispute resolutions, is indicated.

For students, mediation fosters the development of personal and professional skills essential to their personal, academic, and professional success. For judicial affairs and other staff, mediation services provide an effective alternative or supplemental process that can expand their capacities for helping students move forward and benefit maximally from their higher education experiences. Less litigation and more collegiality, respect, tolerance, and effective communication are just a few of the ways mediation brings added value to campus communities. As mediation services are incorporated to become integral components of campus-wide dispute resolution systems and more collaborative processes are established, the number of mediation cases can be expected to increase while the numbers of formal complaints and lawsuits can be expected to decrease.

Case Study: They Used to Like Each Other

Jan and Megan are freshmen in their second semester at a state university in the southern part of Georgia. They are both first-generation college students. They are also roommates in campus housing, and they have been referred to mediation by Residence Life Staff.

Jan is an African American female from New York City. Megan, a Caucasian female, is from a small town in Kansas. Although neither of the students has had close relations or interacted regularly with people from different racial groups than their own, Residence Life staff reports that the students initially bonded well with each other. It appeared that the fact they were both first-generation college students away from their families and long time friends for the first time in their lives caused them to overlook differences between them. They looked to each other for support and security in their new environment.

Lately, however, the two had begun to quarrel frequently and to complain about numerous issues, such as disagreements about when and how long visitors should be allowed in their room, and what time the lights should be turned off for sleeping. Unfortunately, the unresolved issues have caused anger and resentment to emerge between the students. As the anger and resentment have intensified, Jan and Megan have begun to complain to other students, who are taking "sides."

Supporters of both Jan and Megan have begun to suggest that "race" was probably the cause of the conflict between them. The residence halls are full. So separating Jan and Megan by assigning them different rooms is not a viable option.

QUESTIONS FOR DISCUSSION

1. How would you determine whether mediation is suitable for resolving this dispute?
2. What additional information do you need from Residence Life staff?
3. What would you tell Residence Life staff about mediation to help facilitate the mediation referral process?
4. Assuming that you would decide to mediate this case, what would you do to make sure the students understand mediation, and that they are comfortable with participating?
5. As a mediator, would you address the "race" perceptions in this case? Why or Why not?

REFERENCES

Beeler, K. D. (1986). Campus mediation: A promising compliment to student judicial processes. *The College Student Affairs Journal, 7*(1).

Bush, B. & Folger, J. (1994). *The promise of mediation: Responding to conflict through empowerment and recognition.* San Francisco: Jossey-Bass.

Hayes, J., & Balogh, C. (1990). Mediation: An emerging form of dispute resolution on college campuses. *NASPA Journal, 27*(3).

Inlow, L. (Ed.). (2006). *Summer institute on conflict management in higher education: Campus mediation.* Atlanta, GA: Consortium on Negotiation and Conflict Resolution.

Marske, C., and Vago, S. (1980) Law and Dispute Processing in the Academic Community, *Judicature, 64*(4), 165–75.

McCarthy, J. (1980). Conflict and mediation in the academy. *New Directions for Higher Education, 32.*

Moffitt, M. and Bordone, R. (Eds.). (2005). *The handbook of dispute resolution.* San Francisco: Jossey-Bass.

Powell, C. (2009). *Mediation, diversity, and justice in the workplace.* Unpublished doctoral dissertation, University of West Florida, Pensacola.

Rule, C. (1994). Collegiate mediation programs: A critical review. *The Fourth R, 50,* 36–37.

Serr, R. and Taber, R. (1987). Mediation: A judicial affairs alternative. *New Directions for Student Services, 39.*

Todaro, C., Brattle, C., and Stafford, J. (2002). Mediation: An effective way to restore collegiality and shared governance in dysfunctional university departments. *Conflict Management in Higher Education Report, 3*(1).

Van Hoorebeek, M., Gale, C., and Walker, S., (2011). The role of mediation within university protocols concerning student complaints and appeals. *Multicultural Education & Technology Journal, 5*(3), 209–220.

Warters, W. (1998). *The history of campus mediation systems: Research and practice.* Paper presented at the Reflective Practice in Institutionalizing Conflict Resolution in Higher Education, Georgia State University, Atlanta.

Warters, W. (2000). *Mediation in the campus community.* San Francisco: Jossey-Bass.

Wing, L. (2002). *Social justice and mediation.* Unpublished doctoral Dissertation, University of Massachusetts, Amherst.

Chapter 10

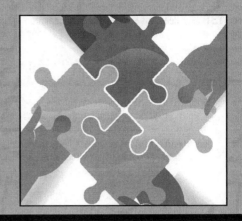

The Process of Mediation in Gang Disputes

Bruce C. McKinney

One of the more important points for advocating mediation to resolve disputes is that it is most effective when the disputing parties have a *continuing pattern of interaction*. People are usually not too concerned at digging into issues with other disputants when they know they will never see the other disputant again. However, when disputing parties know they will have to continue to interact with the other disputant, mediation becomes a more viable option. The fact that mediation does not identify a "winner" or "loser" in the conflict makes it especially useful for mediating disputes involving youth gangs. Gangs who will continue to interact for issues such as turf and self-respect only prolong the agony when there is a clearly identified winner or loser. The fact that mediation empowers disputants is especially important for gangs. Gangs who feel disrespected and powerless are more prone to lash out with violence. Once a gang loses face, many see violence as the only proper response. The use of mediation which addresses all of these issues makes it a much better option for reducing gang violence than other forms of dispute resolution.

THE YOUTH GANG PROBLEM

Youth gangs are not just problems for big cities. Older Americans might recall the 1961 film *West Side* Story which presented an almost romanticized view of the *Jets* and *Sharks* who fought mainly for turf. However, the Department of Justice concludes that local, indigenous gangs are the major cause of gang problems (Maxxon, 1998) that are much more serious than any activity of the *Jets* and *Sharks*. While violent crime and property crime rates have decreased dramatically over the past decade (Federal Bureau of Investigation, 2011), gang violence continues to increase, especially in urban areas (Howell, Egley, Tita, & Griffiths, 2011).

Currently there are an estimated 29,400 gangs in the U.S. with over 756,000 gang members, and gang related homicides increased more than 10 percent from 2009 in cities with of populations of more than 100,000. (Egley & Howell, 2012). Local youth gang problems in the United States have increased steadily. In 1970, only 19 states reported youth gang problems, now all 50 states plus the District of Columbia report gang problems (Howell, 2010). Of the more than 700 homicides that occurred in Loss Angeles and Chicago in 2010, *more than half were reported to be gang related* (Egley& Howell, 2012). The summer of 2012 was a murderous one in Chicago. While crime is down overall by 10 percent, shootings in the city are up 30 percent which the city blames on gang violence. In one weekend in March, 49 people were shot and ten died (Daly, 2012). On June 28, seven year-old Heaven Sutton was selling candy with her mother, when gangs down the street opened fire. Heaven died after being struck by a random bullet, another victim of collateral damage from gang violence.

Though the type and nature of youth gangs can vary as much as the geography from where they exist, the National Youth Gang Center defines a youth gang as

a self-formed association of peers having the following characteristics: three or more members, generally ages 12 to 24; a name and some sense of identity, generally indicated by such symbols as style of clothing, graffiti, and hand signs, some degree of permanence and organization; and an elevated level of involvement in delinquent or criminal activity. (National Youth Gang Center, 2006).

While a gang from New York City may have many differences from a gang in rural Kansas, Moore (1998) identifies five conditions within a community that must exist before a gathering of individual youths becomes an organized gang: (1) ineffective and alienating family and school systems, (2) too much free time that is not consumed with prosocial roles, (3) lack of employment, (4) a place to congregate. The major reasons youths join gangs are ones any adolescent can identify with: socialization and protection (Decker & Van Winkle, 1996; Pererson, Taylor, & Esbensen, 2004). If these reasons are combined with an environment with few or no extracurricular activities, obviously there would be a greater tendency for an individual to join a gang. However, as Peterson et al., (2004) conclude, youths are far more likely to be a victim of a violent crime while in a gang.

In an attempt to answer the question "What are the characteristics of individuals who join gangs?" the U.S. Department of Justice's research concluded that gang members are socially inept, have lower self-esteem, sociopathic tendencies, a high level of interaction with antisocial peers, and a low level of interaction with prosocial peers. (Esbensen, 2000). The wide variety of offenses committed by youth gangs are enough to cause any community concern, especially those in large cities. The most common offenses committed by large city gangs are drug use, drug trafficking, and violent crime (Howell & Decker, 1999). The use of a firearm is a major result of gang violence. In 84 percent of the gang-problem jurisdictions reported at least one use of a firearm by one or more gang members in a crime of assault (Egley & Arjunan 2002). However, the problems associated with gangs in school settings, though less frequent than on the city streets, are still a cause for concern. Gottfredson and Gottfedson (2001) found a -.49 correlation between school safety and presence of school gangs, and there was an increased amount of victimization in schools with gang members present. Chandler, Chapman, Rand, and Taylor (1998) reported that between 1989 and 1995 the percentage of students reporting the presence of gangs at their schools nearly doubled. Additionally, Chandler et al., found a strong correlation between the presence of gangs in schools and the presence of drugs and firearms at these schools. Their study listed the reasons why students concluded that there were gangs in their schools: (1) the gang had a name, (2) had a recognized leader, (3) had their own identifiable territory, (4) turf was tagged or marked with graffiti, (5) there were identifiable violent acts committed by the gang, (6) clothing was identifiable with gang membership, and (7) they were aware of gang member tattoos (Chandler et al., 1998).

REACTIVE APPROACHES TO GANG PROBLEMS

While it is only speculative that the existence of gangs in schools may increase, it seems a logical conclusions with schools cutting extracurricular activities as states try to balance budgets. The Great Recession has probably led to an increase in gang behavior. One poll reported that 67 percent of those surveyed believed that the recession has had a direct bearing on the increase in gangs in the United States (Daniels, 2010). What is most alarming about gang activity in schools is that measures to curb gang violence and activities are largely reactive and not proactive. Howell and Lynch (2000) identified typical security steps schools used as measures against gangs: (1) security guards, (2) school staff supervising hallways, (3) metal detectors, (4) locked doors during the day, (5) requiring visitors to sign-in, and (6) locker checks. The National Institute of Justice (Kenney & Watson,

1999) call this process called "Target Hardening" and offer common criticisms of this approach (1) an oppressive security environment might worsen relations between educators and the police, and (2) such an environment might harm the functional of the educational process in schools.

While such measures may protect students during the school hours, they do nothing to prevent gang violence after school is dismissed. The Federal Bureau of Investigation's 2011 *National Gang Threat Assessment Report* while impressive for its thorough analysis of gangs in the United States, never mentions any suggestions for proactive measures to reduce gang violence in the United States. Of course all law enforcement agencies in the U.S. are more or less reactive and not proactive with respect to gang violence. Proactive strategies seem to the domain of private organizations such as The Aquarius Project and CeaseFire (to be discussed later in this chapter).

MEDIATION AND GANG DISPUTES

With the plethora of studies reporting the success of peer mediation programs in schools, it is interesting that the two agencies that are responsible for much of the published literature on gangs in the United States—the U.S. Department of Justice's Office of Juvenile Justice and Delinquency Prevention and the National Youth Violence Prevention Resource Center—do not report on any studies on the result of school mediation programs for the reduction of gang-related problems. In fact, there are few if any studies on the use of mediation to curb gang violence. The prevailing thought seems to be one of gang prevention with programs such as G.R.E.A.T. (Gang Resistance and Education Training) modeled after the drug resistance program D.A.R.E.[1] There are many publications available that discuss programs to solve problems in schools, but once again these do not involve any material on mediating gang disputes.[2]

One of the few published studies on the use of mediation as a gang prevention strategy was published over twenty years ago (Mendelsohn, 1991). Mediation was used to solve problems between two gangs in which violence had escalated to the point that several people were stabbed and beaten. One gang was predominantly female, the other male. The two groups discussed the two issues that were causing problems between the gang—gender and cultural problems—and were able to reach a mediated agreement that lasted over a year. Tabish and Orell (1996) reported on the use of mediation between gangs at a middle school in Albuquerque, New Mexico. The results were promising. They concluded that the formal mediation process when used between two rival gangs, it markedly curbed inter-gang violence and made the campus a safer place for the student body and adult population. This school did not use student mediators, but mediators from the New Mexico Center for Dispute Resolution.

CONSIDERATIONS FOR GANG MEDIATION

While metal detectors might reduce violence in the halls of schools, they do not prevent future violence by gang members once off school property. It is hoped that administrators realize that gang mediation should be seen as a proactive process to reduce gang problems, and are not an attempt to throw water on a fire after it has already begun. An important initial question to consider when planning mediations involving gangs in schools is whether to use student mediators or professional adult mediators? The New Mexico study, when there were mediations between individual gang members, student peer mediators were used which were drawn from a long standing and successful peer mediation program. However, when mediations were needed for disputes between two groups of gang members, professional adult mediators were employed. Because of the potential for violence while mediating gang disputes, adult mediators with extensive mediation experience *and knowledge of local gangs should be employed.* Mediators who have training in social services and experience dealing with delinquent youths would also be good candidates for gang mediations. Mediators should not be made up of school administrators, but qualified mediators from community mediation centers or professional mediators who are viewed as neutral by the gang members.

While mediation might not be a panacea for all gang problems, it certainly could be an extremely effective preventative and proactive measure for gang related problems. While a plethora of books have been devoted to community mediation, family mediation, etc., there is a void of information when it comes to the mediation of gang-related conflicts. The most comprehensive guide for mediating gang disputes is presented in *The School Mediator's Field Guide* (Cohen, 1999). There are some basic tenets of mediating disputes that involve gang members which will be discussed, but first there are several important decisions that must be made before gang mediation can be implemented.

GANG MEDIATION PROCEDURES

First and foremost, if gang mediation is to be successful, mediators must work with community-based agencies that have experience in dealing with gangs. These agencies can serve vital functions for mediators by helping them learn about the gangs they will work with, arrange preliminary meetings between gang members and mediators, and help with the follow up and support of mediated agreements (Cohen, 1999). Perhaps the most important variable in gang mediation is trust between gang members and mediators. Simply put, trust must be based on mutual respect. If the mediators do not show respect for the gang members, they should not expect trust to be reciprocated defeating the mediation before it begins. Intake procedures are probably even more important when mediating gang disputes. Since each side will usually be represented by more than one individual, the mediators should learn of the specifics of the dispute before the disputants meet face-to-face. If the dispute between the gangs is hostile, it is best to give parties a chance to vent in a preliminary intake than in the open mediation session (Cohen, 1999). During this intake the mediators can judge the severity of potential for violence between the two parties, and assign security personnel as needed. As Cohen (1999) points out, when conflicts are between two groups, it is too risky to begin the mediation without any knowledge of the dispute. This is especially true for gang mediations. Additionally, mediators can use preliminary sessions to demonstrate their neutrality.

The following should be covered during the preliminary meeting between the mediators and the disputants: (1) A discussion of the mediation process and determination as to whether mediation is appropriate for the current dispute. (2) An analysis of the urgency of the conflict—what will happen if the dispute is not resolved? (3) If appropriate, encouragement to use mediation to resolve the dispute (Cohen, 1999). It is also easier for the mediators to get parties to agree to the ground rules before the mediation, so hostile remarks will have a lesser chance of being aired during the mediation. It is essential that the ground rules of mediation be clearly stated and enforced when the mediators introduce the process. As one gang mediator says, "Some of these kids in gangs have never followed rules. They do not know what rules are for. Even when you state them, they will break them to challenge you."[3] If the mediators allow gang members break rules that are not enforced, chaos and perhaps physical violence could follow.

SPECIAL CONSIDERATIONS FOR GANG MEDIATIONS

In general, community mediations are usually held at mediation centers across the country where a safe environment is taken for granted. However, issues of security are the most pressing concerns for the location of mediations involving gang disputes. This is essential for the protection of both the mediators and the disputants. If either feels threatened, the success of the mediation is questionable. To achieve a safe environment, Cohen (1999) recommends the following: (1) the implementation of a "no weapons" policy, and informing all disputants that they will be frisked before the mediation begins; (2) the prohibition of wearing gang-related clothing; (3) encouraging spokespersons from the gangs to appear, not all gang members; (4) security personnel located outside or inside the mediation room, and (5) the escorting of gang members to "safe zones" after the mediation has concluded. This information must be communicated to, and agreed upon by all participants in the mediation before the process begins.

Gang disputes that cause problems in both rural and urban areas are usually caused by gang members of high-school age. An important question to be considered is whether or not gang mediations should take part on a school campus or at another site perceived as neutral to gang members. One problem with allowing gang mediations on school grounds is the reluctance of school administrators to allow this type of intervention. By allowing gang mediation on school grounds, administrators are admitting that there are gangs in their schools—something administrators might not like to admit. Simply being identified as a gang member (e.g., wearing gang colors or tattoos) may warrant suspension. If the dispute is between gang members who attend the same school, the local school may be perceived as a neutral site. If the dispute is between gang members who attend different schools, a neutral site independent of the schools is preferable.

As with other types of mediation, confidentiality is an issue that mediators must deal with effectively. If a mediator learns of crimes committed or other laws broken, what are their moral and/or legal responsibilities? Does their state allow mediators with the same privilege as given to attorneys and their clients? These questions are crucial if the gangs have previously engaged in violent or illegal behavior. Therefore, the expediency of the mediation must be carefully assessed by the mediators, as well as the consequences of not holding mediations when the consequences are clearly identified. While models of mediation may vary, the traditional mediation model (introduction, explanation of mediation, defining the conflict, seeking solutions, reaching agreement) may be employed in gang mediation.

It is not recommended that the traditional seating arrangements be employed in gang mediation. There should be as much physical space as possible should be allowed between the opposing gangs. Additionally, any instruments that could be used as weapons should not be allowed in the mediation room—this includes pencils and pens.

When agreements are reached in gang mediation, they must involve all gang members. This may take time to allow gang representatives to discuss the agreement with their respective gang members. If this is not done, the empowering aspect of mediation will not be recognized by all gang members, and agreements might fall apart. However as with any mediation, mediators must not pressure gang members into agreement that they feel they do not own. Another important aspect in the agreement is to determine if the agreement reached is realistic based on past behaviors. If two disputing gangs reach an agreement that does not seem tenable based on past events, the mediators should test this with the disputants. While there are few published resources on gang mediation, it does not mean the problem is not being actively addressed. Two organizations who strive to reduce gang violence will now be discussed.

THE AQUARIUS PROJECT

The Aquarius Project, a highly successful gang mediation program in San Jose, California, is based on the city of Boston's Operation Cease-Fire, deals with gang disputes that have life and death consequences. This program was initially conceived to stop gun violence in Boston through the "Streetworker Program" as part of "Operation Cease-Fire." Staff members in this program are trained in conflict resolution and gang mediation, and are available to gang members and their families to mediate gang dispute and truces, and act as a go between for gang members and existing governmental and community programs. Because of the volatile nature of the gangs they deal with, the Aquarius Project utilizes some practices that are different from what might be considered a typical mediation. Aquarius is an intervention, prevention and suppression program aimed to deter gang violence, and works in collaboration with the Santa Clara County District Attorney's Office, the Public Defender's office, and Santa Clara County Probation Department. The program is also associated with the San Jose Mayor's Gang Prevention Task Force and the San Jose Police Department. The stated mission of the Aquarius Project is

to provide effective violence and gang intervention and health promotion services, thus building youth capacity to protect their safety and establish them on a path toward independence and self-sufficiency while protecting community safety (Aquarius Project Web Page, 2012).

Hewitt R. Joyner, III, the Chief Operating Officer and President of the Aquarius Project in San Jose, says that the most important thing in mediating gang disputes is the ground work before the actual mediation. This is needed to find out as much as possible about the nature of the gang, its members, and the type of dispute to develop a rapport with at least one of the gangs in the dispute. This involves getting information from a variety of sources that have had contact with the gangs before (e.g., their neighborhood, parents, schools and churches). This includes a home visitation with gang members before the mediation to find out about such information as how the gang members live, if they are religious, do they have parents—and if so, the nature of that relationship. This is a proactive program with the purpose of stopping gang violence before, during, and after it starts. When gang members arrive for the mediation, they are searched and are seated at a separate table from the other gang. The number of mediators and law enforcement officers at the mediation always outnumber the number of the disputants, as Joyner says, "The gang members need to respect who we are and the fact that we can always be more aggressive than they are."[4] An important aspect of this type of mediation is reality testing because the "what ifs" have deadly consequences: lives may be lost of the mediation does not take place correctly. This project does not allow any more than three disputants from each side during the mediation. Disputants are told to only discuss the current dispute and not bring up other complaints from past grievances with the other gang, because as Joyner states, "when you're dealing with gang disputes, you're dealing with past and current murders and violence, this isn't your Betty Lou and Suzzie Cue hair brush issue, you're dealing with gang members!"[5] This project is aimed more at violent gangs who contribute to the large number of criminal offenses committed by gangs. According to Joyner, out of over a 100 clients who have used the Aquarius Project, only two have been shot and there have been no fatalities.[6]

Unfortunately the Aquarius Project has run into problems with city officials and law enforcement because collaborative conflict management (which is at the heart of mediation) is something these officials do not seem to comprehend.[7] This project also has had problems that confront many mediators: those who have not been trained in gang mediations have little understanding of the process. As with any social program, another big problem Joyner has faced is lack of community involvement.[8]

CeaseFire

Chicago has a robust operation known as CeaseFire that strives to reduce all violence in Chicago and views gang violence as public health problem and advocates the use of a public health model to prevent gang violence.[9] The main goal of CeaseFire is to prevent violence utilizing intervention and community-mobilization in some of Chicago's most dangerous communities. It was created in 1999 by the Chicago Project for Violence at the University of Illinois at Chicago School of Public Health. This project was founded in 1995 by Dr. Gary Slutkin, and epidemiologist who believes that violence is a public health issue that can be countered by changing the behavioral norms associated with violence. The activities of this program is organized into five core components which address not only those who could be involved in shootings (e.g., gang members), but also the community at large. These components are: (1) street-level outreach, (2) public education, (3) community mobilization, (4) faith community involvement, and (5) law enforcement. The underlying assumption is that certain behaviors or "inputs" are responsible for violence or "outputs." Much of the program's day-to-day activities are spent targeting the inputs that cause violence in an attempt to eliminate negative outputs (Skogan, Hartnett, Bump, DuBois, 2008).

The crucial front line workers in CeaseFire are "the interrupters" and outreach workers who establish a rapport with gang leaders and what the project defines as highest-risk individuals such as: (1) a person with a history of carrying weapons, (2) an individual recently released from prison for a violent act, (3) those involved in street activity, (4) those known to be a member of a violent street organization, (5) individuals between the ages of 16 to 25, (6) a recent victim of a shooting, and (7) persons with a history of violence/crimes against people.[10] These individuals work alone or in pairs and walk Chicago's streets at night mediating both gang and other types of disputes before these disputes result in violence.[11] If there is a shooting and it is gang related, they provide nonviolent alternatives to gang leaders and associates of the shooting victim in an effort to interrupt the cycle of retaliatory violence so often found in gang life styles (Ritter, 2009).

Many of the interrupters are former gang members themselves who have served time in prison which gives them more credibility in mediating disputes. The Chicago police have partnered with CeaseFire in an attempt to reduce the rising violence in Chicago in the summer of 2012 (Gold, 2012). Frank Perez, the National Director of CeaseFire notes that it is only a small percent of the target population that is involved in the current violence wave in Chicago.[12] The individuals who may become shooters and perpetuate the cycle of violence are the people Cease-Fire hopes to reach (Ritter, 2009); in 2010, CeaseFire mediated 498 conflicts in Chicago that most likely saved many lives. The success of the program is evident by the fact that many other cities (e.g., Baltimore, New Orleans, Philadelphia, San Juan, Puerto Rico, and several states in New York State) are adopting this proactive approach to prevent violence in their cities (Hardiman, 2011). In the summer of 2012 at the United States Conference of Mayors 80th Annual Meeting in Orlando, mayors adopted a resolution in support of the CeaseFire model.[13]

CONCLUDING COMMENTS

Gang mediation is probably the least studied and least understood of all the forms of mediation. Yet the consequences of not resolving gang disputes can have deadly consequences. While reactive measures (e.g., metal detectors) may give those in school a feeling of protection from gang violence, they do little to present gang violence outside of the school. The gang problem in the United States is rising, not declining. Until more effective measures of *preventing* gang violence are implemented, the crisis of gang-related criminal offenses will continue not only in the inner city, but in more suburban areas as well. Programs such as the Aquarius Project and CeaseFire seem to be successful to this end, and provide much more promise for reducing gang violence than simply reacting to it.

Because of its philosophy of empowerment and recognition embedded in mediation, it would seem as a possible effective measure in reducing gang-related problems. Even more important, mediations between gangs are seen as proactive measures, not an attempt to pour water on a fire that has already been burning. With the success of such programs like the Aquarius Projec and CeaseFire, it seems that mediation can be a much more viable measure of dealing with gangs. The alternative will only be a rise in gang-related problems. The success of mediation in resolving a wide variety of disputes is widely published and understood, why more attempts like the Aquarius Project are not implemented to reduce gang problems is a troubling question. Our children deserve better.

Case Study: The Street Wizards and the Castle Boys

The Castle Boy's turf is located in an eight block square area bordered by Franklin Street, Market Street, South Quincy Street, and Oak Street. This area is "tagged" with their blue and gold colors with "CB" painted on many buildings, fences, and billboards. This is a Hispanic gang, and they have controlled this area for over ten years. Two people have been murdered since the Castle Boys took control of this area: one was an unfortunate tourist who because lost and wandered onto their turf looking for directions; the other was a member of their rival gang the Street Wizards who was caught tagging while on their turf.

The Street Wizards turf begins on the other side of Main Street. The Wizards, an African American gang, once occupied some of what is now the Castle Boys turf. However, with the massive influx of Hispanics into the city—many who have joined the Castle Boys—the Wizards decided to give up a two block area of their former turf and move four blocks south of Main Street. This created a two block buffer between the two gangs which is now referred to as the Demilitarized Zone (or DMZ). However, each gang sees the DMZ as an extension of their territory. Though they do not occupy it, violent incidents have occurred when a rival gang member was seen in the DMZ. However, if no one from either gang encroaches on this territory, the gangs are willing to accept this as a buffer between their two gangs.

Though the Castle Boys and the Street Wizards are violent enemies, they respect each other's turf, and are well aware of the consequences of trespassing onto another gang's turf. However, a new and more volatile set of circumstances occurred when a playground was built in the DMZ. There are many younger children—brothers, sisters, offspring—of both gangs who want to use the new playground. Two weeks ago a fight broke out between opposite gang members who accompanied the children to the playground. Additionally, members of the Street Wizards tagged the playground with their black and orange colors, angering the Castle Boys who then tagged the playground as well. Because of these problems, the playground in the DMZ is now used very little because people in the neighborhood see it as an extremely dangerous environment and they are afraid to let their children play there. The children and younger siblings of gang members are upset because they all liked the playground and want to continue to use it. However, it is now a matter of pride between the two gangs as to who can claim the playground as their turf. Saving face is very important to each gang, and both gangs feel that it would be destructive to gang morale and pride if they conceded the playground to the other gang. Additionally, members of both gangs indicated that they would lose respect for their gang leaders if they did not try to claim the playground as their own.

QUESTIONS FOR DISCUSSION

1. Do you think this conflict be resolved through mediation? Why or why not?
2. If this dispute is mediated, what information should the mediators try to discover during preliminary session with each gang?
3. What are the underlying issues in this conflict?
4. Which gang members should appear in the mediation?
5. What topics of discussion should the mediators try to avoid?

NOTES

[1]For an explanation on a G.R.E.A.T middle school component, see http://www. great-online.org/corecurriculum.htm.

[2]See for example, Crawford D., and Bodine, R. (1996). "Conflict Resolution Education: A Guide to Implementing Programs in Schools, Youth-Serving Organizations, and Community Juvenile Justice Settings: Program Report." Office of Juvenile Justice and Delinquency Programs, U.S. Department of Justice, and Safe and Drug-Free Schools Program, U.S. Department of Education.

[3]Hewitt Joyner, III, June 30, 2006, personal interview.

[4]Ibid.

[5]E-mail correspondence with Hewitt Joyner, III, July 9, 2012.

[6]E-mail correspondence with Hewitt Joyner, III, July 23, 2012.

[7]Ibid.

[8]Ibid.

[9]CeaseFire Web page, (2012). Available from http://www.ceasefirechicago.org.

[10]E-mail correspondence with Frank Perez, July 25, 2012.

[11]PBS Frontline produced an award-winning documentary about the CeaseFire Chicago program available on PBS Frontline's web site, "The Interrupters." Frank Perez, the National Director of CeaseFire stresses that the interrupters do not use Chicago Police and do not employ Guardian Angles in these teams.

[12]Frank Perez, July 3, 2012, personal interview.

[13]CeaseFire Web page, "Mayors Affirm Support for CeaseFire Prevention Model." Available from http://ceasefirechicago.org/featured/nations-mayors-affirm-support-ceasefire.

REFERENCES

Aquarius Project-'Web page (2012). Available from http://www.aquariusproject. org/about-us.html.

CeaseFire Web page, (2012). Available from http://www.ceasefirechicago.org.

Chandler, K. A., Chapman, C. D., Rand, M. R., & Taylor, B. M. (1998). *Students. Reports of School Crime: 1989 and 1995.* Washington, D.C.: United States Departments of Education

Cohen, R. (1999). *The School Mediator's Field Guide.* Watertown, MA: School Mediation Associates.

Daly, M. (2012). Chicago gang shootings spikes as the city tries to cope." *The Daily Beast.* Available from http://www.thedailybeast.com/articles/2012/04/17/ chicago-gang-shootings-spike-violent-crime-statistics-as-the-city-tries-to- cope.html.

Decker, S. H., and Van Winkle, B. (1996). *Life in the Gang: Family, Friends, and Violence.* New York: Cambridge University Press.

Egley, A., Jr. (2005). "Highlights of the 2002–2003 national youth gang survey." *Juvenile Justice Bulletin.* Washington, D.C.: U.S. Department of Justice, Office of Juvenile Justice and Delinquency Programs.

Egley, A., Jr., and Arjunan, M. (2002). "Highlights of the 2000 national youth gang survey." *Juvenile Justice Bulletin* Washington, D.C.: U.S. Department of Justice, Office of Juvenile Justice and Delinquency Programs.

Egley, A., and Howell, J. C. (2012). Highlights of the 2010 national youth gang survey." *Juvenile Justice Bulletin* Washington, D.C.: U.S. Department of Justice, Office of Juvenile Justice and Delinquency Programs

Ebensen, F. (2000). "Preventing adolescent gang violence." *Juvenile Justice Bulletin.* Washington, D.C.: U.S. Department of Justice, Office of Juvenile Justice and Delinquency Programs.

Federal Bureau of Investigation (2011). "Crime in the United States, 2010." Washington, DC: U.S. Department of Justice.

Gold, J. (2012). Chicago police to partner with anti-violence group CeaseFire to curb shootings. NBCNEWS.com. Available from http://usnews.msnbc.msn. com/_news/2012/06/27/12423957-chicago-police-to-partner-with-anti- violence-group-ceasefire-to-curb-shootings?lite.

Gottfredson, G. D., and Gottfredson, D. C. (2001). *Gang Problems and Gang Programs in a National Sample of Schools.* Ellicott City, MD: Gottfredson Associates, Inc.

Hardiman, T. (2011). CeaseFire: Success beyond Chicago. *Huffington Post.* Available from http://chicago.blackyouthproject.com/2011/02/ceasefire-success- beyond-chicago.

Howell, J. C. (2010). Gang prevention: An overview of research and programs. *Juvenile Justice Bulletin.* Washington, D.C.: U.S. Department of Justice, Office of Juvenile Justice and Delinquency Programs.

Howell, J. C., and Decker, S. H. (1999). The youth gangs, drugs, and violence connection. *Juvenile Justice Bulletin.* Washington, D.C.: U.S. Department of Justice, Office of Juvenile Justice and Delinquency Programs.

Howell, J. C., and Lynch, J. P. (2000). Youth gangs in school. *Juvenile Justice Bulletin.* Washington, D.C.: U.S. Department of Justice, Office of Juvenile Justice and Delinquency Programs.

Howell, J. C., Egley, A., JR., Tita, G. E., and Griffiths, W. (2011). U.S. gang problem trends and seriousness, 1996–2009. Washington, D.C.: Bureau of Justice Assistance, U.S. Department of Justice and U.S. Department of Justice, Office of Juvenile Justice and Delinquency Programs.

Kenney, D. J., and Watson, S. (1999). Crime in schools: Reducing conflict with student problem solving. *Research in Brief.* Washington, D.C. National Institute of Justice.

Maxson, C. L. (1998). Gang members on the move. *Juvenile Justice Bulletin.* Washington, D.C.: U.S. Department of Justice, Office of Juvenile Justice and Delinquency Programs.

Mendelsohn, D. O. (1991). Mediation: A gang prevention strategy. *MCS Conciliation Quarterly, 10,* 5–6.

Moore, J. W. (1998). "Understanding youth street gangs: Economic restructuring and the urban underclass." In M. W. Watts (Ed.), *Cross-Cultural Perspectives on Youth Gangs and Violence* (pp. 65–78), Stamford, CT JAI.

National Youth Gang Center, (2006). *Frequently Asked Questions Regarding Gangs.* Available from http//www.iir.com/nygc/fac.htm.

Peterson D., Taylor, T. J., and Esbensen, F. (2004). Gang membership and violent victimization. *Justice Quarterly, 21,* 794–815.

Ritter, N. (2009). CeaseFire: A public health approach to reduce shootings. Washington, D.C.: National Institute of Justice Journal Number 264.

Skogan, W. G., Hartnett, S. M., Bump, N., and Dubois, J. (2008). *Evaluation of CeaseFire—Chicago.* Chicago: Northwestern University.

Tabish, K. R., and Orell, L. H. (1996). "Respect: Gang mediation at Albuquerque, New Mexico's Washington middle school." *School Counselor, 44,* 65–70.

Chapter 11

Faith-Based Disputes and Mediation Intervention

William D. Kimsey
Sallye S. Trobaugh

Faith-based organizations, like synagogues, temples, churches, and others, create a reality for their membership, which defines a member's worldview and how the organization governs through interlinked systems of symbols, schemas, and standards. Talk, dialogue, and negotiation at all levels, including interpersonal, group, and organizational shape believers' identity and experience. This shared reference sustains the substance of group and individual identity. Social and religious contexts provide for experiences where believers reify virtues, priorities, and ideals of their faith culture (Goldberg & Blanke, 2011; Bercovitch & Kadayifci-Orellana, 2009; Said & Funk, 2001; Said, Funk & Kunkle, 2003); normative practices make social interaction meaningful.

Deep-seated standards provide boundaries for achieving individual growth and transformation promised by faith-based organizations. Individual behavior must derive from and reflect organizational beliefs and higher-level cognitive schemas such as ideologies, orthodoxies, orientations, and more. Compliance with organizational values is implicit in all activities of the group. Yet, the premise of choice coupled with conviction often creates defensive communication patterns when faith-based members debate and dialogue amongst themselves. Members with minority opinions risk persecution within the organization if they do not represent the "official" position.

Faith-based organizations typically operate in religious paradigms, which impact all aspects of group and organizational life, including setting values, solving problems, resolving conflict, and more. Conflict in faith-based organizations often is tempered with unspoken tenets threatening rupture among member believers and severance of relationship with deity, both critical for definition of self, others, and worldview. Uncertainty, which surrounds faith-based disputes, coupled with difficulty of not knowing precisely the best way to respond often starts a conflict avoidance cycle that may create an appearance of submission to organizational values when just the opposite is true.

The purpose of this chapter is to present a framework for understanding faith-based conflict and resolving believer disputes through mediation. A seven-phase model of believer conflict is described with a comparative discussion of facilitative and transformative mediation practices. Examples of ways the authors have used the conflict schema and different experiences serving as mediators in faith-based organizations are presented.

A SCHEMA FOR FAITH-BASED MEDIATORS

The seven-phase model of conflict identifies patterns of conflict behavior individuals may choose when their commitment to the organization and its members is disturbed, distressed, or deteriorating. The model hypothesizes that there are points within the seven phases in which organizational leaders can resolve developing problems in the organization.

Critical moments in the conflict process present opportunities for intervention. Organizational leaders and mediators will intervene when conflict resolution is most likely to be successful. Use of mediation in key conflict phases can reduce or prevent destructive outcomes.

The attributes of the seven-phase model as presented by Kimsey, Trobaugh, McKinney, Hoole, Thelk, and Davis (2006) include worldview, frame of irony, relational dialectics and conflict phases. Figure 11.1 presents a schema of the model.

Worldview constitutes values, attitudes and behavior, which provide meaning for an individual (Kimsey & Fuller, 1998).

The War on Terror demonstrates the power of religious paradigms for spawning different groups with similar visions about what people should believe and how they should live such as the Hezbollah or the al-Qaeda both declaring jihad against the Capitalist and Judeo-Christian worldviews.

Worldviews are reinforced by systems that justify individual beliefs. Frame of Irony deconstructs challenges to worldview by dissembling thoughts, making assertions or performing actions that negatively project the motivation behind a chal-

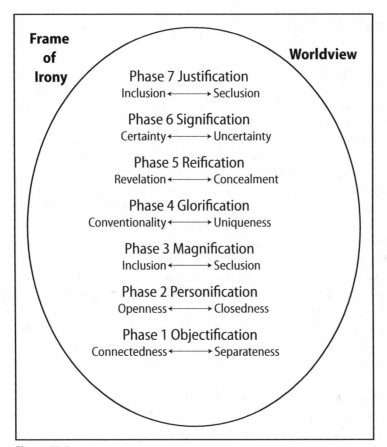

Figure 11.1

The Seven-Phase Model of Conflict

lenge. For instance, if inquiry is made why the religious leader lives a higher standard of living than the believer members, the inquiry is met with rebuke suggesting the intent behind the question reflects a critical spirit that harbors jealousy. The frame of irony serves the purpose of deflecting reasonable inquiry for finding the truth thus ensuring the existing worldview.

Relational dialectics create push-pull contradictions inherent in engaging frames of irony and making challenges to existing worldviews. Unified by interdependence, the dichotomous predispositions coexist in a nexus of tensions which achieve resolution by negating each other. The interplay between relational dialects, including *Connectedness-Separateness, Predictability-Novelty, Openness-Closedness, Inclusion-Seclusion, Conventionality-Uniqueness, Revelation-Concealment* and the frame of irony creates a link where the interdependence with the opposite impulse and independence from the opposite impulse occurs. The following describes the seven phases of conflict in faith-based organizations.

SEVEN PHASES OF CONFLICT

Phase 1: Objectification. The first step involves the believer objectifying self and others. Objectification is the base step for ultimately proving that one is right. When the believer objectifies he or she projects an independent reality, making another individual impersonal. In other words, people are put in categories or boxes. For example, a woman, whose name is Elizabeth, teaches Sunday school at a church and has been doing so for over twenty-five years; she is now 83. The church elders hired a young, new minister, Bob, who through his inexperience promptly dismissed Elizabeth because, in his interpretation of the Bible, women should not be teaching. The minister used his interpretation of the Bible to justify his actions—dismiss the Sunday school teacher, whom Bob has now framed as an object and does not acknowledge as a person. A dialectical tension occurs in Phase 1: Objectification, when the individual believer attempts to achieve connectedness by agreeing with the organization's worldview while at the same time attempts to speak out, knowing such boldness may pose a threat of separation.

Phase 2: Personification. The second step, Personification, starts with the believer's casual conversation with other members of the group without disclosing his or her position. Interpersonal discussion focuses now on personal deficits of others who are not like-minded, particularly those in leadership. Elizabeth, in the above example, could have challenged the minister's actions, but instead starts talking to friends and parents of children whom she has taught, asking for their opinions about her dismissal. Likewise, Bob responds to friends' and members' inquiries about the dismissal citing the Bible as his authority for the action all the while marking who agrees or disagrees with him. The relational dialectic in this phase exemplifies openness-closedness: "Do I personify by openly disclosing my position or do I remain silent and closed, not voicing my dissatisfaction?"

Phase 3: Magnification. The third step, Magnification, involves the act of enlarging the rightness of one's position by complimenting others who express support. Using the same example above, having focused on personal deficits in Personification, a choice for creating facts out of unwarranted perceptions is the focus. Both the minister, Bob, and the member, Elizabeth, can spiral into detracting obvious shortcomings of one another, e.g. making comments like "He seems very legalistic about administration" or "It's really great to have more men involved in church work." The goal here is to convince oneself and other like-minded believers that what has been attributed in Personification not only exists but is supported by fact—fact often taken out of context or overstated or used as puffery. The relational dialectic of *Inclusion-Seclusion* surfaces at this point where the supportive communication achieves inclusion and defensive communication creates seclusion.

Phase 4: Glorification. Step 4, Glorification, is the act of exalting, glorifying, and venerating, often characterized by self-elevation. For instance, the glorifier talks about other spiritual experiences and notes how wonderful, powerful, and anointed the other leaders were that led that organization to fame and blessing. Likewise, alliances emerge for the purpose of recognizing those who have been suffering under the same injustice caused by the worldview and frame of irony set in place by the other side. In the case with Bob and Elizabeth, Bob has a few men in the Church, whom he trusts, who will pray through the difficulty created by his position on women in leadership. Elizabeth, who has seen the minister's type of disingenuous acceptance of women in other churches, knows that women, in general, may harbor ill feelings over being treated as "second-class" citizens in the Kingdom of God. Also, she can prove Bob's scriptural position is too narrow. The relational dialectic for the Glorification phase is *Conventionality-Uniqueness*.

Phase 5: Reification. Reification is creating a reality, which is believed to be true by producing the behavior and actions to support that truth. In Reification, the believer creates situations that provide evidence for his or her worldview whether in error or not. It is in this phase of Reification that the believer may become more entrenched in imagination and no longer examines the accuracy of his or her actions. At this stage of the conflict progression, the believer is convinced of the rightness of his or her understanding of what is happening. It is not uncommon to see self-fulfilling prophecy expanding and being assigned greater importance than necessary. This is often the place where the believer forms his or her own frame of irony for the purpose of defending positions. For instance, Bob, who "knows" he is called of God to be positional about the place of women in the Church, and Elizabeth, who knows God has used her to touch a lot of people's lives through her teaching Sunday School, may use every example and expression of their individual work as a "see, God is in what I am doing" attitude. The dialectical tension in Reification is *Revelation-Concealment;* the believer can go along with the revelation and demonstrate the appropriate behaviors or secretly conceal disbelief. Bob and Elizabeth want the rightness of what they are doing individually to be revealed to others, while at the same time discrediting the claims of their opponent.

Phase 6: Signification. Assigning meaning for the purpose of drawing conclusions that support judgments and evaluations that have been made in Phases 1–5, is the role of Phase 6, Signification. Examples of Signification could be that the organization is beginning to suffer because of the growing disagreement between two factions that are now taking sides in the biblical interpretation Bob has placed on his action. Everything that does or does not happen in the lives of leadership or membership is used to provide proof that the individual believer, the one who assigns meaning, is right. Power derived from earlier phases makes it punishing for the believer to change his or her course, and the fundamental judgments made early in Objectification and reinforced in Phases 2–5 cannot be deserted. Justification must now be achieved; too much has been committed, too much has been ventured, and too much is public. Elizabeth and Bob point to the illnesses, problems, and crises that occur in the other's life as proof that the other is out of God's will and therefore out of God's blessing. The dialectical tension of Signification is

Certainty-Uncertainty; everything must happen in a manner that is in line with the "truths" of the believers and if that does not happen, the seeds of uncertainty are sown.

Phase 7: Justification. The final phase of the believer conflict, Justification, involves exoneration for the purpose of normalizing assertions made earlier when no real information was present to sanction the positions taken. Phases 1–6 sequentially build to a critical mass for achieving assent to the position of the believer. A mindset of "I told you so" prevails. The goal that the believer is exact, fair, and has the heart of deity on the matters in dispute is now revealed to those objectified. Examples of this could involve being part of a plan to challenge the organization's leadership; to initiate prayer with other members for the purpose of resisting the other side's agenda; or even going to court to repossess the assets of the organization. In this stage, the believer is ready to take action and to fight for what he or she believes. Everything at this point is made right by winning battles; a win-lose approach concerning who is right and who is wrong is the mindset (Fisher and Brown, 1988). When the believer reaches Justification, it is often difficult to reason and turn him or her from a course that could easily take on a life of its own. In short, a movement bringing forth a new worldview for the organization could result if enough believers of a similar mentality come together as a power. In our example, both Elizabeth and Bob have now talked to enough members at all levels of the organization during the previous six phases. The results culminate in a conflict episode where there is a "showdown" to prove who is right, even to point of splitting the church. Bob is convinced he is right because Elizabeth's actions now prove she is a power-seeking troublemaker. Elizabeth is sure she is right because Bob has proven that he is a legalistic, insensitive leader with chauvinistic values. The dialectical tension associated with Justification is *Inclusion-Exclusion:* You are either with us or against us; since we have the truth, we will watch you lose. Moving to the *Win-Lose* framework allows the conflict to be brought into the open and for the first time more clearly defined.

The seven-phase model of conflict presented in this chapter identifies a conflict continuum that mediators and organizational leaders can use to conceptualize conflict (Kimsey, et al, 2006, p. 497) (see Figure 11.2 Hypothesized Conflict Model Continuum).

When Objectification is high, the believer may be intense in judgment, but he or she is likely to be alone still in their thinking. If leadership in the faith-based organization can resolve the issue, the conflict can be contained before growing and spreading. Within the phase of Personification, leadership also has the opportunity and ability to resolve the believer's issues, prior to critical mass growing. When members are in the process of magnifying, glorifying, or reifying, it is likely that outside mediation may be necessary. A group of like-minded believers is forming and may be resistant to the other side's attempts to solve the issue, especially if Glorification is high or the conflict is with the leadership. Problem solving and transformative mediation practices are choices available to organizational leadership.

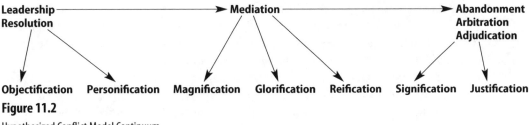

Figure 11.2
Hypothesized Conflict Model Continuum

Problem solving is recommended for non-faith related issues while transformative is best for faith related issues. When a cadre of believers has reached the point of Signification or Justification, the likelihood of successful mediation quickly diminishes. All egos are involved and too much face would be lost even in a win-win situation.

FAITH-BASED MEDIATION PRACTICES

A facilitative process, using a mediation procedure, in most instances, is perhaps the only real means of achieving reconciliation among believers. Guilt accumulated as the believer passes through each of the seven phases of believer conflict creates a critical moment during which it is imperative that intervention helps believers reframe their positional, win-lose ploys to principled, win-win approaches (Sandford, 1989; Fisher & Ury, 1991). If this does not occur, the guilt resulting from fragmenting the group will not only hurt the believer but could eventually harm the organization (Cloud & Townsend, 1999).

It is essential for the individual believer to recognize that conflict is omnipresent. The believer's testimony, regardless of the person, is all about resolving conflict as the individual progresses through life cycles, starting with conception and birth and ending with death and release.

The requirement for interdependence compels believers to be in fellowship, and the expressed struggles now focus on commitment to relationships and commitment to positions, e.g. doctrine (Lulofs & Cahn, 2000). Empowering the individual believer to have high concern for both relationship and individual goals is a natural consequence of engaging doctrine and the body of faith members. It is here where the believer must make a choice to work through conflict resulting from competing worldviews, frames of irony, and difficult people while not separating themselves from the faith-based organization (Kimsey & Fuller, 1998).

Key elements in achieving principled win-win resolutions should include a) separating other believers from the problem, b) focusing on interests, not positions in believer conflict, c) proceeding independent of trust and dependent on faith, d) achieving transparent communication with other believers for the purpose of finding options achieving mutual gain, and e) insisting on outcomes separate from individual will—yielding to principle not pressure (Fisher & Ury, 1991).

Mediation is facilitated, principled discussion with an emphasis on achieving win-win outcomes by using a neutral intervener for the purpose of equally empowering the believers to solve problems resulting from competing worldviews, frames of irony, and difficult conflict styles. The mediation procedure provides a framework for achieving the above-identified key elements in win-win resolution. The following are discussions of problem solving and transformative mediation practices used to help believers be true to themselves and allowing for what their doctrine requires while navigating organizational pressure to conform. *The Promise of Mediation: Responding to Conflict Through Empowerment and Recognition* (Bush & Folger, 1994/2005), *Mediator Communication Competencies: Problem Solving and Transformative Practices 5/e* (Kimsey, McKinney, Della Noce, & Trobaugh, 2005) and other mediation texts provide elaboration of the concepts presented.

PROBLEM SOLVING MEDIATION IN FAITH-BASED SETTINGS

The first step, *Introducing the Process,* involves establishing a positive communication environment. Believers in conflict and mediators meet and reach agreement, through discussion, about schedule, procedure, rules, and other matters necessary for satisfactory interaction. The purpose in the first step of mediation is to create a setting in which believers can pursue a clear and open discussion of the issues in dispute. Before meeting with believers, mediators should a) review available information about the dispute, b) discuss potential problems or difficulties, c) discuss roles, duties, and responsibilities, and d) become familiar with the physical setting selected for the mediation.

Other responsibilities of the mediator or, when appropriate, mediators should a) welcome the believers and affirm his or her choice to use win-win approaches in problem solving mediation, b) clarify the purpose of mediation, c) explain the procedure and the mediator's role and function, d) describe the potential for private caucus sessions with the parties, e) discuss confidentiality and note-taking, and f) establish rules for interaction and secure agreement from the parties.

At the conclusion of the opening phase of a mediation session, the members and the mediators should be acquainted and comfortable with each other, understand and agree to the process for discussing the conflict, feel confident that they will be treated fairly and ethically, and know that the conflict and the process are owned by the believers.

The second step, *Defining the Conflict,* provides an opportunity for each believer to disclose, as fully and as completely as possible, his or her perception and understanding of the conflict. Each member will describe the conflict from his or her perspective. The parties' description will be unrestrained and uninterrupted. The mediator will summarize each believer's descriptions and ask for elaboration, clarification, or explanation necessary for developing a complete and accurate understanding of the conflict.

The procedure in this step includes: a) each member, in turn, describes the conflict from their perspective, b) believers are encouraged to identify facts, share their feelings, and describe their desired outcome, and c) the mediator summarizes each parties' description. At the conclusion of the Defining the Conflict Step, the parties and the mediators should have a complete understanding of the conflict— the facts, and the feelings—and have identified a tentative agenda of issues to resolve.

Step 3, *Solving the Problem,* focuses on gaining consensus regarding relevant issues and develop strategies, procedures, and solutions, acceptable to all members which will allow the believers to reach successful agreement. The purpose of Step 3 is to generate positive communication interaction while creating a supportive environment.

Procedures for the Solving the Problem Step require the mediator to a) facilitate identification of issues in conflict, b) prioritize issues for discussion, c) pursue discussion of interests and positions concerning each issue, d) encourage members to dialogue relevant to issues under discussion, e) provide periodic summary of progress and positive reinforcement, and f) caucus when necessary to overcome impasse or explore ideas privately.

At the conclusion of the Solving the Problem Step; the members and mediators should have reached an oral agreement concerning each issue, be satisfied that all dimensions of each issue have been considered; be satisfied that the believers have been given full opportunity to participate in the discussion; and be confident that the strategies, procedure, and solutions are fair, ethical, and practical.

The last step, *Implementing the Agreement,* provides a device to insure, to the degree appropriate and possible, that the believers accept responsibility for implementing their agreement and providing documentation, if necessary, of that commitment. The purpose of Step 4 is to bring the mediation session to a close and provide for some documentation of what has been agreed and what has been resolved.

Procedures for facilitating the Implementing the Agreement Step are for the mediator to a) write a statement of agreement, if needed, in clear and precise language and b) specify who is agreeing to what, when, and how. At the conclusion of this step, the members and mediator should achieve some closure with specific understanding of what is resolving the conflict and be satisfied with the steps taken for resolution.

It is in facilitated discussion where the individual believer now has a greater appreciation for his or her conflict over worldview, frame of irony and difficult believers. Engaging the conflict using a principled win-win procedure like mediation allows all involved to find individual growth in their faith experience while engaging the relational dialectics inherent in organizational pressures for conformity. The promise of mediation achieved through empowerment and recognition provides the believer the opportunity for solving problems in several of the seven phases of believer conflict while transforming the individual believer according to his or her faith structure. Transformation of the inner person for believers is a lifelong pursuit and a lifelong challenge, and most faith-based organizations provide some approaches for achieving those goals. The following section describes how transformative mediation works.

TRANSFORMATIVE MEDIATION AND FAITH-BASED ORGANIZATIONS

Transformative mediation is defined as "a process in which a third party works with parties in conflict to help them change the quality of their interaction from negative and destructive to positive and constructive as they explore and discuss issues and possibilities for resolution" (Bush & Pope, 2002, p. 83). The goal of a transformative mediator in faith-based organizations is to help believing members identify the opportunities for empowerment and recognition shifts that arise in their own conversation, and to choose whether and how to respond to these opportunities (Della Noce, Bush, & Folger, 2002, p. 51). Thus, competent mediator practice focuses on (1) fostering empowerment shifts by supporting each believer's efforts at deliberation and decision making at every point in the session where choices arise, and (2) fostering recognition shifts by supporting, but not forcing, each member's freely chosen efforts to achieve new understandings of the other believer's perspective (Bush & Pope, 2002, p. 84). This means that the transformative mediator maintains a dual goal focus throughout the mediation process.

The transformative model presumes that transformation of the interaction is what matters most to members—even more than a tangible settlement agreement (Della Noce, Bush, & Folger, 2002, p. 51). Success is measured not by a settlement agreement, but by member shifts toward empowerment and recognition. The mediator observes these shifts in the believers' interaction.

The mediator in a faith-based organization begins the mediation session by having an opening conversation with the believers. A transformative mediator relies on the metaphor of conversation to convey to the members the nature of the process in which they are taking part. The opening conversation between the mediator and the believers emphasizes empowerment and recognition. Transformative mediators focus attention on the conversational quality of the members' interaction; emphasize believer autonomy, choice, believer-to-believer communication and understanding; and frame settlement as one of a number of possible valuable outcomes.

The transformative mediator listens to the members' conversation with an ear to opportunities for empowerment and recognition. The mediator "punctuates" the conversations occurring in the mediation. The mediator does not lead the discussion; the believers lead the discussion. The transformative mediator does not intervene each time he or she hears an opportunity in the conversation; the mediator remains quiet and allows for silence and space so the members hear and respond to each other.

When appropriate, transformative mediators use three kinds of responses: reflecting, summarizing, and questioning. Reflection is powerful in supporting both empowerment and recognition. Mediator reflection amplifies the conversation for each believer; the members hear and understand what is being said. Mediator reflection confirms and elicits an immediate affirmation.

Mediator summary amplifies and clarifies the developing conversation between the believers. The summary makes the believers' conversation an entity unto itself; it includes the differences revealed and the choices offered, more "visible" so the members can make clearer choices about what to do. The parties respond to the mediator's summary by moving the conversation forward and often in new directions.

Mediator questioning and checking-in are used when members request help. While transformative mediators favor open-ended questions, "checking-in" is a particular use of a closed ended question. A check-in focuses on a decision about the mediation conversation itself, e.g., "You just said . . . is that what you want to do now?" or "Did I miss anything, what are you really wanting done?"

Mediator questions provide opportunities for a believer to elaborate on and get clearer about what he or she has said. Questions stimulate recognition shifts by letting the non-speaking member hear different elaborations of what the believer is saying, which may lead to new understandings.

Check-in allows a member to correct a mediator reflection or summary, and maintain some control. Mediator check-ins emphasize decision points and support recognition shifts by allowing each believer to become aware of the choices and priorities of the other, as decisions are faced and made in different ways.

Separate meetings are used often between the transformative mediator(s) and one member. Separate meetings help believers think through goals, resources, options, alternatives, and consequences. The mediator helps a believer to explore new information, to consider what new understandings he or she could extend to the other, and to explore whether there is something else that may need to be disclosed. The transformative mediator suggests separate meetings by checking-in with the members.

In recessing and resuming after separate meetings, the mediator discusses what is happening and why. The mediator instructs how information shared in separate session is handled, e.g., if there are confidentiality issues. The mediator facilitates the conversation, during separate session, about what a member wants to share, and how he or she might do so. Finally, the mediator summarizes what has happened in the joint session before adjourning and after starting in a subsequent session.

At the conclusion of a transformative mediation, believers have a better understanding of each other's position, what is wanted, and where they would like to go. Because of the emphasis on conversation, the members have openly clarified their perceptions and with new understanding can proceed to a more harmonious relationship. Out of the *Nova Harmony* they are better equipped to continue.

SELECTING BEST MEDIATION PRACTICE

Criteria for selecting the appropriate mediation practice, problem solving or transformative, are suggested as follows:

Criteria	Practice
✳ Faith related problems	Transformative Mediation
✳ Non-faith related problems	Problem Solving Mediation
✳ Compounded issues	Either Mediation Approach

A compounded issue may combine these mediation practices. Analyze the parts; the faith portion and non-faith portion may each be isolated, proceed then to mediate separately.

In order to assist understanding for making a selection of mediation practice, which is best suited to the issues, the following examples are offered.

Dispute Category	Mediation Practice
1. Philosophies	Transformative
2. Redemption/Sin	Transformative
3. Abortion/Right to Live	Transformative
4. Same Sex Marriage	Transformative
5. War/Peace	Transformative
6. Administrative	Problem Solving
7. Communication	Problem Solving
8. Education	Problem Solving
9. Divorce	Problem Solving
10. Marriage & Family	Problem Solving
11. Worship/Traditions	Either
12. Political Responses	Either
13. Community	Either
14. Medical vs. Faith Healing	Either
15. Sacraments	Either

Faith-based members in low-context societies typical of Western countries often associate with people in short time increments across a variety of contexts. Language, knowledge, and rules define how members in faith-based organizations problem-solve and build community. Relationship development for faith-based members is often driven by deterministic thinking emphasizing personal achievement. Judeo-Christian worldviews not uncommon in Western psyches are, generally speaking, empirical, cause-effect, linear, solution oriented, individualistic, and motivated toward managing the individual rather than the group. The drive toward solution inherent in the facilitative, problem solving mediation practice often assumes a low-context individualistic approach to conflict resolution.

High-context societies found in Eastern countries typical of Asia or the Middle East are often characterized as placing emphasis on process and ceremony over content and structure. They are less direct and give less information in written form. Emphasis on group identity, setting strong boundaries over who is or is not accepted and the importance of "face" creates complex frameworks making problem solving techniques difficult (Ting-Toomey, 2005). The transformative method, being non-directive, member driven, allows for more conversation which is consistent with high-context signification of situations and relationships. Faith-based organizations rely on high-context events and rituals which serve to justify choices made for the group and the believer member. Problem solving mediation may achieve outcomes typical of transformative practices, e.g. empowerment, recognition, etc.; yet the transformative process often is longer in duration, mediator authority less noticeable, outcomes may appear less clear and, perhaps even less controllable than problem solving. This is evident, particularly, with a first time introduction to transformative. Faith-based leaders favor transformative practices over problem solving mediation when the issues of the conflict are over values, beliefs, or doctrines and not about disputes over administration.

CONCLUDING COMMENTS

With practice, discerning which mediation method to use will become clearer. The believer's choice for faith-based mediation is usually difficult to initiate for the members who are more comfortable thinking that working on their issues separately without confrontation will make the problems go away. Therefore, many times there will be approach/avoidance with the idea of mediation for fear of escalation of the conflict. The parties' concern may be that open discussion through mediation may expose their true position and somehow make them appear to be less worthy in the eyes of deity, when in reality the very opposite holds true. Mediation offers an organized direct approach to solving issues without either party losing.

Case Study: Charismatic versus Seeker Sensitive Focus

A non-denominational church with a charismatic focus, approaching the celebration of their 15th year anniversary has been considering for some months how best to move forward and meet the evangelistic goals in their strategic plan.

The charismatic focus has been on praise and worship, experiencing the gifts and visitation of the Holy Spirit and allowing prophecies to be spoken on Sundays. Many meetings become very emotional and uplifting for the congregation and validates that God is present and blessing this group. Emphasis is on the biblical mandate to win the lost at any cost; weekend morning services are directed toward reaching the un-churched. However, the administration and many members of the governing body have concluded that the evangelistic goals can be best met by changing the focus from charismatic to a seeker-sensitive orientation with a more traditional church atmosphere. Citing that the highly emotionally charged atmosphere has been proven in sister churches to scare away new members, the decision is announced for consideration.

This positioning had been discussed in private throughout the membership for months. The final announcement came forth with the following rationale. God is tired of us proclaiming the truth on street corners, like the man with a loudspeaker. In fact he will go as far as to say that Christians who try to witness to their friends and preach the gospel to them are down right annoying. Our Church needs to be purpose driven and we need to make our Church so appealing that the whole world will want to be part of it. We don't need to drive Jesus down the visitors' throats; we'll let people decide for themselves as our Church meets their needs. But we need to get them through the Church's doors first.

Shortly after the announcement of the Church's new direction, conflict erupted among different groups: the praise and worship team over songs and style of presentation, Sunday school teachers over programs and materials, youth group leaders seeking appropriate direction, the finance committee on budget allocations, and other staff. Reports began streaming into the administrative staff regarding increased disagreements and divisions. The congregation was splitting right before their eyes. The administrative board is split on administrative issues. The board of elders is split on spiritual issues and doctrine.

Seeking the outside counsel of the Community Mediation Service, their problem was broken down into two types of conflict. The first was administrative issues, the second category was spiritual. The mediation service recommended the administrative board meet first to mediate conflicts over finance, programs, and staff issues. Secondly, the administrative board would agree to allow the elders to mediate on behalf of the spiritual issues related to worship service, sermons, youth group issues, doctrine, and the prophetic direction of the Church.

Questions for Discussion

1. Where in the Seven-Phase Model of Conflict would you say the Church presently finds itself? Why?

2. What style of mediation practice, problem solving or transformative, best fits the conflicts? Why?

3. If mediation is not successful, what methods of negotiation could be used to reach a satisfactory solution?

References

Bercovitch, J., & Kadayifci-Orellana, S. (2009). Religion and mediation: The role of faith-based actors in international conflict resolution. *International Journal, 14,* 175–204.

Bush, R. A. B., & Folger, J. P. (1994/2005). *The Promise of Mediation: Responding to Conflict Through Empowerment and Recognition.* San Francisco: Jossey-Bass.

Bush, R. A. B., & Pope, S. G. (2002). Changing the quality of conflict interaction: The principles and practice of transformative mediation. *Pepperdine Dispute Resolution Law Journal, 3*(1), 67–96.

Cloud, H. & Townsend, J. (1999). *Boundaries: When to say yes, when to say no, to take control of your life.* Grand Rapids, MI: Zondervan Publishing House.

Della Noce, D. J., Bush, R. A. B., & Folger, J. P. (2002). Clarifying the theoretical underpinnings of mediation: Implications for practice and policy. *Pepperdine Dispute Resolution Law Journal, 3*(1), 39–65.

Fisher, R., & Brown, S. (1988). *Getting together: Building a Relationship that Gets to Yes.* Boston: Houghton Mifflin Company.

Fisher, R., & Ury, W. (1991). *Getting to yes: Negotiating Agreement without Giving In* (2nd ed.). New York: Penguin Books.

Goldberg, R., & Blancke, B. (2011). God in the process: Is there a place for religion in conflict resolution? *Conflict Resolution Quarterly, 28*(4), 377–398.

Kimsey, W. D., & Fuller, R. M. (1998). A path model of world view, intolerance and violence. *Peace Research: The Canadian Journal of Peace Studies, 30*(4), 56–69.

Kimsey, W. D., McKinney, B. C., Della Noce, D. J., & Trobaugh, S. S. (2005). *Mediator Communication Competencies: Problem Solving and Transformative Practices* (5th ed.). Boston: Pearson Custom Publishing.

Kimsey, W. D., Trobaugh, S. S., McKinney, B. C., Hoole, E. R., Thelk, A. D., & Davis, S. L. (2006). Seven phase model of conflict: Practical applications for conflict mediators and leaders. *Conflict Resolution Quarterly, 23*(4), 487–499.

Lulofs, R. S., &, Cahn, D. D. (2000). *Conflict: From theory to Action* (2nd ed.). Boston: Allyn and Bacon.

Said, A. A., & Funk, N. C. (2001). The role of faith in cross-cultural conflict resolution. A paper presented at the European Parliament for the European Centre for Common Ground, September, 2001.

Said, A. A., Funk, N. C., & Kunkle, L. (2003). Cross-cultural conflict resolution. In N. N. Kittrie, R. Carazo and J. R. Mancham (Eds.), *The Future of Peace in the Twenty-First Century.* Durham, NC: Carolina Academic Press.

Sandford, J. L. (1989). *Why Some Christians Commit Adultery.* Tulsa, OK: Victor House, Inc.

Ting-Toomey, S. (2005). The matrix of face: An updated face-negotiation theory. In W. B. Gudykunst (Ed.), *Theorizing about Intercultural Communication.* Thousand Oaks, CA: Sage.

Chapter 12

Business Disputes

Jerry Bagnell with Aubrey Waddell

Aubrey Waddell, J. D. provided the Case Study, Questions for Discussion, and a review of and additions to the model and sequence of events for business mediation.

Business disputes include those between vendor and purchaser, merchant and customer, service providers and their customers, doctors and their patients, and even authors and their publishers. Anytime there is a business transaction between two or more parties, a dispute might arise about the quality or work or service performed, the time to complete a project, or delivering merchandise to a store by a certain date. Certainly, you can think of many other examples.

Conflict is normal. Harmony is abnormal. That reality endures in any relationship personal or business. Whenever two or more parties enter into a personal or a business transaction disputes can occur because of unrealized expectations; i.e., one party thought that a certain pattern or event would occur. The other party may have had very different expectations. When business is transacted or shortly afterward, these unrealized or unstated expectations can lead to misunderstandings and conflict.

Although business might have at one time been based upon a handshake or a verbal exchange of expectations and promises, today even the smallest business might use a written contract to memorialize the planned or expected transaction. Misunderstandings resulting in conflict because of handshake deals would seem to be the most common dispute. In fact, even with written contracts, business disputes often occur. An initial step in resolving any business conflict is to determine whether there was a legal contract to provide a product or service.

The basics of a legal contract are quite simple. There must be an ***agreement*** and ***something of value must be exchanged.*** The thing of value can be either a tangible item or product such as a car, or it can be a service such as going to the hairdresser for a shampoo and cut.

The two elements comprising an agreement are an ***offer*** and ***acceptance*** of the offer. A contract does not have to be written. Some people believe that a notarized statement is a contract. A notarized statement only attests to the fact that the parties who signed it are in fact who they represented themselves to be. If the two elements comprising an agreement are present, a handshake deal can be a valid contract. If you take Fido to a groomer to be washed but the groomer also trims the dog's nails and includes that service on the bill you receive when you pick up Fido, you can refuse to pay that portion of the bill for the nail trim because there was no agreement for that additional service.

If you put an item on lay away at a store, the exchange of something of value consists of your completing the purchase agreement by paying the balance due and the merchant giving you the item.

To keep things simple, we will not discuss delay of acceptance or what happens if the product or service exceeds the agreed upon amount in an agreement. We will use a scenario involving a manufacturer and a contractor hired to perform a service for the manufacturer in a case study to follow later.

WHY IS THIS TYPE OF DISPUTE SUITABLE FOR MEDIATION?

Business disputes can range from a simple misunderstanding to a breach of contract. Either situation can result in protracted litigation to determine who is at fault and what penalties or compensation, if any, might be appropriate. We have all seen television ads for personal injury attorneys or those who offer to sue someone for malpractice that you have dealt with, such as a doctor who botches an operation or a medical product supplier whose product has caused injury or death. The ad might even say there is no expense for you if the attorney does not prevail when taking the case to court. What often appears in such small print that you can barely see it, or so quickly that you are not able to read it, is that the attorney may not accept your case. Why would an attorney waste time and money on a case that has no merit? You may think you have a valid complaint but the matter may not rise to the level of applicable law.

Attorneys can be sanctioned by the court for filing frivolous lawsuits. You may want your pound of flesh or your hour in court, but there must be a legal basis to litigate a dispute. As we will explain later, arbitration and mediation provide an opportunity to resolve disputes that do not have to conform to any specific legal standard.

Although some business disputes might be handled in small claims court, many disputants are seeking more than token compensation for a transaction that they believe entitles them to a substantial amount of money. These cases can take years to resolve and the parties may incur substantial attorneys' fees. Even if an attorney accepts a case based on a contingency fee, for example 30% of the overall settlement, there may still be delays and unexpected costs when trying to resolve the matter.

Some disputants offer an incentive such as a payment to the other party if that party agrees to accept the payment and not proceed with the case. The intent of this practice is to save both time and money for either or both parties. An example might be an insurance company agreeing to pay a claim even if the insured may not be at fault, just to avoid the time and expenses of a protracted legal battle.

WHAT DOES THE CURRENT MATERIAL SAY ABOUT MEDIATING THIS TYPE OF DISPUTE?

Because even when a conflict starts as a minor dispute, any disagreement disrupts the businesses involved and distracts them from their normal business routine. It means they must devote time and effort to matters unrelated to the activities that produce profit. The stress of being sued can be overwhelming. It can affect parties mentally and physically. Because of the potential loss of money and the time it might take to resolve a dispute, some believe the best solution is one that results in a quick solution, even if not an ideal one.

One of the fastest ways to resolve a business dispute is to use mediation. Mediation is sometimes preferred over litigation or arbitration because arbitration or litigation produces winners and losers. No one likes to lose.

Arbitration may not be included in the contract between parties. Parties might agree to arbitrate but cannot be required to if there is no such provision included in the contract between them. Many businesses include arbitration clauses in contracts to avoid the time and expense of litigation. One benefit of arbitration is that the matter is settled. However, that does not mean that either party might be satisfied with the arbiter's decision. Such a decision does not have to be based upon the law or legal precedent. It may simply be based on what the arbiter believes is fair, reasonable, or appropriate. Arbitration may or not be confidential. Confidentiality may be a part of the settlement. For example, one party agrees to accept a certain amount of money and not disclose the nature of the complaint or the settlement. This is a frequent result in cases involving sexual harassment in the work place.

Litigation is very costly, takes years in some cases, and just like arbitration produces winners and losers. Litigation is not private so reputations may be adversely affected. The matter in dispute becomes known to the public. That might have been a goal of one party to the dispute; i.e., to make the public aware of a product or service that can cause harm or the workmanship of a contractor that is shoddy or fails to meet minimum standards of construction.

Even if the matter is dismissed by the court, damage to the reputation of either or both parties may occur. That can have long-term effects on a business. The public may remember that a contractor was charged with fraud even after he or she is found not guilty. Just the threat of a lawsuit may motivate a party to seek a way to resolve the issue without the public spectacle of a court battle.

Although litigation might result in a settlement based on applicable law, it does not guarantee that either party will be satisfied with the result. Remember that the court bases decisions on the law or legal precedent, not fairness as either party might subjectively define it.

Another consideration is that a litigant's definition of their day in court may be based upon a lack of knowledge about what a court will consider as relevant. In most cases, an attorney representing a party speaks on behalf of the client. The party may not get to say what they think or feel is important. Even in small claims court, rules of evidence may apply. For example, "Another customer told me that happened to her too" is hearsay and will not be considered by the court.

Mediation is less costly and the confidentiality of the process preserves the reputations of the parties and their relationships whether business related or interpersonal. However, mediation is a voluntary process. Although courts can order a case to mediation, the parties cannot be compelled to agree on a settlement.

Mediation is faster than litigation because there is no waiting for a case to be docketed. Considerations for choosing mediation include *voluntariness* and *confidentiality* as well two other concepts called *self-determination* and *informed consent. Informed consent* relates to *voluntariness* and means that the parties understand and accept the rules or guidelines used by the mediator. They do not have to agree to settle their dispute, but they agree to follow the rules prescribed by the mediator and make a good faith effort to settle.

Self-determination means simply that the parties themselves can create a solution that satisfies both their objective and subjective considerations. They might include terms and conditions not found in the law but that satisfy either or both of their interests.

Mediation produces an outcome that the parties are fully aware of in advance because they create it themselves. The mediator merely records the terms of the agreement. That agreement may then be used by attorneys to prepare whatever legal documents are necessary to implement the terms of the agreement.

If parties use either litigation or arbitration, the outcome is uncertain until announced by the court or the arbiter. Even the most experienced attorney cannot guarantee that a court will decide a matter in a certain way. Predictions of adjudicative outcome might sound attractive in advertising but if the parties want a certain outcome, mediation provides them with a process to achieve a mutually satisfying result rather than waiting for a decision that may surprise and displease either or both of them.

Although some parties may argue about the objective or actual value of a product and service, many argue about the subjective value; i.e., what does it represent to them from an emotional point of view. If a jeweler damages a watch while repairing it and offers to replace it with one of equal value, the owner may not believe that is a fair or reasonable way to compensate him or her for the loss. Consider that the appraised value of a gold pocket watch manufactured in 1940 can be determined in a dollar amount. However, if the watch was one that your father left you in his will, the subjective or emotional value cannot be reduced to a dollar amount based on an appraisal or an offer to provide you with a replacement.

Considering the example of your father's watch, would it be worth the time and expense to litigate the matter? Do you want to pay an attorney several hundred dollars to litigate the matter even if he or she agrees to do so on a contingency fee basis? The insurer for the jeweler may propose a monetary settlement rather than take the matter to court as an option that saves time, money, and prevents damage to the jeweler's reputation with the public. The contract between you and the jeweler might require you to submit the matter to arbitration. That means that a third party will decide whether you or the jeweler will prevail. Mediation will provide you with a way to explain the emotional basis for your claim, will be confidential, and can produce a timely and expedient solution to the dispute. You and the jeweler decide how to resolve the matter.

Here are some other considerations for choosing a dispute resolution process:

1. Don't take it personally. It's only business. That sounds like good advice but every dispute is based upon facts and feelings. Facts can be proven or refuted. Feelings are not right or wrong but can significantly influence the parties to a dispute. Reputations are not easily defined in terms of dollars. How much is your reputation or your privacy worth?

2. Fractionate complicated disputes. Try to solve convoluted matters one item at a time rather than hold out for a comprehensive settlement. This simple idea is one of the most useful conflict management tactics. Conflicts can be broken down from one big mass into several smaller, more manageable conflicts. It simply makes the components of large conflicts more approachable by parties who are trying to manage their disputes. It also involves making small conflicts out of larger ones. Almost all conflicts can be made smaller without being trivialized.

3. Consider your alternatives in sequence. What can you do to attempt to resolve the matter other than threatening to take the other party to court? Your first option is to negotiate with the other party yourself in a one-on-one manner. It is confidential and costs you nothing in terms of money. It may take time and effort but there is no other cost. If you are unable to resolve the matter that way, consider using a mediator as a go between to facilitate the negotiation. Those two options give you control over the outcome. If you want someone else to make the decision for you, arbitration and litigation are the remaining options.

TRAINING AND EXPERIENCE NEEDED TO MEDIATE CORPORATE DISPUTES

A Bargaining-based (Evaluative) Model that focuses on problem solving is used for most business disputes. Business mediators tend to be practicing attorneys or former judges that have subject matter expertise about the matters in dispute. Some are independent contractors who limit their practices to mediation. They cannot be members of the same firm or in any way associated with either of the attorneys who represent the parties to the dispute. If they have served as a mediator for clients represented by either or both of the attorneys for the current dispute, they should disclose that relationship so that the clients will understand and accept that, as mediators, they have no stake or interest in the outcome of the dispute.

Business mediators emphasize efficiency and acceptance of the realities of the legal system or precedents. They caucus frequently, and use shuttle mediation to discuss the strengths and weaknesses of their clients' positions, and to influence them about options the attorneys feel are in their clients' best interests. They often offer substantive ideas for settlement based upon what they believe would be the most likely outcome of litigation. To move the parties toward settlement, they tend to exert significant direct pressure and use other directive techniques.

Business mediations may involve multiple parties who are each represented by attorneys. That makes those cases very different from a case with one mediator and two disputants. Some mediation conducted by attorneys is often a facilitated four-way where the mediator shuttles back and forth between the parties.

Critics of the Bargaining-based (Evaluative) Model used by most business mediators might cite the following as major limitations that affect the resolution of issues and the durability or future viability of any settlement. Here are pros and cons:

A. The mediators' agenda and directiveness may undermine the parties' autonomy and the durability of the agreement if an ongoing relationship is a factor. The Facilitative Model frequently used by attorney or non-attorney mediators for situations such as divorce where ongoing relationships are a significant factor, would not be appropriate for business disputes because facilitative mediators may be unable to meet the parties' needs or expectations for assistance with substance, such as subject matter expertise or knowledge of legal precedents.

B. The Transformative Model used for workplace disputes between employers and employees such as allegations of discrimination, sexual harassment, or hostile environment as defined by Title VII of the Civil Rights Act of 1964, emphasizes empowerment and recognition rather than problem solving. The underlying assumption is that achieving those goals will enable people to resolve their issues. Feelings and emotions are considered. Business mediators focus on the financial, contractual, and operational aspects of disputes.

C. The business mediator's failure or unwillingness to pay attention to emotional and communication dynamics may result in outcomes perceived as unjust or that hurt less powerful participants. Unless a business is owned by one person, emotions are usually not relevant. What would shareholders think is in their best interest? The very nature of business disputes tends to be about financial and contractual matters rather than meeting the emotional needs of the parties. Communication dynamics may be relevant if they led to a misunderstanding about what one party could expect from the other relating to a tangible product or a service that was performed.

D. Business mediators may leave unexplored the parties' potential for growth, change, and healing. The latter considerations are not the focus of the Bargaining-based (Evaluative) Model. If the parties want those matters to be considered, they should use a Facilitative mediator. Remember, one important consideration for choosing a dispute resolution process is "do not take it personally. It's only business." Easier said than done!

Although there is no formally prescribed model or sequence of events for business mediations, the following steps are usually followed:

1. Prior to the commencement of business mediation, attorneys for the parties typically prepare a "Mediation Statement" for review by the mediator. This statement describes facts from a particular party's point of view, and often contains some legal argument to support that party's position. These are held in confidence by the mediator, and are not shared with the other party.

2. A typical business mediation begins with the mediator introducing himself or herself to the parties. This is followed by an opening statement by the attorneys. These statements may be similar to an opening argument presented in court. Since the mediator is usually an attorney, the attorneys for the parties may refer to applicable law and precedents as well as explaining their clients' positions and interest in legal terms.

3. Once the attorneys have finished their presentations, the parties themselves may make a statement. Although they have been prepared by their separate and individual attorneys, the mediator should listen to what their positions are and the interests underlying those positions. The parties are not expected to have a comprehensive knowledge of the applicable law. They merely explain the situation from their perspective in laymen's terms.

4. During the mediator's introduction, he or she will also typically explain some ground rules. These often include:

   a. That the materials submitted to the mediator and the discussions had during mediation are confidential, and cannot be used against either party in any subsequent lawsuit.

   b. How long the mediation will last, and when the mediator may determine that the parties have reached an "impasse."

     Some professional mediators believe that an "impasse" is not a situation in which the parties are "stuck," but is one when the mediator does not know what to do next. A highly skilled and experienced mediator does not use the term "impasse" when encouraging the parties to continue working to resolve their dispute. He or she might say, "You seem to be stuck temporarily. What can either of you do to move forward?" That provides the parties with the mediator's expectation that there is still a possible resolution that they can achieve by continuing to work toward it collaboratively.

    c. What type of follow-up the parties can expect from the mediator should the dispute not be resolved during the day or days the mediation is taking place.

5. The mediator meets separately with each party for a **caucus** and each party's attorney to gather sensitive information, explore interests underlying or motivating what they are demanding, clarify their concerns, explore possible proposals for resolution, and facilitate reality testing; i.e., can any proposed agreement actually be implemented? There may be more than one caucus with each side. The attorneys may caucus with each other without the parties to determine if they should have an additional caucus or caucuses with the parties.

6. Occasionally, if the parties are not overly combative, the mediator may ask them to jointly discuss settlement potential, or clarify misunderstandings. Usually this happens only when the parties are VERY close to actual settlement.

7. Typically, parties who resolve their dispute during mediation will, assisted by their attorneys, draft a **settlement agreement** term sheet that sets forth the critical points of their proposed agreement. This term sheet is then expanded upon and finalized in a settlement agreement drafted for the parties by their attorneys.

HOW DOES A MEDIATOR PREPARE FOR THIS TYPE OF MEDIATION?

In addition to reviewing the mediation statements prepared by attorneys for the parties, business mediators will often research and review case law and precedents that would be applicable for the matter in dispute. He or she might also research the nature and content of mediated settlements relating to similar disputes.

WHAT ARE SOME TYPICAL AND UNIQUE PROBLEMS ASSOCIATED WITH THIS TYPE OF MEDIATION?

Hopefully, the parties are not as emotionally charged when mediating a business dispute. Mediators always have to consider the best interests of the company they represent. Companies interest are defined by the interests of shareholders not necessarily those of the parties to a dispute Settlement may be the preferred outcome for the company and their shareholders as a whole, although the individuals involved in a dispute may have "an axe to grind" or be overly litigious.

CONCLUDING COMMENTS

Mediating business disputes saves time and money. It also gives the parties an opportunity to create a mutually satisfying outcome rather than one imposed by the court or determined by an arbiter.

Any delay in resolving business issues has an immediate and significant effect on the profitability of a business. Not being able to conduct ongoing business with the public can be devastating. Even if a business can maintain a daily operation, any profit will be significantly diminished by the cost of protracted litigation.

Mediation provides businesses with an opportunity to not only save money for resolving legal issues in court, but also preserves the reputation of the businesses involved in the dispute because mediation is a confidential process that provides an expeditious resolution for most business disputes.

Case Study: ABC Construction vs. Track Shoes R Us

Track Shoes R Us (TSRU) is a retailer that sells running shoes, clothing, and workout gear. It has been extremely successful and has rapidly expanded its presence in malls around the country. Last year, it opened five new stores in the span of three months.

This year TSRU hired ABC Construction (ABC) to "build-out" another new store in the best shopping mall in the Southeast. ABC agreed to a fast-paced construction schedule so that the new store could open before the holiday shopping season.

ABC estimated that construction would cost about $100K, but told representatives of TSRU that cost overruns were always possible—even likely—when something like this had to be done so quickly. TSRU representatives said they understood, and agreed that any additional costs would be discussed when and if they arose. ABC and TSRU signed a contract for $100K and completion of all work in three months.

Construction was fast and furious. TSRU repeatedly told representatives at ABC, verbally and by email, to do everything they had to do to make sure the store was open before November.

And, sure enough, all of the construction was completed on time. There were no problems with the quality ABC's work, and the stores were already doing a profitable business at each location.

Soon after the grand openings were over, ABC sent a final bill to TSRU in the amount of $200,000—twice the original estimate and twice the stated contract price. ABC told TSRU that it would be forced to file a lien on the shopping malls if they were not paid in full. A lien that resulted from TSRU's store construction would be a violation of TSRU's leases, and could mean they would be sued by their landlords or be forced to leave each of the malls. TSRU had over $250,000 invested in the new store's fixtures, inventory, and advertising.

TSRU told ABC through Sue Yew Moore and Associates there was no chance it would pay $200,000 for the work. TSRU hired Oliver, Wendell, and Holmes to represent them, and has filed a lawsuit for the additional $100,000 owed.

The parties agreed that before spending substantial dollar amounts in legal fees, they would mediate in hopes of settling the dispute. The mediator is Will U. Settle, a retired judge with more than 35 years of legal experience in matters such as those that are in dispute between the parties.

QUESTIONS FOR DISCUSSION

1. What is TSRU's best argument that it does not owe the additional money to ABC?
2. What is ABC's best argument in favor of being paid in full?
3. How do you think the parties ended up in this predicament?
4. What might the parties have done differently in defining their expectations for this transaction?
5. What should the mediator ask each party in order to determine whether settlement is possible?
6. What are the risks to the parties if they do not settle the dispute, but rather continue to litigate?

Chapter 13

Transformative Mediation and United States Postal Service

Julius Z. Frager

In 1994, Jossey-Bass published a book written by Robert A. Baruch Bush and Joseph P. Folger called "The Promise of Mediation." In a presentation at the annual meeting of the Academy of Family Mediators in Eugene, Oregon in July of the same year, one of the authors stated that what was important in mediation was not whether or not a case was settled or resolved, but whether the participants were transformed as individuals. Yes, as a Family Mediator, I knew of situations when a couple came to me for help in the dissolution of their marriage that there had been a transformation of the wife from the time she first met with me and until the couple had reached their Agreement. When I first met the wife, she would have low self-esteem, have no job or a job where she would never be able to support herself financially, and be fearful of her future. By the end of the process, she felt good about herself, took pride in her new job, felt she would be able to be self-supporting, and looked forward to the future. But this process took 6–9 months and was just a by-product of the process. Couples came to me to reach an Agreement, not transform!

This could have just been another book, but the Hewlett Foundation and the Surdna Foundation provided funds for trainers to expand the theory and develop a program to teach one how to practice "transformative" mediation.[1] Then, Cindy

Hallberlin convinced the United States Postal System (USPS) to test this model in the Panhandle of Florida in 1994. The results were better relationships between employees and management and fewer charges of discrimination from the employees. As a result, in 1998, the USPS started rolling out a mediation program for the whole country to deal with discrimination claims called **REDRESS®** that stands for "**R**esolve **E**mployment **D**isputes **R**each **E**quitable **S**olutions **S**wiftly".[2] Training sessions were held to teach (current mediators) how to mediate using the Transformative Model. Mediators were required by their contract to use only the Transformative Model. Mediators were instructed that it was not the mediator's responsibility to get the parties to reach an Agreement, but the Parties' decision. Did the USPS really mean this?[3]

TYPES OF CASES MEDIATED UNDER AND ACCESS TO USPS REDRESS® PROGRAM

Technically,[4] the **REDRESS®** program is available to all USPS employees on a voluntary basis as part of its process to resolve Equal Employment Opportunity (EEO) Complaints. Because there is paperwork that the employee has to fill out indicating when and why they were discriminated against, all cases involve a situation where either the employee does not feel that they were treated fairly and their complaint was not resolved through the grievance process[5] or else the Postal Service has taken some action which the employee does not like (such as placing a warning in the employee's file that is required before the employee could be terminated). Nothing prohibits an employee from claiming discrimination at the same time that their Union representative has filed a grievance.[6] This program is also available to management employees who are not represented by a Union.

TRANSFORMATIVE MEDIATION VERSUS OTHER MEDIATION MODELS

Definition of Mediation: Mediation can be defined as a neutral third party facilitating negotiation between two or more parties. There are basically two ways to negotiate: a.) Competitively, where you are trying to impose your views and solutions on the other party, or b.) Collaboratively, where the parties are trying to reach a voluntary (without threats), mutually acceptable solution that meets the needs of both parties.

Evaluative Mediation in a Competitive Negotiation: When a mediator is facilitating a Competitive Negotiation, this is frequently referred to as an "Evaluative"

Mediation model. This type of mediation is often used when each party is represented by separate and independent attorneys. Frequently, each attorney will send a brief to the mediator before the mediation begins outlining the legal strengths of their case and why they believe their party would prevail in Court. When the mediation actually begins, the attorney for each party gives opening remarks stating their party's perspective about the factual situation and why the party's position is correct (and maybe why the other party's position is wrong). There could be some additional discussion in a joint session, but normally the parties are separated into different rooms and the mediator shuffles between the rooms relaying information and trying to apply pressure to both parties by pointing out the weaknesses in their cases, their potential downside risks if they go to court, and the cost to them if they continue in the litigation mode to go to court. All of these things are done in an effort to move the parties towards an agreement. The parties quickly realize that the mediator is not on their side, and they will usually control what they want the mediator to hear or believe. At times, the mediator may call them back into joint session to allow them to discuss certain issues or settlement options. During the mediation, the mediator is controlling the process of what happens, when the parties are in joint session or in caucus, and when shuttling between the parties. The mediator is also controlling what each party hears that the other party says or wants. In caucus, the mediator may even be telling the parties what they should be agreeing to do. All of these strategies of trying to impose your solution on the other party are representative of what happens in a Competitive Negotiation.

Facilitative Mediation in a Collaborative Negotiation: When a mediator is facilitating a Collaborative Negotiation, the mediator will decide who speaks, what topics are to be discussed, and in what order the topics will be discussed. A normal progression would be checking each party's perception of the factual situation of what happened, determining what the issues and differences are between the parties, identifying the issues and needs of each party, brainstorming for possible solutions that would meet the needs of both parties, developing a mutually satisfactory resolution that is determined by the parties without advice or pressure from the mediator, and then deciding how both sides will insure that the agreement is carried out and what are the consequences or steps if there is a problem. If the mediator would like to speak to either party in private, the mediator would call for a caucus, where the mediator would meet with each party separately. If the mediator can hear truthfully and understand what each party needs, then the mediator is in the unique position of being able to suggest solutions that might work for both parties. In both models success is considered achieved when the parties sign a settlement agreement. However in the Facilitative model, although the mediator is controlling the process, the mediator should never be telling either party what they should be doing. It is the parties who control this decision making process, without any pressure from the mediator. Any agreement in a Facilitative model must be made voluntarily and work for both parties, not one party at the expense of the other. The mediator may use various tools while in caucus such as:

a. Ask a party questions to help the party and the mediator obtain clarity for him or her on what the party really wants or needs.
b. Ask questions to help the party determine whether or not the expectations of the party are realistic.
c. Coach either party about how they might express themselves to the other party in a more effective manner. Since this is done while in caucus, the mediator avoids appearing to be favoring one of the sides.
d. Act as a sounding board for either party, listening and reflecting back what the mediator hears. This could also allow a party to "let off steam" without doing it in front of the other party which would possibly not be constructive.

In facilitating a Collaborative Negotiation, the mediator is focused on there not being a power imbalance between the parties so that each party has access to the same information, understands what his or her options are, the consequences of those options, and that a free will decision is made about how they would like to resolve their differences. The belief is that if a voluntary decision is made under the above conditions, then the parties will carry out the terms of their settlement. The goal of the Facilitative process is for the parties to reach a settlement agreement that seems fair to both of them.

Questions: If you are a party preparing for mediation, are you going to be honest in caucus with the mediator and tell the mediator what you want, what is most important to you, and how much you are willing to compromise? How might your willingness to be honest with the mediator differ based upon whether the mediator is facilitating a Competitive Negotiation as opposed to a Collaborative Negotiation?

Evaluative Mediation Compared to Facilitative Mediation: In both an Evaluative and a Facilitative mediation, the underlying premise is that the mediator is smarter than the parties. By controlling the process and knowing techniques of mediation, the mediator can "almost manipulate" the parties to help them reach an agreement that they would be unable to reach on their own. In the caucus during a Facilitative mediation, if the mediator has established a trusting relationship with a party, where the party feels that the mediator is trying to help the party meet his or her needs, then there is a higher likelihood that the party will share honestly what the party wants and needs as opposed to posturing about what the party wants (as in the Competitive context). The mediator then has an opportunity to be able to hear how far each party is willing to compromise in order to reach a settlement and can suggest a solution that might be acceptable to both parties. In facilitating a Competitive Negotiation, the mediator's focus is on the parties reaching a settlement without regard to their relationship after the agreement, other than to insure that the terms of the settlement will be implemented. In facilitating a Collaborative

Negotiation where any agreement has to be mutually acceptable and voluntary, the parties are not engaged in trying to impose their solution on the other party. This then allows the parties to have a positive relationship after the mediation has ended.[7]

TRANSFORMATIVE MEDIATION

Bush and Folger believe that parties have the capability of resolving their differences without manipulation or interference from the mediator. They believe in the power of the individuals to resolve their differences in Transformative Mediation because of the dynamic effects of *empowerment* and *recognition.* "In simplest terms, *empowerment* means the restoration to individuals of a sense of their value and strength and their own capacity to make decisions and handle life's problems. *Recognition* means the evocation in individuals of acknowledgment, understanding, or empathy for the situation and the views of the other."[8] In the Transformative Model, the mediator only focuses on the moment, what is being said, and how to "highlight" it for the parties to assist them in their *empowerment* and *recognition.* Whether an agreement is reached or not is the responsibility of the parties, not the mediator.

In the Transformative model, although a caucus can be requested by either party or the mediator, it is usually requested by a party who:

a. Wishes to discuss something <u>privately</u> with their "Support Person" that may or may not include the mediator;
b. Wants to tell something to the mediator which they feel is important for the mediator to understand; or
c. Is seeking input or feedback from the mediator.

The goal of transformative mediation is to help each party have a clearer understanding of their situation and each other's perspective. The hope is that they will change how they interact with the other person and that this relationship change may enable them to resolve their dispute. In short, under the Transformative model, not only do the parties control the decision making, but also the parties control the process of what happens, when it happens, what is discussed and deciding if they want to settle or not.

Questions: If mediation is the facilitation of negotiation and you can only negotiate either competitively or collaboratively, then what type of negotiation are you facilitating in Transformative mediation? How could you negotiate in a Transformative manner without a mediator and how would you do it? How do the caucus and the mediator's role differ between the three models of mediation?

TRAINING AND EXPERIENCE NEEDED TO QUALIFY AS A MEDIATOR FOR USPS

Persons who are or were former Postal Service employees, and persons who are or have been arbitrators for the Postal Service, are not eligible to be a mediator. Any person wanting to be an applicant for the Postal Service Rooster[9] must have completed a three-day mediation course (minimum of 24 hours) that included extensive role-playing, AND completion of at least ten (10) mediations as lead or co-mediator, AND evaluations from a qualified source. If an applicant meets the minimum criteria above, then the applicant is specially trained in Transformative Mediation through a two day, 20-hour course. Upon completion of training, the applicant's Transformative Mediation skills are analyzed in a pro bono mediation session. If judged competent by an EEO Alternative Dispute Resolution (ADR) Specialist personally observing the applicant conducting a **REDRESS**® mediation, then the applicant may become part of **USPS REDRESS**® roster. As of March, 2012, there were over 1,000 mediators throughout the country on the roster and the USPS was not accepting any applications at that time.

STEPS IN A REDRESS® MEDIATION

A. If a postal employee believes that they have been discriminated against because of race, color, religion, national origin, sex, age (40+), physical or mental disability, or in retaliation for engaging in an EEO-protected activity, they must first call an EEO ADR Specialist at the Postal Service requesting counseling. The postal employee has the choice of traditional EEO counseling or participating in the **REDRESS**® mediation program.

B. An EEO ADR Specialist tries resolving the issue by talking with the employee and the supervisor and/or the supervisor's manager against whom the employee is complaining. The employee will be requested to fill out and send in a form indicating why the employee felt he or she was discriminated against and a brief description of the facts.

C. If traditional counseling is not successful or if the employee wants to go directly into **REDRESS**®, then the EEO ADR Specialist sets up a **REDRESS**® session usually at the location of where the employee works during the employee's shift[10] within two or three weeks. The supervisor or manager against whom the complaint is filed is required to participate in the **REDRESS**® mediation.

D. The EEO ADR Specialist then selects the mediator from the approved rooster.[11]

E. The employee can decide not to participate in **REDRESS**® and file a formal complaint with the Equal Employment Opportunity Commission (EEOC).

F. Both the employee and the supervisor are allowed, but not required, to have a "support" person or "representative" at the mediation. The support person does not have to work for the Postal Service or have any special credentials. The support person for the supervisor is usually his or her manager. The support person for the employee is usually a union representative, but could also be a family member or a co-worker.

G. The **REDRESS**® mediation is one session and all mediators are paid the same flat amount regardless of the length of the session.

H. At the end of the session there is one of three results:

1. **Settlement Agreement**—A written agreement is signed by the parties that cannot be in violation of any contractual rules between the union and the Postal Service.[12] If the employee believes that the Postal Service has not carried out the Settlement Agreement, the employee has to give notice within 30 days of violation and the issue is reinstated.

2. **Withdrawal**—The employee feels that the issue has been resolved, no longer exists, or that the parties feel that there is no need for a formal resolution. The employee loses all rights in regard to this complaint even if an informal (verbal) agreement is not carried out.

3. **No Agreement**—The parties could not reach a Settlement Agreement and the employee does not want to withdraw his/her complaint.[13] The employee then has 30 days to fill in papers to file a formal complaint with the EEOC or they lose their rights.[14]

INFORMATION RECEIVED AND PREPARATION FOR REDRESS® BY THE MEDIATOR

Once you have been called by an EEO ADR Specialist and accept a **REDRESS**® mediation for a specific time and Postal location, your information packet is sent to you via email (now). After each person's name will be a description such as "Counselee" (for the employee who filed the complaint), counselee's representative, supervisor, manager, or supervisor's representative. If either the counselee, or the supervisor against whom the complaint has been lodged, wishes to change their support person, they must give at least 24 hours advance notification to the EEO ADR Specialist or else the new support person cannot participate without the other party's approval. If the counselee's designated support person is not available to attend the **REDRESS**® mediation, then the counselee must find a replacement (giving 24 hours advance notification) or proceed with the **REDRESS®** without the support person. Failure by the counselee to cancel the mediation at least three business days in advance may jeopardize the counselee's ability to have the **REDRESS**® rescheduled.[15] In the information packet that the mediator receives are: an Agreement to Mediate form,[16] a **REDRESS**® Settlement Form,[17] a Withdrawal Form, a No Agreement Letter,[18] and a **REDRESS**® Invoice. In the cover letter with the above information is the statement: "The claim(s) raised in the EEO process for this mediation request is as follows: . . . ." A typical description would be "Age, Retaliation." Unless the EEO ADR Specialist has volunteered further information regarding this case, this is the only information that the mediator receives about the case.

Questions: In Transformative Mediation, how might having more information about the situation before starting help? How might having more information ahead of time, create a bias within the mediator for or against one of the parties? How might this affect the mediator's ability to listen?

The preparation as a mediator is therefore making sure that you have all of the forms listed in the cover letter, making sure that the forms appear to be filled out correctly, filling out any information that you can ahead of time regarding your invoice, making sure you know how to get to the location for the mediation, and making a note so you know who the parties are. When you arrive early (you're requested to be there 15 minutes ahead of time), you then get to see the room and setup where the meeting will be heard.

TYPES OF PROBLEMS ENCOUNTERED USING TRANSFORMATIVE MEDIATION IN REDRESS®

Physical Environment: Your Postal Service mediation usually takes place at the location where the employee who filed the EEO Complaint works during the employee's regular shift. If this is at a large Distribution Center where the mail is sorted, it probably has a meeting/multi-purpose or lunchroom which employees are used to accessing. If this is at a local branch Post Office or in a small town, the only available room may be the facility manager's small office that has a desk and some chairs. Although you may be able to close the door for privacy, on the other side of the wall could be where the public is gathering to purchase stamps.

Question: What type of problems could these arrangements create and how would you deal with them?

Potential Perception that you are Part of Management:

1. This is the Postal Service's process. An EEO ADR Specialist has probably already talked with the counselee/complainant and the supervisor and/or manager trying to resolve the issue. Now this same person, who is part of management, is going to be arranging for selecting a mediator, usually without any input from the complainant as to which mediator will be chosen.

2. The complainant pays nothing to participate in this process (and in fact is paid for their time during the **REDRESS**®). The mediator is paid by Postal Service and selected by the Postal Service. (The system that the Postal Service uses to select mediators for resolving the complaints[19] has changed over time.)

3. When the mediator arrives for **REDRESS**®, the mediator is usually instructed to ask for the Facility Manager or an EEO ADR Specialist. As a result, employees may notice that conversations are occurring between the mediator and management before **REDRESS**® begins although instructions are now given for the mediator to avoid discussions with either side before the session begins.

4. The EEO ADR Specialist is partially compensated based upon how the **REDRESS**® Mediation is resolved, but they are supposed to be only an "Observer" and evaluate how well the mediator is using the Transformative Mediation model. Some observers will state in the beginning that they are there only to observe and say nothing for the balance of the **REDRESS**®. Some observers will be willing to be used as a "resource" in answering questions from either of the participants (or the mediator) about what type of solutions are possible or what steps are next if there is no agreement. A few observers will become actively involved in participating in caucuses with the participants in order to facilitate a settlement.

Questions: How might the behavior of the observer affect the perception of the mediator by the participants? Which Observer type of actions should the Postal Service encourage or discourage? What do you think about the Postal Service tying an EEO ADR Specialist's pay to the results of **REDRESS**®*; is it or is it not consistent with the Transformative Mediation model? If the EEO ADR Specialist selects the mediator, what would you do as the mediator if the observer calls for a caucus and meets with both sides without you, resulting in an agreement?*

Creating an Atmosphere for a Conversation between Equals: The problem is trying to create "space" for a mutually respectful and open communication between "equals" when the complainant is always the subordinate and will be again after the meeting. The complainant is many times fearful of retaliation or of how they will be treated by their supervisor or manager after the **REDRESS**® mediation.

Question: If you, as a complainant, had to accuse your supervisor or manager of discrimination to get into the **REDRESS**® *process, and feel you were treated unfairly, what could you say or do in order to minimize the supervisor's or manager's negativity towards you?*

Fear that the **REDRESS**® Process Will Be Abused: If an employee has been issued a warning or punishment and that employee files an EEO Complaint against management, management fears that if they reverse their warning or punishment for one person, then everyone being disciplined will be filing a complaint to try to overturn their discipline.

The supervisor's manager sits as the support person for the supervisor: Many times the supervisor's manager sits as the support person for the supervisor or the manager is named in the complaint along with the supervisor. If an agreement has to be reached, the manager may need to be there because the supervisor may not have the authority to solve the issue. This has the possibility of two different types of problems:

1. The supervisor may feel uncomfortable in revealing to the complainant what the manager instructed the supervisor to do. The supervisor may fear that he or she would be in trouble with their manager if they revealed what orders they were given. Since the supervisor does not want to be seen as a poor supervisor, he or she may respond defensively, be less willing to open up truthfully, and avoid admitting mistakes that they made.

2. The manager might believe that what the supervisor did was not good management practice but does not want to put the Postal Service in a bad position or undermine the supervisor in front of their subordinate. Thus, the manager might not be willing to acknowledge to the complainant that the complainant is correct and that the supervisor is in error. (Usually this is dealt with in private caucus between the manager and supervisor, with the manager "suggesting" to the supervisor how the issue should be resolved and how the supervisor should be changing his or her habits.)

Management is Required to Participate in **REDRESS®**: This presents opportunities for individuals to change (transform) their interactions with others. Disputing parties can make their own decisions and gain perspective over their situations. The parties set their own agenda and decide what to discuss. The mediator supports the process, summarizes discussions, clarifies issues, and promotes confidence in making decisions. The mediator achieves this by "reflecting," "summarizing," "checking in," and by asking "open ended questions." Anything outside of that scope does not fit into the transformative framework. The mediation is considered successful when the parties participate in interactive communication that results in a clearer understanding of their situation and each other's perspective. Often, this leads to resolution of the dispute.

What will a transformative mediator refrain from doing? Transformative mediators will not direct the content of the mediation, will not "gather" information for settlement purposes, and will not take an active role in the decision-making process. Instead, they support the parties with the process. They will not push the parties towards settlement, even if they believe they "know" how the case can fairly settle. "Forced" settlements do not resolve the underlying conflict. They will not suggest whether one party's viewpoint has more merit than the other's. They will not comment on the strength or weakness of either party's case or on the status of the law or company policy. Transformative mediators will not discourage the parties from exhibiting their emotions. Seeing the other party's emotional response may allow parties to better understand the impact of their words and actions.

WHAT ONE TRANSFORMATIVE MEDIATOR ACTUALLY DOES IN REDRESS® MEDIATIONS

Confidentiality versus Uniformity and Quality Control of REDRESS® Program: Since one of the prime rules in mediation is that the process is confidential, unless someone is endangered, how could the USPS insure that the mediators were using the same Transformative Mediation Model? To address this issue, the Postal Service used a small group of trainers to roll out the program so that everyone would receive the same training. Years later, there was an Advanced Training called **REDRESS®** II to refresh their mediators' training and incorporate changes that had occurred as the Transformative Mediation model was enhanced. During the beginning years, there were questionnaires that were filled out by all participants, the mediator, and any observer that were sent to Lisa Bingham at Indiana University Bloomington (see Footnote 2). The results were summarized and then returned to each Area EEO ADR Specialist giving feedback not only as to how the participants perceived the experience, but also responses to questions that were asked to determine if the mediators were acting in the manner required for Transformative Mediation. Many of the questions were designed to determine if the mediator was trying to control the process, tell the participants what they should be doing, or exerting any pressure on the participants' decision making process. However, (maybe because of confidentiality), results were given to the Area ADR Specialist for the total group of their mediators without any specific names. Thus the only way that an EEO ADR Specialist had for evaluating a particular mediator was from either direct observation, (which was not frequently after you had been "approved"), or if participants made comments back to them.[20] There is also the issue of whether a mediator behaves in the same manner if being observed. Further, you have the variables of the skills and knowledge of the EEO ADR Specialist who is observing you.[21] I know that I may not have followed 100% the USPS description of the Transformative Model, but I believe that I followed 100% of the spirit of the Transformative Model. What follows therefore is just my personal description of what I try to do and why. I make no claim as to it being correct or whether this is Transformative Mediation as intended, and I have no direct knowledge of what other Transformative Mediators for the Postal Service actually do.

Setting up the Physical Environment: Although the Postal Service will move a **REDRESS®** from the counselee's/complainant's work location if there is no privacy, I try to insure that the physical arrangement is such that there is no difference between the seating for the complainant/support person and the supervisor/manager to indicate that this is not a discussion between supervisor and subordinate, but between people of equal value. Rarely are there any large round tables. Therefore, I try to arrange the seating so that the distance between the complainant and supervisor are about the same as if they were having a personal conversation, while still giving enough space between them so that neither party will feel uncomfortably close. The complainant and supervisor are seated facing each other directly, rather than the other's support person, and closest to me with their support person being further away. This helps the perception that I am not part of management, as the supervisor's manager is not sitting next to me. If the meeting is in the plant manager's office (which is usually small), I will sit behind the desk and put all the participants out in front. If the manager were behind his or her desk, this would be a constant reminder of the superior/subordinate relationship with the complainant.

Introduction Speech to the Participants: My introductory speech usually takes 20 to 30 minutes and is an important opportunity for me to be able to make sure that the participants understand what the **REDRESS**® process is and is not, what the options are for the complainant, what happens if there is no resolution, what my role is and is not in this process, and that I am not part of the Postal Service management (for the complainant's benefit). Below are some of the more salient points that I cover.

1. Check if Participants have been through **REDRESS**® before: If the Participants have not been through the **REDRESS**® process before, then I know that I need to spend more time explaining to them what to expect so that they have a realistic perspective of what will be happening and so that they will feel more comfortable with the process. If some have and some have not been through **REDRESS**®, then I ask permission from those who have, to bear with me while I explain. At the end, I usually ask the ones who have been through **REDRESS**® if I have missed anything. Sometimes, if I know one of the participants has been through **REDRESS**® many times, I may invite them to explain the process. This not only allows me to check their understanding, but also initiates the participants talking to each other, rather than to me. If all participants have been through **REDRESS**®, I may ask what they liked and did not like about their previous **REDRESS**® meetings. These questions give me an opportunity to understand their perceptions of the process, to be alerted to any major issues that they might have had with the process in the past, and to be able to clarify anything that I do as a mediator that might address their concerns. My goal is to not only explain the process, the rules, the choices, etc., but also to try to avoid having anyone bored at the start.

2. How I am compensated: To help the complainants understand that I am not part of management, I explain to them that I get the same pay regardless of the length of the **REDRESS**® or the results of the **REDRESS**®.

3. Belief in the ability of individuals to solve their problems: It is important for the participants to hear that Bush and Folger (2005) believed in the power of individuals to solve their problem. I point out that in Facilitative Mediation, although the parties make the decisions, the mediator controls the process and uses many skills to help the parties reach an agreement. This implies that the mediator is smarter than the parties because they could not solve the problem on their own and the mediator could manipulate them to reach an agreement. However, in the Transformative Mediation, the mediator not only does not control the decision-making, but also does not control the process. By emphasizing that the Postal Service believes in their ability to solve their issues without "interference," this not only empowers them to feel good about the process, but also helps reinforce that I am not there as part of Management to get an agreement.

4. My job: Typical comments by me would be: "As opposed to other styles of mediation, my job is not to get you to reach an agreement. This is your responsibility, if you feel that it makes sense. My job is solely to help you hear and understand the other side's perspective AND have clarity for yourself. If I am to help you hear the other side's perspective, then I have to understand what you are saying. If I do not understand something or something does not make sense to me, then I will be asking questions not to challenge you, but to help me understand. If I can not understand, then I can not help the other side understand your perspective."

5. Implications of **REDRESS**® being filed: My normal comments would be (addressing the complainant first): "I want you to know that by filing your complaint that you have accused your supervisor of having discriminated against you. I have never met a supervisor who believes that they discriminated, and thus the supervisor usually feels attacked, hurt, and/or defensive." (Then addressing the supervisor): "I don't know if the complainant actually believes that you legally discriminated against him or her. However, I do know that complainants do feel that they were not treated fairly or else they would not have gone through the trouble of filing the paperwork to get into the **REDRESS**® process." At this point I am usually catching from the corner of my vision complainants nodding their heads in agreement with my statement, and I know that I have started in connecting with the complainants. I then continue addressing the supervisor, "I am therefore asking that you not feel so defensive and just focus on what can be done so that the complainant will feel that he or she is being treated fairly." By these statements, I hope that both participants feel that I understand their situation and feelings, and hope to help them understand the other's perspective, to build their trust in me, and to lower the potential emotional level of their conflict.

6. Calling for a Caucus: I ask both participants if they understand what a caucus is. If one of them responds affirmatively, I then ask them to explain so that the other participant can hear. I do this to minimize my always being the authority telling them the answers and to encourage them to talk to each other. If something is

missed, then I will add whatever was missed. In the end, they understand that either of them or I can call a caucus for a private discussion with them and their support person. If either of them calls a caucus, it is their choice as to whether or not they want me to be part of their caucus. Further, I cannot repeat anything said while I am in the caucus without their approval in advance. Regardless of who calls for a Caucus, I will be available to meet with both Participants separately. *I also advise them that I rarely ever request a Caucus.*

7. <u>Options at the end:</u> The claimant is reminded that at the end of the **REDRESS®**, the claimant will have to choose one of the following three options:

   a. **Withdrawal of Complaint:** This means that the complainant believes that his or her issue has been resolved and the complainant is prohibited from pursuing the EEO complaint in the future for any action that occurred prior to the Withdrawal of Complaint.

   b. **REDRESS® Settlement Agreement:** This is a formal agreement where each side states what will be done to resolve the EEO Complaint. No agreement can be in contravention with any contract between the Union and the Postal Service. If the agreement is not kept by the Postal Service, the complainant must notify the Postal Service in writing within 30 days of the alleged breach of the agreement.[22]

   c. **No Agreement Letter:** The mediator signs a letter stating that both participants appeared for their scheduled mediation, but they were unable to resolve their dispute.[23]

Consequences if no agreement reached: Although the mediator is prohibited from giving any legal advice, this does not stop me from indicating to them that if no agreement is reached and if they feel that they want to file a formal complaint with the EEO Commission, they should consider consulting with an attorney as to the validity of their discrimination claim and to be sure to relay to the attorney the Postal Service's perspective of the problem.[24]

Have they read the Agreement to Mediate? The Agreement to Mediate is sent to all participants before the mediation session. I have usually covered all of the issues, but it provides me with an opportunity to emphasize that the purpose of **REDRESS®** is not to build a case to file with EEO Commission, (recording is prohibited and I discourage note taking as this comes across as confrontational), but to have the participants hear each other to see if they can mutually resolve their problem(s).

Any Questions? If not then everyone signs: After everyone there, including the mediator and any observer, has signed the Agreement to Mediate, then I remind the participants that I am not there to control their decision making or the process about what they discuss when. I then request them to begin talking to each other.

Facilitating the REDRESS®: In Transformative Mediation, I believe that my role consists of two parts: (1) <u>To Help the Participants Hear the Other Side's Perspective</u>: I try to assist each participant to be able to see, feel, and/or understand the situation from the other person's viewpoint. In a normal conflict, we are usually rebutting the other person's arguments in our head before they finish talking. This prevents us from hearing the other person as a human being who has a problem and prevents us from being able to understand how the other person perceives his/her problem. Usually, we are more focused on, "They are wrong and here is why!" (2) To Help Participants Gain Clarity for Themselves: I try to allow each participant to gain clarity for him/herself as to the reality of the situation so that he/she can make a rational decision as to what their best choices and options are. I want to encourage each participant to make decisions less emotionally for what is in their best interest. Reacting emotionally hurts their ability to hear the other side's perspective and to think logically. I focus on trying to understand (by listening), what is motivating the individual and to determine if their actions are in accordance with their motivation(s). If not, then I focus on trying to gain clarity (for my own understanding), of how their motives and needs are or are not resolved by various actions or solutions. By the participant helping me understand, the participant frequently achieves clarity for him/herself.

What I Focus on Doing: As a Mediator using Transformative Mediation, I am focused only on **Listening with Empathy.** Some people may describe this as "Active Listening," but I believe it is more. I want to not merely be able to repeat back what a participant said but I want to also be able to: (1) understand what they are saying factually, (2) perceive how they view the situation, (3) understand how they view themselves (which is usually in a positive light), (4) comprehend what is motivating their actions, and (5) feel and internalize their emotions as if this was happening to me. This means not only internalizing what is happening with the speaker, but also internalizing how the listening participant is reacting.

Techniques Used in Joint Session: Because I am focused on listening to what is being said and NOT trying to figure out how the participants are going to resolve their differences, I try to hone in on important things that I am hearing spoken or feeling from the body language. I am therefore:

1. Frequently summarizing to make sure I have correctly heard what was said or felt. In choosing what I highlight (facts and/or emotions), I am emphasizing what seemed important to me before the other (listening) participant responded. If the speaking participant has talked for a while, my summarization helps the listening participant remember the salient points (in case they were focusing on rebutting instead of listening). In addition, my summarization may help bring organization or clarity to the speaking participant's thoughts and perhaps give them an additional perspective about the facts or their feelings that had not consciously occurred to them.
2. Asking for an explanation if I am not sure what one party means or if what is being said raises a question in my mind. Hopefully, the question that I am asking is similar to what the listening participant is wondering. If correct, then I am helping the listening participant better understand the perspective of the speaking participant.

3. Asking one participant what they would do or how they would want the other participant to act if their roles were reversed. This question forces them to think from the other participant's perspective and at the same time gives the other participant good information of what they could do to minimize or avoid the other participant feeling that he/she is not being treated fairly.

4. Breaking in and requesting a further explanation to help me understand the cause of the agitation if a participant (usually the complainant) is becoming highly agitated. The response from the complainant gives me an opportunity to summarize what caused the agitation and allows the supervisor to hear what they were or were not doing that caused the claimant to be upset. The agitated participant becomes calmer as he/she feels that they are being heard. Further, it is hard to stay agitated if you are trying to respond to a request for additional information to better understand from the mediator who is not the source of your agitation. At the same time, the supervisor does not have to react in kind for what was said at an emotional time by the complainant.

5. Trying to facilitate a conversation between the participants where they can hear each other's perspective without having to react in a defensive emotional manner as they had in the past. By highlighting through summarizing what was said or through non-threatening, information-seeking questions for clarification, the hope is that misunderstandings and poor communication will be replaced with empathy and understanding of the other participant's situation *(recognition)*. By facilitating a conversation where the subordinate (complainant) is treated respectfully as an individual who's thoughts are valued, and where the subordinate is given an equal opportunity to decide how a resolution might be achieved *(empowerment),* it is hoped that the conflict interaction changes from one that has been negative (destructive) to one that is positive (constructive).

6. Caucuses: As opposed to other mediation models where the caucus is frequently used by the mediator to try to move the parties to an agreement, in the Transformative Mediation Model, I see my role as solely being a resource to help them gain clarity for themselves, not to persuade them. Therefore there is no need for me to call a caucus. The caucus is to enable the participant to have a private discussion with their support person and/or gain my input if they feel it might be helpful. If asked in caucus, I will give my opinion of what I hear happening and what strategy or options that I would consider if I was in their situation. This is not done to tell, pressure, or persuade them, but to help them gain a perspective of a possible new alternative that might work for both participants based upon my perception of where each party is. By engaging in a conversation with the participant as to why a course of action might or might not work for them, the participant gains clarity about what options would work best for the participant that might also be acceptable to the other party.

Question: Do you think what I am doing is following the Transformative Mediation Model as defined by Busch and Folger and why? If no, does it follow the spirit of what they are trying to achieve and why?

How I know when it is time to end the **REDRESS**® *and what I say:* At some point in the discussion, it will become apparent that everyone has said everything that they want the other participant to hear. To insure my conclusion is correct, I will say to both participants, "Is there anything else that you would like to say to the other person?" If there is, then they get a chance to say it. If not, then it is time for the complainant to make one of their three choices. At this point, it is usually fairly obvious, based upon the comments of both of the participants, of whether or not there is a possibility of reaching a Settlement Agreement. If not clear, then the question to the complainant is: "Do you want to propose a solution?" or "What would you hope to achieve at the end of this mediation?" This question may be followed by, "Do you want to have a caucus with your support person before replying?" This allows the support person, who is not as emotionally involved, to have the opportunity to give the complainant their advice and perception of what the complainant should do. If invited to the caucus, the mediator hears what the complainant is really thinking because the complainant is not posturing for their supervisor or manager. In addition, the complainant does not have to worry about saying something that would offend their supervisor or manager, as the mediator has to keep all comments made in caucus confidential. If the mediator is meeting with both participants (which means that the mediator has the trust of both participants), the mediator will be able to quickly understand if there is any common ground for a Settlement Agreement. If no Settlement Agreement is possible, then the issue is whether the complainant withdraws their complaint or the mediator signs a letter of No Agreement. If in caucus with the complainant (at the complainant's request), I will make the statements that if the complainant is considering, but not sure if they want to pursue filing an EEOC Complaint, then they should request a No Agreement. This gives the complainant the opportunity to file the formal complaint with the EEO and nothing requires them to do anything if they decide not to file. On the other hand, if the complainant knows that they are not going to pursue their claim, for whatever reason, I would suggest that they consider withdrawing their complaint because it will be a way of taking away some of the sting and resentment that their supervisor may feel because of being accused of discriminating. If the supervisor now has a better understanding of what the supervisor did that caused the complainant to feel that they were treated unfairly. Then, by withdrawing the complaint, the complainant is taking the first step of trying to repair the relationship with their supervisor. This strategy is very low risk as the complainant has nothing to lose if they are not going to further pursue their EEO Complaint.

Does it really matter if an Agreement was reached or not? According to the Transformative Mediation Model, whether an Agreement is reached or not is unimportant. The important issue is whether both participants have been able to understand the other side's perspective and that there is now better communication and understanding so that there is an improvement in their future interactions. The question then arises as to how the **REDRESS**® system helps if you have a poor supervisor, who is not discriminating legally, but is using some poor supervisory skills with their employees. During **REDRESS®,** the mediator can't make any comments to the supervisor (because the mediator has promised to use the Transformative Model) or later to management (because of the confidentiality in the Agreement to Mediate).[25] The answer that I have received is that if the supervisor continues to receive similar complaints from different subordinates, then hopefully, the supervisor will realize that the problem may be with the supervisor and re-evaluate what they are doing. In addition, since the supervisor's support person is usually their manager, the manager hears the complainant's comments regarding the supervisor's actions. If there are more complaints filed, then the manager has to realize that the problem may not be a disgruntled employee, but a supervisor with poor skills. Thus even if an agreement is not reached, the process is eventually beneficial in improving the relationship between management and their employees.

NOTES

[1]Bush, R. A. B., and Folger, J. (2005). *The promise of mediation: The Transformative Approach to conflict,* Revised Edition, San Francisco: Jossey-Bass Acknowledgments (p. ix).

[2]Nabatchi, T., and Bingham, L. B. (2001). Transformative mediation in the USPS REDRESS® Program: Observations of ADR specialists. *Hofstra Labor and Employment Law Journal,* Vol. 18, p. 399.

[3]Although the mediators were paid originally by their hourly rate and later by a flat fee, which did not vary with the results, the USPS ADR (Alternative Dispute Resolution) Specialist's compensation was affected by the results.

[4]Many employees will allege an Equal Employment Opportunity violation to get into the REDRESS® program even though they know that they were not legally discriminated against. If they file a complaint alleging a violation, they are allowed into the REDRESS® program.

[5]A grievance has to be filed by the employee's Union representative for a violation of the USPS' contract with that particular Union. The grievance goes through various steps as it works its way up the hierarchy of the Postal Service and the Union. If not resolved between the parties, then the issue goes to an Arbitrator for a binding decision.

[6]*Question: Do you think this is giving the employee two chances to win their case?* The rules for the REDRESS® program say that grievances are not allowed to be discussed in the REDRESS® program, but if the EEO complaint of discrimination is discussed and settled in the REDRESS® program and if a Union representative signs off, then the grievance can be dismissed.

[7]The facilitative model is therefore the most popular model to use when a continued relationship is required after the mediation such as in family issues where

there are children involved and the parents will be required to cooperate with each other for the benefit of their child.

[8]Bush and Folger, p. 22.

[9]From USPS Publication 102—Mediating Postal Disputes.

[10]All Postal Service employees are paid during the REDRESS® mediation. This is also usually during the time that the supervisor or manager is supposed to be working, as well as the employee. If the employee's representative is also an employee (or union representative), they also get paid even if it is not during their regular work shift.

[11]The process of which Mediator is selected and how has changed over time. It used to be that a Regional EEO ADR Specialist, who knew the mediators skills, would make the decision based upon the needs of the case, the skills of the mediator, and the distance the mediator had to travel. Parties could also request certain mediators on the rooster. Now (March, 2012), it is computerized. The specialist has to call the mediator who is closest to the location which is generated by the computer. If the mediator does not respond in a timely fashion or is not available, then the computer spits out the next name. This is done to save money because the uniform policy is now to pay any mediator who has to travel more than 50 miles one way to reach the mediation location.

[12]There are a lot of rules regarding seniority for bidding for jobs or which of three shifts that you work. Seniority may be lost if you transfer to a different location. The rules that are in each union's contract cannot be overridden in a Settlement Agreement.

[13]The employee may request No Agreement if he/she thinks or is not sure if they want to proceed to file a formal complaint with the EEOC. However, sometimes the employee knows that they have no legal case of discrimination, but are so upset at management because they could not get what the wanted out of the REDRESS® that they request No Agreement.

[14]I have been told that, historically, 60% of the cases settled (Settlement Agreement or Withdrawal) at the REDRESS® session and another 20% of the cases never proceeded to a formal complaint.

[15]This provision is to prevent a counselee from canceling the REDRESS® mediation at the last minute because they cannot get the representative that they want to attend the mediation.

[16]Agreement to Mediate form is signed by all parties attending, including the mediator and any observer (EEO ADR Specialist). The form states this is voluntary process to see if the parties can reach a resolution; the parties cannot subpoena the mediator or observer to testify what has been said; the mediator or observer will not report anything said unless one of the participants "makes a genuine threat of physical harm, reports criminal activity occurring on postal property, reports fraud or abuse of postal property or suspected child or elder abuse"; the session is not to be recorded; and that any documents prepared for or during the mediation are for settlement purposes only and may not be subpoenaed.

[17]REDRESS® Settlement Form has all the "legal conditions" preprinted and there are blank spaces and pages to fill in the agreement that is reached.

[18]The No Agreement Letter is only signed by the mediator and states that the parties appeared at the scheduled mediation, but could not resolve their dispute.

[19]In 2011, the Postal Service switched to a computer-generated system for selecting mediators based upon their proximity to the hearing location. I assume this was done to save money as the Postal Service pays for mileage if the mediator's travel is more than 50 miles one way. Under the original system, the EEO ADR Specialist for the local area, who knew the skill level of the mediators, was able to select the mediator who they felt was more qualified for the more difficult cases. *Question: If the new system results in fewer settlements or transformation of relationships, has the Postal Service really saved money?*

[20]At the end of my REDRESS® mediations when copies of the paperwork were being made for the participants, I frequently encouraged the participants to give feedback to the ADR EEO Specialist about the mediation, whether positive or negative. I also sometimes asked (if applicable), how their mediation with me compared to previous mediations with other mediators and what they liked or disliked.

[21]Some of the older and more experienced in Labor Relations EEO ADR Specialists were excellent in understanding the process and balancing what was needed to transform the relationship and dynamics between the parties. However, there were also a few who were flagrantly violating the transformative mediation concept themselves in the interest of trying to get everything settled.

[22]The statement of noncompliance may include a request that the terms of the settlement agreement be specifically implemented or that the complaint be reinstated so that the Complainant can then file a formal complaint with the EEO Commission.

[23]Some of the claimants will select the "No Agreement" even though they know that they have no valid claim for discrimination or that it does not make economic sense for them to pursue a formal EEO complaint. (This could be because no attorney will take the complainant's case on a contingency fee basis, the claimant is not willing to pay for an attorney's time to pursue the case, or any settlement collected would be less than the cost of pursuing the claim.) Historically, I have been told that approximately 40% of the total complaints result in No Agreement and half (20% of total claims) of the No Agreements are never pursued formally and are therefore barred from future actions. Many times, even though the complainant knows that they have no legal discrimination claim, they will refuse to withdraw their complaint because they are upset at their supervisor and/or they are unhappy that their problem was not solved.

[24]Many times a case sounds great when you hear only one side's perspective. However, this frequently changes when you hear the other side of the story. If the claimant can objectively relay both sides' perspective, the attorney can make a better evaluation as to the strength of the claimant's case.

[25]If I have established a good relationship with the supervisor, I may give a suggestion in caucus or after the REDRESS® session has ended with nobody around, about what they might want to try to do differently. I base this upon my educational training and experience of having run a company with over 1000 employees.

Chapter 14

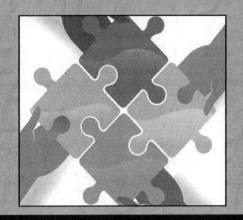

Conclusion

Bruce C. McKinney

It always amazes me when individuals react with shock when they are part of a conflict—as if conflict was an unnatural occurrence. In fact, conflict is a natural part of life. It would be more realistic to be *shocked when there is an absence of conflict.* With our own personal needs and egos, we are always going to encounter conflict in our daily lives. What is abnormal (at least to me) is that most people live their lives with no formal instruction in conflict management. That creates the perfect need for mediation. I remember watching a program a few years ago where three very intelligent and wealthy people—a nurse, a lawyer, and an attorney—were in disagreement over who should pay for the repair of a small bridge leading to their houses. Mediation would have been a perfect vehicle to manage this dispute. Instead the conflict spiraled out of control and two people ended up dead.[1] For reasons such as these, Jerry and I will always be proponents of mediation, and besides this book being about mediation, we hope that it can help spread the word about the promise of mediation (with apologies to Bush and Folger for using their title in this remark).

As we wrote in the first edition of this book, during years of teaching students in the classroom about mediation as well as presenting a number of programs throughout the United States, we have been unable to find a source we could refer students to that would answer many of their basic questions about mediation. Five years later this still seems to be the case. There are many more "how to" books for mediators, but few that contain contributions from both scholars and practitioners.

We hope that you have found the second edition *Readings and Case Studies in Mediation* to be a source of information about much more basic questions such as, "What happens to couples who choose to proceed with a divorce mediation?" or "Can you really mediate with gangs?" Our focus was on "what's it all about" rather than how to perform specific tasks in mediation. We are certain that experienced practitioners will find some of the contributing authors' comments to be very basic but are equally certain they will acknowledge that they have provided those same answers to students and other interested persons throughout the years they have practiced.

The authors have always enjoyed and welcomed the curiosity of people who bring enthusiasm and an open mind to our classrooms and trainings. As you have read each of the chapters of this book, we hope your experience has been much like someone wandering the aisles of a store containing lots of interesting items. Some of you may have just been looking, others may have had a specific item you were searching for; we hope that you may have found it in this book.

Whether you just wanted to find out how divorce mediation differed from victim/offender mediation, or you wanted to see if there was a better way to handle conflict at work, our contributing authors were pleased to show off their wares and not be too concerned about a scholarly analysis of their opinions. However, as you may have noticed, some of the chapters present more research than others. This is intentional—we wanted both scholars and practitioners to contribute to this book, and we think it is a nice blend of experiential and academic information about mediation. The term "practice wisdom" is often used to describe the lessons learned by seasoned practitioners. If those who seek such wisdom have spent some time as practitioners, what they learn will have some relevance. On the other hand, for those who may seek the answer to some academic question about mediation, they will find plenty of answers in this text. Those who are merely curious and want to decide about becoming practitioners or consumers of mediation services often hesitate to ask what they are afraid might be perceived as naïve questions. This book is an attempt to help those people as well.

We hope that you recognized that our authors anticipated even the most basic questions and answered them in a manner that was easy to understand and inspired you to look even further into the profession of mediation. If we have aroused your interest, if we have even tickled your curiosity, we have succeeded in accomplishing our goal for producing this text.

Certainly, there are many more questions to be answered and many more books available to peruse for those answers. This writer's favorite book on "how to" mediate is *Mediation Theory and Practice* by McCorkle and Reese (Allyn & Bacon, 2004). Several years ago if you did a search for a mediation text on a site like Amazon.com, you would not find my books on the topic. Now there are over 45 texts on Amazon's site. Clearly mediation is not going away. I have been an advocate for mediation ever since I was first introduced to the process at James Madison University in 1988. In 2010, I found myself at the other side of the mediation table as a disputant in a conflict that, to put it mildly, was not helping my blood pressure. I went into the mediation with a mindset (that is probably typical of any disputant) that I welcomed the intervention, but I doubted it would succeed. I could not have been more wrong. The experience left me as an even stronger advocate for mediation. Whether you are a serious mediator or an interested disputant, we hope we have not dampened your passion for mediation and that by sharing our insights and opinions, you have been inspired to begin your journey down that road. Trust the process, it works!

NOTE

[1]This program is still available on *NBC Dateline's* web page. This program is called "The Trouble on the Hill." It is a perfect video to begin a mediation class when discussing conflict. It is available on YouTube and may be purchased from Amazon.com.